Rethinking Mary in the New Testament

Rethinking Mary in the New Testament

By Edward Sri

Ignatius Press
San Francisco

Augustine Institute
Greenwood Village, CO

Ignatius Press Distribution
1915 Aster Rd.
Sycamore, IL 60178
Tel: (630) 246-2204
www.ignatius.com

Augustine Institute
6160 S. Syracuse Way, Suite 310
Greenwood Village, CO 80111
Tel: (866) 767-3155
www.augustineinstitute.org

Cover art: *Madonna*
by Giovanni Battista Salvi, Il Sassoferrato (Italian, 1609–1685)
Restored Traditions. Used by permission.

Cover Design: Lisa Marie Patterson

© 2018 by Ignatius Press, San Francisco,
and the Augustine Institute, Greenwood Village, CO
All rights reserved.

ISBN: 978-0-9997592-9-5

Library of Congress Control Number 2018936338

Printed in Canada ∞

To Mary

Contents

Abbreviations

AER – *American Ecclesiastical Review*

CBQ – *Catholic Biblical Quarterly*

CCC – *Catechism of the Catholic Church*

CSEL – Corpus Scriptorum Ecclesiasticorum Latinorum

EphMar – *Ephemerides Mariologicae*

EstMar – *Estudios Marianos*

JBL – *Journal of Biblical Literature*

JSNTSup – *Journal for the Study of the New Testament* Supplement Series

LXX – The Septuagint

MNT – *Mary in the New Testament*

PG – Patrologia Graeca

PL – Patrologia Latina

1QH – Qumran Scroll on Thanksgiving Hymns

1QS – Qumran Scroll on Community Rule

VTSup – *Vetus Testamentum* Supplements

Introduction

At first glance, the New Testament picture of Mary seems surprisingly limited. She appears only in a few accounts, and apart from some of the scenes narrating Christ's infancy, she is more of a background figure, just one member in a large supporting cast. Other characters such as John the Baptist, Peter, the Pharisees, and the Sadducees emerge more prominently in Christ's public ministry than the mother of Jesus does.[1] So when one compares the number of New Testament references to Mary with the amount of Marian doctrine and devotion that has developed over the centuries, the contrast is striking. One can understand why those approaching the Scriptures from outside the Catholic Tradition might wonder why the Catholic Church gives so much attention to Mary.

But let's start with one common point on which biblical scholars of various faith traditions tend to agree. In recent decades, Protestant, Catholic, and Orthodox Scripture commentators have increasingly recognized at least this about Mary: that she appears in the New Testament as a faithful disciple, a woman permeated by the Word of God.[2]

She is the first in the new covenant era who receives God's Word with joy and acts upon it (Lk 1:38). She is blessed because she has believed (Lk 1:44–45). She ponders the events of her Son's life in her heart (Lk 2:19, 51) and encourages others to carry out his instructions (Jn 2:5). She remains with her Son at the Cross when other disciples run away (Jn 19:25) and lives with the community of disciples in prayer in the days leading up to the descent of the Holy Spirit (Acts 1:14). From the Annunciation to Pentecost, she stands in the New Testament as a model disciple.

Nowhere, however, do we see her devotion to God's Word more than in her hymnlike prayer known as the Magnificat (Lk 1:46–55). As commentators have often noted, these verses draw heavily from various passages in the Jewish Scriptures to form a beautiful "pastiche of texts taken from the Old Testament."[3] Indeed, the Magnificat gives us a window into Mary's soul: through these words we see a woman whose whole life seems shaped by the Word of God. Consider Pope Benedict's observation about what Mary's Magnificat tells us about her relationship with God's Word.

> Here we see how completely at home Mary is with the Word of God, with ease she moves in and out of it. She speaks and thinks with the Word of God; the Word of God becomes her word, and her word issues from the Word of God. Here we see how her thoughts are attuned to the thoughts of God, how her will is one with the will of God. Since Mary is completely imbued with the Word of God, she is able to become the Mother of the Word Incarnate.[4]

Mary is a good biblical model for how we should approach God's Word in Scripture, and her own example should guide our study of what the Bible says about her. In other words, if we want to understand correctly what the New Testament reveals about Mary—who she is, what her role is in God's plan of salvation, and how she might relate to Christian disciples today—we should be immersed in God's Word as she was. For, as we will see in this study, the passages in which Mary does appear are often packed with allusions to the Jewish Scriptures and shaped by the narrative strategies, historical contexts, and theological aims of the sacred writers. Paying close attention to the way the New Testament authors present the Mother of Jesus—allowing ourselves to be "imbued with the Word of God" when examining her portrayal in the biblical texts—will bear much fruit in shaping an understanding of Mary that is truly scriptural. And, at times, it may even help us see a clearer trajectory between the Mary presented in the New Testament and a number of Marian beliefs that developed over time in the Church.[5]

The main emphasis of this book is on examining what the New Testament itself conveys about the Mother of Jesus. Hence, the focus is on exegesis—that is, drawing the meaning "out of" (*ex*) the biblical text—as opposed to eisegesis, in which the interpreter puts his or her own meaning into (*eis*) the text. Moreover, while we will at times draw upon insights from the Catholic Tradition, our primary aim is to demonstrate what can be gleaned from a careful investigation of how the New Testament writers describe the Mother of Jesus and her role in God's plan of salvation. Such a study can tell us much about her identity and mission and can even shed valuable biblical light on some traditional beliefs about Mary—more light than many studies on Mary in the Bible from the last fifty years suggest.

Minimal Mary

On one hand, some scholarship on this topic has tended to see little continuity between the Mary presented in the New Testament and the Marian beliefs developed by the Church in later centuries. Although the Church came to view Mary as the *Theotokos*, the spiritual mother of all Christians, a powerful intercessor, and the Immaculate Conception, and had given her titles such as "Queen of Heaven," "New Eve," and "Ark of the Covenant," it is often held that there is little to no basis for these Marian beliefs in the New Testament itself. Take, for example, the groundbreaking 1978 ecumenical work *Mary in the New Testament*. While the authors make several good observations about the Marian texts of the Bible (insights upon which we will draw later in this book), they tend to reach minimalist conclusions about what the New Testament actually reveals about Mary. They critique, for example, interpretations that suggest Luke's infancy narrative is presenting Mary in light of Old Testament images such as Daughter Zion or the Ark of the Covenant[6] or that view Jesus's words at the Cross, "Woman, behold, your son," as recalling the "woman" of Genesis (Eve) or pointing to Mary's role as spiritual mother of all faithful disciples[7]— even though, as we will see, there are strong exegetical grounds for these traditional interpretations.[8] They also dismiss the common Catholic understanding of Gabriel's greeting Mary with the word *kecharitomene* (traditionally translated "full of grace") as pointing to Mary's personal holiness (Lk 1:28). According to these authors, this view is problematic because it points to Mary's "personal possession of grace and privileges"—an interpretation that "reflects later Mariology" and clearly goes "beyond the meaning of Luke's text."[9] Although the authors of this ecumenical work raise fair concerns about some interpretations that read too much Marian theology into the scriptural texts, we will see that there are more foundations for these and other Marian beliefs in the New Testament itself than they acknowledge (see chapters 2, 3, 9, and 20).

Minimalist conclusions are found not just in Protestant authors and ecumenical works, but also in some Catholic scholars, even those who are genuinely attempting to demonstrate biblical support for Mary's important role in salvation history. Take, for example, Ignace de la Potterie's wonderfully insightful *Mary in the Mystery of the Covenant*, which has much to offer for our understanding of Mary in the New Testament. Even in this excellent work, however, there are times when de la Potterie seems overly cautious in his evaluation of how deep the scriptural roots for traditional Marian interpretations go. For example, he seems hesitant about how much Scripture can be used to demonstrate that Mary is being revealed as the mother of the Immanuel child of Isaiah 7:14 or as a New Eve figure (related to the prophecy of Genesis 3:15).[10] In regards to the traditional interpretation that John's Gospel portrays Mary as the New Eve when Jesus calls her "woman" at Cana and Calvary (Jn 2:4; 19:26), de la Potterie critiques this view for being "totally traditional": "Neither at Cana nor at the Cross is there the slightest hint of the Genesis account."[11] We will see, however, that the strong creation themes in John 1 (e.g., "In the beginning . . .") are not completely abandoned in John's account of the Wedding Feast at Cana or at Calvary, and that John does intend the reader to understand Mary in light of the woman of Genesis (see chapters 17 and 20).

Theological Deductions

On the other hand, there are some commentators who have turned to the Scriptures to uphold these and other traditional Catholic views about Mary, but at times do so without demonstrating exegetically that the New Testament writers themselves were presenting Mary in these ways. This tendency can be found in some Catholic Marian devotional books and popular works on Catholic apologetics that attempt to defend the Church's Marian doctrines using Scripture primarily as a source of proof texts for preconceived ideas about Mary but not as "the soul of sacred theology" truly shaping our understanding of her.[12] But it can also at times be found in Catholic scholars who make the primary point of departure for their treatment on Mary the method of *theological deduction*. In this approach, the Scriptures are used to make secondary deductions about Mary. The scholar notes how the New Testament reveals a certain truth about Mary, and then draws an inference from that revealed point, but without demonstrating how that inference is something the New Testament itself is making.

Joseph Fenton, for example, in his article on the biblical teaching about Mary's queenship, starts by showing how Luke's account of the Annunciation to Mary clearly presents her as the mother of Israel's king and asserts that Mary, as the king's mother, would be the person who is most closely connected with the king. Then Fenton argues for Mary's queenship by making the following logical deduction: "And, since the office of a queen, in the proper sense of the term, is precisely that of the woman most intimately associated with the king in the government and the direction of his own realm, Mary's position with reference to Our Lord constitutes her as a true and perfect queen in the kingdom of her Son."[13]

Notice how Fenton begins with the divinely revealed truth of Mary's being the mother of Christ the King but then makes the secondary logical deduction that she must be the queen. Also notice how the model of kingship and queenship is taken not from Scripture but from the kingdoms of this world. Such an approach might shed some light on Mary's royal office, but it remains a step removed from the New Testament portrayal of Mary. It fails to demonstrate how the New Testament *itself* is presenting Mary as queen. As I stated in an earlier academic monograph that looked more extensively at the relationship between exegesis and theology, this approach of theological deduction "applies logic *to* the biblical texts, instead of building more closely upon the logic found *in* the texts."[14] A more thorough examination of the biblical understanding of kingdom and queenship—especially the ancient Jewish scriptural tradition of the queen mother (in which the mother of the king reigned as queen)[15]—and the ways Luke presents Mary in light of that queen-mother tradition would shed more helpful light on this topic.

"Extra-Biblical" Typology

We can see something similar when commentators attempt to make typological connections between Mary and various figures and symbols in the Old Testament, such as Eve, Queen Esther, Wisdom, and the Temple. Although some interpreters clearly show how those typologies (or prefigurements) are connections that the New Testament authors themselves are making, in many cases the commentators have not persuasively demonstrated that the New Testament is actually portraying Mary in light of these figures.

Along these lines, the Pontifical Biblical Commission (PBC), an international body of Scripture scholars that advises the Church, makes a subtle but important point regarding biblical typology. Its 1994 pronouncement *On the Interpretation of the Bible in the Church* states that an authentic typological sense of Scripture is found in the associations made by the New Testament writers themselves:

"The connection involved in typology is ordinarily based on the way in which *Scripture* describes the ancient reality.... Consequently, in such a case one can speak of *a meaning that is truly Scriptural*."[16] With the strongest cases for biblical typology, the connection between the Old Testament type and the New Testament reality is not based simply on the way extra-biblical authors reflected on Old Testament people, places, and events. Rather, it is based on the way subsequent *scriptural texts* describe those ancient realities.[17] Hence, the PBC gives special attention to Scripture as the criterion for determining an authentic typological sense.[18]

With this background, let's consider, for example, the treatment of Mary as the Ark of the Covenant in Stefano Manelli's biblical Mariology book, *All Generations Shall Call Me Blessed*. When making the case for interpreting Mary as the new Ark of the Covenant, Manelli starts by pointing out various similarities between the Ark of old and the Mother of Jesus. Just as the Ark carried the Word of God on tablets of stone, so Mary carries the Word of God in her womb. Like the Ark, which contained the rod of Aaron, the first High Priest, so Mary carries the one who is "the root of Jesse." And just as the Ark of old held the manna from the desert, so Mary carries the one who is the Bread of Life, the Eucharistic Christ.[19]

For many Catholics, these points from Manelli offer beautiful typological connections and ones that we should carefully ponder. But these associations remain at the level of spiritual interpretations made by the theologian. Manelli in this work does not demonstrate that the *New Testament authors* are making these connections. This distinction should not downplay the important contributions such spiritual interpretations can make to our understanding of Mary. But these "extra-biblical" typologies remain a step

removed from the actual New Testament presentation of
Jesus's mother. A more thorough examination of Luke's
account of the Visitation could take interpreters further.
As some Protestant and Catholic scholars have pointed out,
Luke's Gospel portrays Mary's visit to Elizabeth in ways
that recall certain events surrounding the journey that the
Ark of the Covenant made to Jerusalem in 2 Samuel 6.[20]
Manelli mentions this point, but only in passing. He doesn't
develop it. Scholars who start with the New Testament's
presentation of Mary and clearly demonstrate how *Luke*
is portraying her in light of the Ark of the Covenant in
2 Samuel 6, on the other hand, offer a stronger foundation
upon which Manelli's spiritual typologies can be built.

Conclusion

In this book, we will see that the New Testament reveals
more about Mary than has been commonly appreciated in
contemporary scholarship. But the approach we will take is
not about apologetics. It's about exegesis. It does not intend
to offer a response to every objection to Catholic beliefs
about Mary. Rather, it aims to help us understand who
Mary is according to the biblical authors. Certainly, in some
cases we will see New Testament passages clearly presenting
Mary in ways that demonstrate traditional Marian beliefs.
But in other cases we will find the Scriptures simply offering important foundations from which a line of continuity
within the development of Marian doctrines in the Church
can be more fully appreciated. At other points we will
simply discover fresh perspectives into Mary of Nazareth
herself—who she was, what she was going through, and
how her own walk as a disciple can shed light on ours today.
Most of the conclusions we make about Mary in the New

Testament will be drawn not merely from theological deductions or "extra-biblical" typology, as illuminating as those approaches may be at times. Our focus will be on what the New Testament itself—in the literal sense—can contribute to our understanding of Mary. Like Mary herself, may we "keep and ponder" the mysteries of God's Word and may this lead us to a deeper appreciation for the Mother of Jesus in Scripture.

Chapter One

Mary's Life before the Annunciation
(Luke 1:26–27)

What was Mary's life like *before* the angel Gabriel appeared to her? Christians throughout the centuries have speculated about her early life, and various traditions have developed about her birth, childhood, and betrothal to Joseph. But the New Testament itself does not offer much information regarding the pre-Annunciation Mary.

Luke's Gospel introduces her in 1:26–27 with only the following brief points:

1. She was living in "a city of Galilee named Nazareth" (1:26);

2. She was a "virgin" who was "betrothed";

3. She was betrothed to a man named Joseph who was "of the house of David" (1:27); and

4. Her name was Mary (1:27).

Admittedly, these seem like very minor details—not much to work with to get a sense of Mary's early life. But actually we'll see there's a great deal of significance in each of these small points. So if you want to get at least a sketch of what

Scripture tells us about Mary's life before that fateful day when Gabriel appeared to her, let's unpack all that can be gleaned from these two short verses.

Anything Good from Nazareth?

First, Mary lives in "a city of Galilee named Nazareth." Mary is introduced as dwelling in an obscure village in Galilee that is estimated to have covered about 60 acres of land and to have had only about 480 people at the start of the first century.[1]

But Nazareth was not only small in its size; it was small in its significance in Jesus's day. The village itself is never mentioned in the Old Testament. Moreover, the writings of the first-century Jewish historian Josephus as well as those of the ancient Jewish rabbis do not even mention this place. Though other larger, more well-known cities such as Jerusalem (Lk 2:22); Rome (Acts 2:10); or Phoenicia, Cyprus, and Antioch (Acts 11:19) receive no introduction in Luke and Acts, Luke, three times in his infancy narrative, introduces Mary's village as being a part of Galilee (1:26; 2:4, 39)—probably because most of his non-Palestinian readers would have never heard of Nazareth.[2]

It's safe to say that Nazareth was not on most people's Top 10 list of expected places from where the Messiah would come. Nathanael's well-known sarcastic comment "Can anything good come out of Nazareth?" (Jn 1:46) reflects the negative views at least some people had about Mary's village. The fact that God chose a young woman from this lowly place to become the mother of the Messiah is astonishing!

This is all the more remarkable when one considers the stark contrast between where Mary resides and where the previous story in Luke's Gospel just took place. Luke's opening scene tells of the angel Gabriel appearing to the priest Zechariah in the Jerusalem Temple, announcing that his barren wife will become the mother of John the Baptist. Think about that: this first angelic visitation takes place in the holiest spot on the face of the earth. Gabriel appears to Zechariah while he's serving in the Holy Place in the Temple, "a veiled doorway away" from the Holy of Holies, where the presence of God's glory had manifested itself (1 Kings 8:10–11).[3]

After that scene, readers are suddenly whisked away from the Holy Temple to the obscure village of Nazareth, where the same angel appears to Mary. Far removed from the holy city of Jerusalem, it's in this humble village of Nazareth that Mary resides. For the reader, the jarring contrast between Zechariah serving in the sacred Temple and Mary residing in "nowhere Nazareth" could not be more pronounced.

Betrothed

Second, Mary is a *virgin* who is *betrothed*. Betrothal represented the first stage of the two-step marriage process in first-century Judaism and is different from "engagement" in modern Western society. At a betrothal in Mary's day, bride and groom formally exchanged consent in the presence of witnesses (cf. Mal 2:14). This forged a legal bond between the two, who would then be considered married. The woman would be called the groom's "wife" (see Mt 1:20, 24), and this union could only be broken by divorce. Any violation of the man's marital rights would be considered adultery.

At the time, Jewish girls were typically betrothed at a young age, as young as the ages of twelve and thirteen. After betrothal, the wife usually remained living at her family home for up to a year. Then the "taking" home of the wife to the man's home, the second step of the marriage process, occurred. It was then that the man's support for his wife and marital sexual relations formally began.[4] So, when we read at this point in the story that Mary is betrothed to Joseph, this means she is legally married to him, but not yet at the second stage of marriage when she would be living under the same roof with him.

This background makes Luke 1:27 all the more striking. In this single verse, Luke twice mentions that Mary is a virgin. This is quite odd. If Mary is a betrothed woman, she would presumably be a virgin since she has not yet arrived at the "taking" stage and consummated her marriage. To note that Mary is betrothed and then say she is a virgin is, in a sense, redundant. So why does Luke mention Mary being a virgin—and not just once, but twice in one verse? He does so in order to draw attention to her virginity in a unique way, as it will play a key part of the story as it unfolds. This emphasis on Mary's virginity here at the very start of the story prepares the way for the angel's announcement of the unique, miraculous virginal conception of the Christ Child that will soon be announced (1:35).[5]

Royal Family

Third, Mary is betrothed to "a man whose name was Joseph, of the *house of David*" (Lk 1:27). Joseph was a common biblical name used in the postexilic period (Ezr 10:42; Neh 12:14; 1 Chr 25:2, 9).[6] Interestingly, Joseph, who is described as being "of the house of David," receives more of an introduction than does Mary, whose name is simply given ("And the virgin's name was Mary" [Lk 1:27]). Mary's family background is not even mentioned. As New Testament scholar Joel Green observes, "Joseph—who has scarcely any role in Luke 1–2 and is only mentioned otherwise in 3:23—receives more of an introduction than Mary, the primary character in the birth narrative. Why? Luke is interested in his royal ancestry."[7] Indeed, this phrase "house of David" was used in the Old Testament in reference to descendants of David.[8] Luke mentions this detail of Joseph's heritage in order to prepare the reader for understanding Jesus as a Davidic heir—a theme that will be developed extensively throughout this Annunciation scene.[9]

Fourth, her name was *Mary*. The name Mary (*Mariam*) is the Greek form of the Hebrew name *Mirium*, which brings to mind the sister of Moses (Ex 15:20), the only woman in the Old Testament to bear that name. Its meaning has been described in various ways, including "rebellious," "myrh," or "bitter sea," but the name itself is likely related to the word *myrm* in Hebrew and Ugaritic, which meant "height," "summit," or "exalted one"[10]—a fitting backdrop for the name of the woman who is about to become the mother of the Messiah and who in the Magnificat will describe herself as being uniquely exalted by God (cf. Lk 1:49; 1:52).

Mary and Zechariah

Surely, these small details from Scripture do not give us an extensive portrait of Mary's life before the Annunciation. She lives in the obscure village of Nazareth in Galilee. She is a young betrothed girl who, at the first stage of marriage, is still a virgin and not yet living with her husband. Her betrothed is named Joseph from the royal family of David. But when these facts from Luke 1:26–27 are considered in light of the previous scene in Luke's narrative, the annunciation of John the Baptist's birth to Zechariah (1:5–25), they shed important light on what Luke intends to reveal about Mary and her Son, Jesus.

On one hand, we will see that the numerous parallels between these two scenes underscore how they are meant to be read in light of each other and how Mary and Jesus, along with Zechariah and John the Baptist, are caught up in a single divine purpose: God's plan of salvation, which reaches its climactic fulfillment with the coming of the Savior.

On the other hand, we will see that the contrasts between these two scenes—and, in particular, the differences between Zechariah and Mary themselves—draw attention to the unique work God is doing in Mary, elevating her to become the mother of Israel's Messiah.

Annunciation Patterns

Let's begin by considering the connections between the two scenes.

First, Luke frames the angel's announcement to Mary with references to Gabriel's appearance to Zechariah. At the start of the account, Luke introduces the angel's appearance to Mary as taking place "in the sixth month" (1:26)—a chronological reference point that comes on the heels of Luke mentioning the "five months" of Elizabeth's keeping herself in hiding during her pregnancy (1:24–25). Luke's mention of "the sixth month" right after the "five months" of Elizabeth's hiding makes a deliberate link back to the previous scene. It shows how Mary's story is a continuation of Zechariah's. The two stories are part of one larger story in God's saving plan.

At the end of the story, Luke mentions Elizabeth's pregnancy again. Gabriel reveals to Mary that the elderly Elizabeth being pregnant is a sign that "with God nothing will be impossible" (1:36–37). In this way, Luke deliberately frames the entire announcement of Mary with connections back to Elizabeth's pregnancy, suggesting that the two stories are mutually interpretive.

Second, notice the extensive parallels between these two birth announcement stories.[11] Both soon-to-be-parents are greeted by the same angel, *Gabriel*, and both are "*troubled*" by their meeting with the heavenly visitor (Lk 1:11–12, 26–29). The angel assures both parents "*Do not be afraid*" (1:13, 30) and proceeds to announce the birth of an unexpected son who "*will be great*" and will play a critical role in God's saving plan (1:14–17, 32–33). Both parents *ask a question* that highlights the human impossibility involved in conceiving a child (1:18, 34), and both receive *a sign* demonstrating God's hand is truly involved in their lives. For Zechariah, the sign is being struck mute for his unbelief (1:20), while for Mary the sign is the announcement that her elderly kinswoman, Elizabeth, who had been barren, is miraculously in the sixth month of pregnancy (1:36). Indeed, the parallels between these two birth announcement scenes make clear that Luke intends them to be read in light of each other.

In addition, both scenes recall the way God or God's angelic messengers announce the birth of a son in the Old Testament (as discussed more in the Appendix). When Abraham or Samson's parents, for example, receive a heavenly message about having a child, there are common elements in those accounts, such as an appearance of an angel (or God himself), the person responding in fear, the announcement of the child's conception, the parent raising a question, and a sign being given to assure them.

But whatever similarities might be found, on one hand, between Zechariah's and Mary's stories and, on the other hand, the other biblical birth announcement stories, Joel Green notes that "these two are more like each other than either is like the other representatives of this form."[12] Green shows how both accounts involve the following progressive components that, in their entirety, are found only in these two announcement scenes and in no other birth announcement scenes in the Bible: "(1) Introduction of Parents; (2) Specification of Obstacles to Childbearing; (3) Encounter with an Angel, Gabriel; (4) Response to the Angel; (5) 'Do Not Be Afraid,' with Address by Name; (6) Promise of a Son; (7) Objection; (8) Giving of a Sign; and (9) Departure of Gabriel."[13]

Moreover, both scenes use similar language, which further demonstrates that each is meant to be interpreted in light of the other. Consider the parallels:

Luke 1:11–20	**Luke 1:28–38**
"Zechariah was troubled" (v. 12)	"She was greatly troubled" (v. 29)
"The angel said to him" (v. 13)	"The angel said to her" (v. 30)
"Do not be afraid" (v. 13)	"Do not be afraid" (v. 30)
"Will bear you a son" (v. 13)	"You will . . . bear a son" (v. 31)
"And you shall call his name" (v. 13)	"And you shall call his name" (v. 31)
"He will be great" (v. 15)	"He will be great" (v. 32)
"Said to the angel" (v. 18)	"Said to the angel" (v. 34)
"And the angel answered him" (v. 19)	"And the angel said" (v. 35)
"Gabriel . . . God . . . sent" (v. 19)	"Gabriel . . . sent . . . God" (v. 26)
"And behold" (v. 20)	"And behold" (v. 36)

In summary, these extensive similarities both in characteristics and in language underscore how the two families (Zechariah's and Mary's) and, most especially, the two sons

(John and Jesus) are, as Robert Tannehill describes, "part of a single divine purpose, which is developing according to the same biblical pattern."[14] These two opening scenes—and the announcement of the two providential sons narrated in them—work together to proclaim the dawn of the messianic age and the fulfillment of God's plan of salvation.

Mary's Difference

However, these wide-ranging similarities make the *differences* between the two accounts stand out all the more.[15] It's commonly noted that Luke emphasizes Jesus's superiority over John the Baptist. Both sons are destined to do great things for Israel, but Jesus is clearly presented as the Messiah-King, while John is the one who will prepare the way for him. Similarly, both sons are miraculously conceived, but Jesus's conception by a virgin eclipses John being conceived by a woman of old age.

But the contrast is not only between Jesus and John; the differences between the recipients of Gabriel's message, Zechariah and Mary, also are telling. Notice the dissimilarities between the two parents:

- **Older Man or Younger Woman:** Zechariah is an *older man* who is "advanced in years"; Mary is a *young woman*, who, being betrothed, may be as young as twelve or thirteen years of age.

- **Priest or Ordinary Israelite:** Zechariah is a *priest* whose priestly family credentials are underscored by Luke. Zechariah is introduced as being from the priestly class of Abija, and his wife is introduced as a descendant of Aaron. In contrast, Mary has no official position in the Jewish religious structure.

She is simply a betrothed woman, whose family origins are not even mentioned.

- **Sacred Function or Ordinary Life:** Zechariah's encounter with the angel takes place while he is performing the most honorable of priestly duties. He is chosen by lot to offer the incense, a role that brought an ordinary priest like Zechariah the closest to the Holy of Holies. By offering the incense, Zechariah would be representing the entire people of God, offering prayers to the Lord on their behalf. By contrast, Mary is not described as serving in any official capacity for Israel or performing any particular duty when Gabriel appears to her.

- **Sacred or Ordinary Place:** The location of the annunciations is also a significant difference. Zechariah's encounter with the angel takes place in *a most sacred location:* in the city of Jerusalem, in the Temple of the Lord, at the altar of incense, which is close to the Holy of Holies. Mary, in contrast, is far from the Jerusalem Temple, dwelling in the insignificant and derided village of Nazareth in Galilee. No specific setting in Nazareth is even mentioned.

- **Sacred or Ordinary Time:** Finally, the times of the annunciations differ. Zechariah receives Gabriel's message during a sacred time of worship at the Temple: the people are united in prayer with the priest who is offering the incense on their behalf. When Zechariah re-emerges from the Holy Place, the people gathered outside realize "he had seen a vision in the temple" (1:22). In contrast, no special time is noted for the Annunciation to Mary, and there is no mention of people gathered after she receives her message. Her Annunciation seems to be a completely private affair in the midst of her ordinary daily life.

But Who Has Greater Faith?

In light of the care Luke gives to introducing and portraying other characters in Luke 1–2,[16] these social, liturgical, and geographical differences are quite significant. The greatest disparity between Zechariah and Mary, however, will be seen in the way they respond to the angel's message. It's here that Mary emerges clearly as the more noble character. While Zechariah is admonished by the angel for his unbelief and muted, Mary responds with model faith and is given further clarification and reassurance about her maternal mission (1:34–38).

Such a contrast between faith and unbelief is all the more remarkable given the way Mary is introduced merely as a virgin in Nazareth, while Zechariah is impressively presented as a righteous priest performing a most sacred function in the most sacred place of the Temple that he could enter. Surely *he* would be the one we would expect to respond in faith!

Yet, as Green observes, "The contrast with Zechariah—a male, an elder, a priest—could scarcely be more stark; he did not believe [Lk 1:20] but she did."[17] Indeed, Mary is presented in Luke's Gospel as a model of faith. "Mary, who seemed to measure low on any status scale—age, family heritage, gender, and so on—turns out to be the one favored by God and the one who finds her status and identity ultimately in her obedience to God and participation in his salvific will."[18]

In his commentary on Luke-Acts, F. Scott Spencer further draws out the contrast between Zechariah and Mary: "A wise, elderly priest faithfully devoted 'to all the commandments and regulations of the Lord' (1:6) should know that the ancient roots of God's covenant people first sprouted with God's gift of a son (Isaac) to a nonagenarian barren woman (Sarah) and her century-old husband (Abraham) (Gn 17:15–22; 21:1–7) and that at another critical juncture in Israel's history, God listened to the prayers of a desperate childless woman (Hannah) in the sanctuary and granted her a son as well (Samuel) (1 Sm 1:1–20; cf. Jgs 13:2–25)."[19]

Mary's announcement, however, is completely unheard of. As Spencer explains, "The bombshell 'virgin birth' announcement that Gabriel drops on Mary has no biblical prototype for her to consider. Long-suffering barren women might miraculously conceive, but they still need a male sexual partner; virgins who do not 'know a man' are, by definition, childless. More so than Zechariah, then, Mary might be forgiven for asking Gabriel for clarification."[20] Her question, moreover, is substantively different from Zechariah's. Zechariah doubts, whereas Mary asks how this birth will be. "Her query is about process, not proof."[21]

With these details about the pre-Annunciation Mary in mind, let's now turn our attention to Gabriel's announcement to Mary by focusing on the very first word the angel speaks to her: "Hail!" or, as we shall see, "Rejoice!"

Chapter Two

"Rejoice!"—Mary as Daughter Zion
(Luke 1:28)

Just one word can tell us a lot about Mary. Consider the very first word spoken to her in the Bible. The angel Gabriel appears to Mary and says, "Hail" (Lk 1:28).

At first glance, that doesn't appear very significant. After all, how much meaning can be found in a simple greeting? But the word here in Greek, *chaire*, literally is a command that means "rejoice." And, as we will see, this is no simple "hello." For those in tune with the Hebrew Scriptures, Gabriel's addressing her in this way would bring to mind the mysterious Daughter Zion figure of the Old Testament and signal that prophecy is coming to fulfillment and God is coming to Israel as King.

In the Old Testament, Daughter Zion is a symbolic figure representing the faithful remnant of God's people. Zion itself was the name given to the citadel of Jerusalem that King David took from the Jebusites (2 Sm 5:6–9), and the term eventually described the whole city (Ps 125:1–2, 147:12; Is 1:27). In the prophetic books, the expression "Daughter Zion" came to be used figuratively as a poetic personification of Jerusalem and the faithful people of Israel who were

13

awaiting the messianic age (Zep 3:14–15; Zec 9:9; or "sons of Zion" in Joel 2:23). The prophecies foretold how the Lord one day would invite Zion to rejoice because the Lord, the King, will liberate the people from their enemies.

The fact that Gabriel addresses Mary with the command to rejoice (*chaire*) is significant. In the earliest Greek translation of the Old Testament (known as the Septuagint), this exact same command (*chaire*) is used in Zephaniah 3:14 and Zechariah 9:9 to call Daughter Zion to share in the future joy that will come when God arrives as King to rescue his people. The only other two places where the word *chaire* is found is in Joel 2:21 and Lamentations 4:21, where in both cases the theme of Zion rejoicing is also in the background.[1]

In Your Womb

First, consider the prophecy in Zephaniah 3:14–15. The prophet commands the people represented by Daughter Zion to rejoice (*chaire*) in the Lord, the King, coming in her midst (literally, "within your walls") to take away their judgment and free them from their enemies:

> Sing aloud, O daughter of Zion;
>   shout, O Israel!
> Rejoice and exult with all your heart,
>   O daughter of Jerusalem!
> The LORD has taken away the judgments against you,
>   he has cast out your enemies.
> The King of Israel, the LORD is in your midst;
>   you shall fear evil no more.

Notice the many striking parallels between what is said to Daughter Zion in Zephaniah 3 and what Gabriel says to Mary in Luke 1. Just as Zephaniah's prophecy summons Daughter Zion to joy, so Gabriel calls Mary to rejoice (Lk 1:28). Just as Zephaniah describes the closeness of God's presence ("the

LORD is in your midst") so does Gabriel, saying to Mary, "The Lord is with you" (Lk 1:28). Zephaniah assures Zion to "fear evil no more," and Gabriel similarly encourages Mary, saying, "Do not be afraid" (Lk 1:30). And Zephaniah foretells the coming of the King of Israel, which is exactly what the angel Gabriel announces is coming to fulfillment in Mary: the King of Israel is coming in the child she will bear (Lk 1:31–33).

These strong connections make one thing clear: Luke wants us to view Mary in light of the Daughter Zion prophecy of Zephaniah 3. Like Daughter Zion, Mary is told to rejoice because the Lord is about to come "in your midst" in the most profound way in history—the Lord is coming within her womb![2] Indeed, this is an important point Luke is picking up on from Zephaniah, because, while the Hebrew word for "in your midst" (*beqirbek*) can mean "within your walls" when it is used in relationship to a city, when the word is applied to a woman (as it is here with Mary) it literally means "in your womb" (cf. Gn 25:23). Hence, Luke reveals Zephaniah's prophecy about the Lord coming in the midst of his people as being fulfilled by the Lord coming in the womb of Mary.[3] In the words of Ignace de la Potterie, Luke presents Mary as "the new city of the presence of God, the eschatological tabernacle of the presence of God among people."[4] Mary, therefore, is being portrayed like Daughter Zion from the prophets. Just as God was expected to come within the walls of Zion, so the Lord is about to dwell within the womb of Mary.

"Your King Comes to You" (Zec 9:9)

Zechariah is another prophet who uses the command *chaire* to invite God's people to rejoice over the king coming to

Jerusalem. He will bring "peace to the nations" and his dominion "to the ends of the earth":

> Rejoice greatly, O daughter of Zion!
>   Shout aloud, O daughter of Jerusalem!
> Behold, your king comes to you;
>   triumphant and victorious is he,
> humble and riding on a donkey,
>   on a colt the foal of a donkey.
> I will cut off the chariot from Ephraim
>   and the war horse from Jerusalem;
> and the battle bow shall be cut off,
>   and he shall command peace to the
>   nations;
> his dominion shall be from sea to sea,
>   and from the River to the ends of the earth. (Zec 9:9–10)

Once again, we can see the parallels with the angel's announcement to Mary here. Just as the prophet Zechariah called Daughter Zion to rejoice over the coming of the King, so the angel Gabriel tells Mary to rejoice, for, as he will soon make clear, the King of Israel is coming to her (Lk 1:31–33). In Gabriel's command for Mary to rejoice, the angel proclaims that the hopes of God's faithful people throughout the centuries—the hopes summed up in these Daughter Zion prophecies—are now coming to fulfillment.

In summary, Zephaniah and Zechariah prophesied that the Lord would one day come to his people as King. On that day, God's faithful people—symbolized by Daughter Zion—will be called to rejoice (*chaire*). For hundreds of years, the Jews longed for these prophecies to be fulfilled. They hungered for the time when they would taste the *joy* of the messianic era. Now, at the Annunciation to Mary, that long-anticipated moment has finally arrived. When Gabriel tells Mary that the Lord, the King, is coming to his people to establish his Kingdom, he opens his message to her with the exact same invitation to joy found in the Daughter Zion prophecies of Zephaniah and Zechariah. Gabriel's initial word in Luke 1:28—*chaire*—heralds the dawn of the messianic age.[5] Indeed, Mary, just as the prophets foretold of Daugther Zion, has much over which to rejoice. As de la Potterie notes, Daughter Zion was given the command to rejoice over the future saving work of God; now, in Luke 1:28, Mary is being given this same command. "The joy which was announced by the prophets in the Old Testament to the people of Israel—the Woman Zion—diffuses itself and comes to be focused on one particular woman, Mary, who unites in her person, so to speak, the desires and the hopes of all the people of Israel."[6]

Chaire: More than Hello?

Not all scholars, however, agree with this line of interpretation. Some view *chaire* in Luke 1:28 not as an invitation to rejoice but as an ordinary greeting and one that does not bring to mind any prophetic texts.[7] It is often pointed out that, although the literal meaning of *chaire* is "rejoice," the word was used as a simple greeting in classical Greek, in the other three Gospels,[8] and elsewhere in the New Testament.[9] Would the original readers of the third Gospel have seen in this word, which ordinarily meant "hello," anything more than an ordinary salutation? This is the question posed by one of the leading English-speaking Catholic biblical scholars of the late twentieth century, Raymond Brown:

> Luke's readers would hear [the word *chaire*] used every day of their lives with the meaning "Hail, hello." If a modern English writer used "Goodbye" in a farewell without any interpretive comment, would his readers recognize that he was giving it its ancient religious value as "God be with you"?[10]

This is a good question. However, we will see that there are good exegetical reasons for concluding that Mary is, in fact, being greeted with an extraordinary call to rejoice over the coming of the King—reminiscent of the way Daughter Zion was called to rejoice. Let's consider four key points.

First, though *chaire* typically does mean simply "hello" in classical Greek and the rest of the New Testament, the way in which Luke's Gospel uses this word is different. For Luke, the context is key: Is it being used in a Greek or Jewish setting? When Luke wants to express an ordinary greeting to a Greek-speaking audience, he uses the Greek word commonly used for this purpose: *chaire*. In fact, the only two occasions in the entirety of Luke-Acts when *chaire* is employed as an ordinary greeting are in non-Jewish contexts: the openings of letters intended for a Greek-speaking audience (Acts 15:23; 23:26).

But in a Jewish milieu, Luke's Gospel never uses *chaire* to express an ordinary greeting. For simple salutations, he instead uses in the background the Hebrew word that serves this purpose (*shalom*), which is translated in Greek as *eirēnē* (Luke 10:5; 24:36).

So, in summary, when Luke wants to express an ordinary greeting, he uses the word *chaire* in Greek settings and *eirēnē* (peace) in Jewish settings. This is what makes his use of the word *chaire* in the Annunciation scene so striking. Mary is not Greek. She's a Jewish woman from the Jewish village of Nazareth. So one would expect Luke to use the word he normally employs for greetings in Jewish settings, *eirēnē*.[11] But the fact that Luke uses the *Greek* greeting *chaire* in Mary's *Jewish* setting is quite surprising—unless Luke had something more in mind than a simple salutation. Along these lines, theologian Joseph Paredes asks, "Why was a

Greek salute used in a Jewish milieu? It would have been more normal to attribute to the angel the Hebrew greeting *shalom* (peace)."[12]

This unusual use of *chaire* has led Paredes and numerous others to conclude that it is not meant to be taken merely as an ordinary greeting in Luke 1:28. Rather, the use of *chaire* in this Jewish context indicates that it should be interpreted literally as an invitation to rejoice—and one that recalls the prophets' call for Daughter Zion to rejoice over the coming of the King.[13]

The Threefold Pattern

But, second, there is much more to the connections between Gabriel's greeting and the Daughter Zion prophecies than just the one word, *chaire*. As Protestant New Testament commentators John Nolland and Joel Green have pointed out, the words the angel uses to address Mary follow the same threefold formulaic pattern found in these Daughter Zion texts: *chaire* + address + divine action as the cause of joy.[14] This threefold pattern can be summed up as follows:

1. First, there is the *call to rejoice* (the command *chaire*).

2. Second, this is followed by *an address*:

Luke 1:28	"full of grace" (*kecharitōmenē*)
Zephaniah 3:14	"daughter of Zion"
Zechariah 9:9	"daughter of Zion"
Joel 2:23	"sons of Zion"
Lamentations 4:21	"daughter of Edom"

3. Finally, a *divine attitude or action is mentioned as the reason for rejoicing*. We can see this in the

three Daughter Zion prophecies that most closely relate to Luke's Annunciation account:

In Zephaniah 3:14–15, the basis for rejoicing is that the Lord, the King, is in their midst, coming to remove their judgment and cast out their enemies.

In Zechariah 9:9–10, the reason for rejoicing is that their King is coming to them to bring peace to the nations and establish his reign to the ends of the earth.

In Joel 2:23–24, the reason for rejoicing is that the Lord is vindicating his people, ending the curse of drought and famine, and blessing the people with rain and a great harvest.[15]

Similarly, Gabriel calls Mary to rejoice because "the Lord is with [her]" (Luke 1:28).

It is, therefore, not only the command *chaire* that links Luke 1:28 with these Old Testament prophetic texts calling Zion to rejoice. The threefold pattern of *chaire* + address + divine action as the cause of joy in Luke 1:28 is also found in the only Old Testament passages where the command *chaire* is found—passages in which *chaire* clearly serves as more than a simple greeting, for these passages invite God's people to rejoice in God's saving action.

Royal Rejoicing

A third reason for viewing *chaire* in Luke 1:28 as reminiscent of the Daughter Zion oracles is that this interpretation fits with the many royal messianic themes in the Annunciation scene. We've seen how the Daughter Zion prophecies centered on rejoicing over the coming of the Lord as King. This exact same theme is emphasized in Luke's account of the angel's announcement to Mary. Luke underscores how Mary is not called to rejoice simply because she's having

a baby, but because her child will be the long-awaited
Messiah-King. As Gabriel goes on to describe, her child is
the one who will be given the "throne of his father David"
(1:32), who will "reign over the house of Jacob for ever"
and whose "kingdom" will have "no end" (1:33)—in other
words, the one who will fulfill the promises God made to
Israel about the everlasting kingdom.[16] This is great cause for
rejoicing, indeed! So if one of the main messages in Luke's
Annunciation scene is that Mary will be the mother of the
Messiah-King, interpreting *chaire* in 1:28 as evoking the
Daughter Zion prophecies fits nicely with this theme. Like
Daughter Zion of old, Mary herself is called to rejoice in the
coming of the King (Zep 3:14–15; Zec 9:9), the King who will
come to dwell in her womb.[17]

Luke's Theme of Joy

A fourth reason for interpreting *chaire* in Luke 1:28 as
"rejoice" is that it also fits with the theme of joy throughout
Luke's Gospel and specifically in the infancy narrative (1:14,
47, 58; 2:10). In fact, the other two birth announcements in
Luke's Gospel—the annunciations to Zechariah and to the
shepherds in Bethlehem—include the theme of joy (1:14;
2:10). If *chaire* in Luke 1:28 is viewed merely as an ordinary
greeting and not as a call to rejoice, the Annunciation
to Mary would be the only birth announcement in Luke
1–2 without the theme of joy. And that would not seem
fitting since Mary has much more cause for rejoicing than
Zechariah or the shepherds do, for she is not simply called
to rejoice over the coming of the Messiah to Israel, but his
coming in her womb.

In conclusion, Luke's Gospel clearly associates Mary with
the exalted "Daughter Zion" of the Old Testament. The joy

announced by the prophets that would come to Daughter Zion is now focused on a single person, Mary. In the words of George Montague, Daughter Zion is "no longer a personification, but a person."[18] Mary stands as Daughter Zion, representing the faithful people of God, being called to rejoice—for the Lord is in her midst. How fitting it is that she who represents God's people is the one who will receive the Lord, the King, coming to dwell in her womb.

Chapter Three

"Full of Grace"
(Luke 1:28)

Gabriel's second word to Mary—traditionally translated "full of grace"—is also packed with rich meaning. It gives us a window into a profound spiritual gift God gave her.

The word in Greek is *kecharitōmenē*, which is related to the verb that means "to grace" or "to favor" or even "to make graced" (*charitoun*). The particular form of this word (a perfect passive participle) describes an action that began in the past and continues to have its effects in the present. As such, *kecharitōmenē* could be translated "you who have been and continue to be graced."[1] This indicates that Mary already had been graced by God, sometime before the angel appeared to her. Gabriel thus refers not to a grace she is going to possess in the future, but to a grace she already has received and continues to experience.

But what is the significance of this grace for Mary? While there are a wide variety of interpretations,[2] for simplicity's sake, we will focus on two general approaches to understanding Mary's being graced in Luke 1:28. On one hand, some conclude that the word *kecharitōmenē* points to an internal reality, to Mary's personal holiness and the life

23

of God dwelling in her soul. On the other hand, some argue that Mary being graced is something only exterior, describing the way God looks upon her with favor, or something primarily functional—a favor God bestows on Mary because she is chosen to be the Mother of the Messiah.

Most interpreters today view *kecharitōmenē* in the merely external or functional way: as referring to the favor God gives to Mary for her maternal mission, not something pointing to her personal holiness. This is why *kecharitōmenē* in Luke 1:28 is sometimes translated "favored one."Along these lines, Brown, in his work *The Birth of the Messiah*, held that translating *kecharitōmenē* as "full of grace" is "too strong." According to Brown, the word refers to the grace or favor of being chosen to be the mother of God's Son, "the grace of conceiving the Son of the Most High."[3] He later concludes, "The favor of God presupposes and is directly oriented to the conception that is about to take place. *Speculation about what other elements might have been present in the favoring of Mary by God is beyond any detectable Lucan interest.*"[4]

But we will see that there are good reasons to conclude that Luke did, in fact, intend for his readers to consider the special grace given to Mary. For Luke, Mary's grace is not just functional, but also personal. It's not just about how God views her with favor, but points to the spiritual effect this grace has upon her. Certainly, this grace must be seen in relationship to her unique vocation as the Mother of God's Son, but this does not mean Luke has no interest at all in drawing attention to the significance this grace has for Mary herself. As we will see, there is, indeed, "detectable Lucan interest" in the special privilege given to Mary.

Let's consider five ways in which this can be seen.

What's in a Name?

We can begin to see this first in the fact that the word Luke uses, *kecharitōmenē*, is in the passive voice. Since passive verbs draw attention to the effect of an act on the recipient, Luke's use of the passive here draws the reader's attention to the impact of God's action in Mary's life and invites us to ponder what it means for her.[5]

Second, the angel Gabriel addresses Mary not with her personal name, but with the word *kecharitōmenē*. Thus, *kecharitōmenē* functions as a new name for Mary.[6] And that in itself is significant. In Scripture, a name expresses the essence of the person.[7] Therefore, *kecharitōmenē* is not just a nickname or title for Mary. It tells us something important about who she is. She is being revealed as someone who has been and continues to be graced. As François Rossier explains, "There is no question of 'a secondary' reality, one that would have touched her only ulteriorly. Rather, it pertains to the very identity of Mary."[8]

Along these lines, no one else in all of Scripture is given the name *kecharitōmenē*. Only Mary is addressed with this exalted title. So when Luke 1:28 is read in light of the whole of Scripture, it becomes clear that Mary stands out in all of salvation history, underscoring the unique divine favor bestowed on her.[9] As Origen concluded, "Because the angel greeted Mary with new expressions, which I have never encountered elsewhere in the Scriptures, it is necessary to comment on this. I do not, in fact, recall having read in any other place in the Sacred Scriptures: *Rejoice, O Full of Grace*. Neither of these expressions is ever addressed to a man: such a special greeting was reserved only for Mary."[10]

Transformation

Third, *kecharitōmenē* is a type of verb in Greek called a causative verb—which usually indicates a change or transformation in the one acted upon.[11] Other similar verbs such as "to bind," "to set free," and "to enslave" imply a change in the one receiving the action. Luke's use of the causative in 1:28 indicates, therefore, that he likely has more in mind than the mere fact that God looks upon Mary with favor or that Mary is favored because she has been chosen to be the Mother of the Son of God. It points to how Mary is being personally impacted by God gracing her, for the causative verb *kecharitōmenē* suggests that Mary has been changed by this grace.

Fourth, and most significantly, the Letter to the Ephesians describes the type of impact this grace has on people's lives. In the only other instance when the New Testament uses the verb *charitóô*, it describes a profound transformation in people's souls. Besides Luke 1:28, the only other New Testament text where this rare verb is used is in the hymn introducing the Letter to the Ephesians, a passage with strong salvific and ecclesiological resonances.[12]

> He destined us in love to be his sons through Jesus Christ, according to the purpose of his will, to the praise of his glorious grace which he freely bestowed (*echaritōsen*) on us in the Beloved. In him we have redemption through his blood, the forgiveness of our trespasses, according to the riches of his grace which he lavished upon us. (Eph 1:5–8)

Notice the saving impact on the Ephesian Christians being graced. They are described as having "redemption" and "forgiveness of [their] trespasses" (1:6–7). Indeed, the verb is associated with the saving, transforming power of grace that makes Christians adopted children of God who are redeemed and forgiven of their sins.[13] By being called *kecharitōmenē,* Mary is being depicted as someone who has already experienced a grace similar to what the Christians in Ephesians 1:6 did—someone who has the life of redemption and has become a child of God.

One important difference, however, between the use of this verb in Ephesians 1:6 and its use in Luke 1:28 is that Luke employs the perfect participle form, *kecharitōmenē,* in reference to Mary—a form that indicates an action that began in the past and continues to have its effects in the present. Therefore, Luke 1:28 is not simply noting that Mary is transformed by grace. Luke is underscoring how Mary *already had been* transformed by God's grace, *even before* Gabriel appeared to her at the Annunciation. In other words, the Bible reveals that the life-transforming grace that brings forgiveness of sins and redemption in Ephesians 1:6–7 is something Mary already received even before the Annunciation.[14] As theologian Paul Haffner explains, "'Kecharitomene' signifies then, in the person to whom the verb relates, that is, Mary, that the action of the grace of God has already brought about a change ... that Mary has been transformed by the grace of God. The perfect passive participle is used by Luke to indicate that the transformation by grace has already taken place in Mary, well before the moment of the Annunciation."[15]

The Graced One

Fifth, the angel says to Mary: *chaire kecharitōmenē*—Rejoice, graced one! This suggests that the grace envisioned in 1:28 should not be seen exclusively as the favor of the divine maternity, but as a cause for joy in itself. This suggests that the angel tells Mary to rejoice because she already possesses a unique grace—one that is given before her role as the Mother of God's Son begins and before her privileged motherhood is even mentioned.[16]

It is no wonder, then, that the Church throughout the centuries has turned to this verse when discussing Mary's Immaculate Conception—the doctrine that Mary was conceived "full of grace," without Original Sin. Though the beautiful word *kecharitōmenē* would not definitively prove this doctrine—(it doesn't mean "you who have been *conceived* full of grace")—it does point to the unique gift of grace that God gives Mary in preparing her to carry the Son of God in her womb and a gift that Mary already possesses even before the angel appears to her ("you who have been graced"). In this way, the angel's greeting Mary with the word *kecharitōmenē* offers a profound window into the utterly unique and profound gift of grace in her soul. God blesses her with his grace in a way no human person has been blessed before as he prepares her to become the Mother of his Son.

Chapter Four

The Mother of the Messiah
(Luke 1:28–33)

After his initial greeting to Mary, the angel Gabriel delivers three important messages to her in Luke 1:28–31. Each statement brings to mind various Old Testament heroes, prophecies, themes, and hopes. And each signals to Mary that God is entrusting her with a crucial mission in his plan of salvation.

Here are the three things Gabriel tells Mary in these verses:

1. "The Lord is with you" (1:28);

2. "You have found favor with God" (1:30); and

3. "You will conceive in your womb and bear a son, and you shall call his name Jesus . . . and the Lord God will give to him the throne of his father David . . . and of his kingdom there will be no end" (1:31–33).

Let's unpack the meaning of these three statements to see how they shed important light on Mary's vocation to be the Mother of Israel's Messiah-King.

What's the Trouble?

After the angel's initial greeting, Mary is described as being "greatly troubled" (Lk 1:29). At first glance, we might assume Mary is "greatly troubled" because she suddenly encounters an angel. After all, if you were in your house and an archangel appeared to you out of the blue, you would probably be greatly troubled, too!

But that's not what Luke's Gospel is drawing our attention to. Luke is careful to state that Mary was greatly troubled "at the *saying*" (*epi tō logō*) of the angel and she "considered in her mind what sort of *greeting* this might be" (Lk 1:29). In other words, Mary is more troubled over the angel's words than the angel's presence.[1] This is why she is pondering in her mind not what kind of being is appearing to her, but "what sort of *greeting* this might be."

But many modern readers may wonder, What is so alarming about the angel's greeting that it would make her troubled?

"The Lord Is with You" (1:28)

Part of Mary's trepidation may be caused by the angel saying to her, "The Lord is with you." This is no ordinary greeting. These words and other similar assurances of God's presence are given many times throughout the Old Testament to people whom God is calling to a great mission, one in which the future of Israel is dependent on how well they will play their role.

God, for example, tells Isaac "I am with you" when assuring the patriarch that he will be blessed with a multitude of descendants (Gn 26:24). God gives the same message to Jacob—"I am with you"—when promising that he will return to his land after fleeing from his brother Esau (Gn 28:15).

Other great heroes of Israel, such as Moses, Joshua, and Gideon, were assured that the Lord would be with them when God called them to lead the people and defend them from their enemies (Ex 3:12; Jos 1:5, 9; Jgs 6:16). David was assured of God's presence with him at the beginning of his dynasty (2 Sm 7:9), and Jeremiah heard these words at the start of his prophetic ministry (Jer 1:8).

All throughout the Old Testament, the message is clear. The expression "the Lord is with you" is used when God summons someone to a formidable task in his saving plan. The person is going to be stretched like never before and will need to rely on God like never before. That's why God or the angel offers the divine assurance that they are not alone in their mission: "The Lord is with you." As one New Testament scholar explains, "This expression *does not define a static presence, but a dynamic power*—The saying 'the Lord is with thee' takes away fear and gives strength." In the context of the Annunciation to Mary, "its effect is blessing for Mary, the people, the world."[2]

So when Gabriel says to Mary, "The Lord is with you," he's saying a lot. He's signaling to her that she is standing in the footsteps of Isaac, Jacob, Moses, Joshua, Gideon, and Jeremiah. Like the heroes of old, Mary is now being called to some great mission in God's plan of salvation.[3] She doesn't know just yet what her mission is, but she would know something big is about to be asked of her. No wonder she is "greatly troubled" (Lk 1:29)!

Fearless Woman

Luke's simple comment that Mary "considered" in her mind the angel's greeting (1:29) tells us something beautiful about her interior response. The word is *dielogizeto*, which comes from the Greek root word meaning "dialogue." It implies a deeper, prolonged pondering, and one that leads to fervent faith.

Though Mary may be troubled by the angel's greeting, she rises above her initial emotional reaction. She does not allow her feelings of being "greatly troubled" to control her and turn her away from what the Lord might be asking of her. Rather, she engages in an interior dialogue with the Word, seeking to understand the Lord's message to her. As troubled as she is, she still remains in dialogue with God's Word.[4]

As Ratzinger explains, "Mary appears as a fearless woman, one who remains composed even in the presence of something utterly unprecedented. At the same time she stands before us as a woman of great interiority, who holds heart and mind in harmony and seeks to understand the context, the overall significance of God's message."[5] We as readers also ponder the meaning and wonder with great anticipation what the Lord intends to do with this young virgin of Nazareth.

"Do Not Be Afraid . . . You Have Found Favor with God" (Lk 1:30)

The angel's next words, "Do not be afraid" (*me phobou*), only add to the suspense. On several occasions in the Bible, the expression is accompanied by the assurance that God is present with the person being addressed.[6] God told Abraham, "Fear not, Abram, I am your shield," when assuring him of his protection and promise to bless Abraham with a great multitude of descendants (Gn 15:1–8). The Lord similarly told Isaac, "I am the God of Abraham your father; fear not, for I am with you and will bless you," when assuring him of the promises made to his family (Gn 26:24). God told the people of Israel as a whole to have no fear because God was with them and they would be rescued from captivity and brought back to the land (Jer 30:10–11; 46:28). Like Abraham, Isaac, and Israel, Mary is now being assured that the Lord is with her and that she is not to be afraid.

Gabriel goes on to give a very significant reason *why* Mary should not fear: she has found "favor with God" (1:30). In the Old Testament, the Lord's favor points to his choice of someone through whom he will accomplish some important work: Noah is spared from the flood and will be the start of a renewed human family (Gn 6:8). Gideon defends Israel against the Midianites (Jgs 6:17). Hannah conceives Samuel in her barrenness (1 Sm 1:18). David gets back the Ark of the Covenant (2 Sm 15:25).[7]

The most important background for understanding what it means to "find favor" in someone's sight is found in the story of the Old Testament hero, Joseph. There, the expression describes how Joseph was viewed as the kind of person who could be entrusted with great responsibility. When Joseph was a slave in Egypt, he "found favor" in his master's sight and was elevated to overseer of Potiphar's house, managing his day-to-day affairs. The book of Genesis says Potiphar "left all that he had in Joseph's charge; and having him he had no concern for anything but the food which he ate" (Gn 39:4–6). Similarly, when Joseph was in prison, he found "favor in the sight of the keeper of the prison" and the keeper "committed to Joseph's care all the prisoners who were in the prison; and whatever was done there, he was the doer of it; the keeper of the prison paid no heed to anything that was in Joseph's care" (Gn 39:21–23). This gives us a sense of what it means for someone to "find favor" in someone else's sight in Scripture. When Joseph found favor in the eyes of his master or the keeper of the prison, that means he was viewed by them with great confidence and trust. Important responsibilities could be entrusted to him.

This tells us much about the significance of Gabriel's words to Mary: "You have found favor with God."[8] This statement not only puts her on par with some of the greatest heroes of the Old Testament, but it also tells us that God is willing to entrust a lot into her care. Like the Old Testament patriarch Joseph, Mary will be given a tremendous responsibility. Indeed, as the narrative will soon reveal, God views her with such favor that he even is willing to entrust his own Son to her.

Mother of the Son of David

What Gabriel unveils next is Mary's mission. She will become a mother. Gabriel says to her, "You will conceive in your womb and bear a son, and you shall call his name Jesus" (Lk 1:30).

But that's not all. Gabriel also announces that Mary will be the mother not of any ordinary child, but of the long-awaited Messiah-King! Indeed, Gabriel describes Mary's child in several ways that recall the promises God gave to David about his everlasting dynasty.

First, Gabriel tells Mary that her child will be called "Son of the Most High" (1:32)—a title that has royal overtones. Since "Most High" was a title for God in the Old Testament[9] and a common divine title in Luke as well,[10] the description of Jesus as "Son of the Most High" would indicate that he is the Son of God[11]—a likely allusion to the Old Testament designation of the Davidic king as God's Son.[12] In this light, Luke's description of Jesus as "Son of the Most High" recalls Nathan's oracle (2 Sm 7:14) and the royal psalms (Ps 2:7; 89:26–27), which both depict the Davidic king possessing a special filial relationship with God.

Second, we can see this even more clearly in the following verses, which offer more direct connections to the promises made to King David and thus bring more attention to Jesus's messianic identity:

> And the Lord will give to him the throne of his father David, and he will reign over the house of Jacob for ever; and of his kingdom there will be no end. (Lk 1:32–33)

Consider the many clear parallels between Luke 1:32–33 and the promises God made to King David in 2 Samuel 7:9–16. Both passages mention a great name, a throne, divine sonship, a house, and a kingdom.[13] That's why Brown can easily demonstrate how Gabriel's words are a "free interpretation" of the oracle of Nathan, which became the foundation for Jewish messianic hopes.[14] He neatly lays out these parallels as follows:

Luke 1	Samuel 7
"He will be great, and will be called Son of the Most High" (v. 32a)	"I will make for you a great name" (v. 9)
"and the Lord God will give him the throne of his father David" (v. 32b)	"I will establish the throne of his kingdom for ever" (v. 13)
"and he will reign over the house of Jacob forever" (v. 33a)	"I will be his father, and he shall be my son" (v. 14)
"and of his kingdom there will be no end" (v. 33b)	"And your house and your kingdom shall be made sure for ever" (v. 16)[15]

With these many allusions to the promises in 2 Samuel 7, Gabriel is clearly presenting Mary's child as the new Davidic King, the one fulfilling the hopes associated with the Davidic dynasty.

Mother of Immanuel

Finally, we also may find an allusion to the Immanuel prophecy of Isaiah 7:14 in this passage, where the angel says to Mary, "And behold, you will conceive in your womb and bear a son, and you shall call his name Jesus" (Lk 1:31). In his work *The Mother of Jesus in the New Testament*, John McHugh argues that this verse is "a virtual citation of the Greek text of Is 7:14"[16]—only the child's name is substantially different (Immanuel versus Jesus). Consider this prophecy from Isaiah in its context:

> Again the LORD spoke to Ahaz, "Ask a sign of the LORD your God; let it be deep as Sheol or high as heaven." But Ahaz said, "I will not ask, and I will not put the LORD to the test." And he said, "Hear then, O house of David! Is it too little for you to weary men, that you weary my God also? Therefore the Lord himself will give you a sign. Behold, a virgin shall conceive and bear a son, and shall call his name Immanuel. He shall eat curds and honey when he knows how to refuse the evil and choose the good. For before the child knows how to refuse the evil and choose the good, the land before whose two kings you are in dread will be deserted. The LORD will bring upon you and upon your people and upon your father's house such days as have not come since the day that Ephraim departed from Judah—the king of Assyria." (Isaiah 7:10–17)

The connections between this prophecy in Isaiah 7 and Luke's account of the announcement to Mary are strong. Joseph Fitzmyer lists seven possible parallels, which can be summed up in the following chart:

Isaiah 7:	Luke 1:
"Hear then, O house of David" (v. 13)	"Joseph, of the house of David" (v. 27)
"Ask a sign of *the Lord*" (v. 10)	"*The Lord* God will give" (v. 32)
"A virgin" (v. 14)	"A virgin" (v. 27)
"Shall conceive" (v. 14)	"Will conceive" (v. 31)
"And bear a son" (v. 14)	"And bear a son" (v. 31)
"Shall call his name" (v. 14)	"Shall call his name" (v. 31)
"The Lord will bring upon … your father's house" (v. 17)	"He will be king over the House" (v. 32)[17]

In addition to these parallels, Joel Green points out one more: Gabriel's greeting "the Lord is with you" echoes the name of the prophesied child in Isaiah 7:14, "Immanuel" (meaning, "God with us").[18] This is why Green and others conclude that Luke is alluding to Isaiah 7:14: "The conjunction of so many points of correspondence between the Gabriel-Mary encounter and Isa 7:10–17 cannot help but produce an echo effect."[19] New Testament scholar Mark Strauss makes a similar point, noting how Luke's description of Mary as a "virgin" (*parthenon*) (Lk 1:27, 34; cf. Is 7:14), his reference to the "son of David" (Lk 1:27; Is 7:13), and his including the greeting "the Lord is *with you*" (Lk 1:28; cf. Is 7:14, "Immanuel")—"all in the context of Davidic expectations— suggest that Luke indeed had Isa 7.14 in mind."[20] We can conclude with confidence, therefore, that in Luke's account of this scene, Mary is being told that she will bear the promised Immanuel child, the one prophesied by Isaiah.

Mother of the Messiah

Think of all that the angel Gabriel has told Mary in just a few verses. "The Lord is with you" signals that she is being called by God to some important mission. "You have found favor with God" indicates that God is entrusting great responsibility to her. Her child being called "Son of the Most High," sitting on "the throne of his father David," and having a kingdom that will have no end reveal that her mission involves becoming the mother not of any ordinary child, but of Israel's long-awaited Messiah-King. Indeed, Mary's vocation is to become the Mother of the Immanuel child prophesied by Isaiah. She is the one "who will conceive and bear a son" and who "shall call his name Immanuel" (Is 7:14).

But there is still more to come. Mary asks an important practical question, which we will consider next: "How will this be, since I do not know man?" (Lk 1:34). This question gives us two important insights. First, it prompts Gabriel to reveal something even more amazing about Mary's child—that he is not only Israel's King, but also the holy Son of God who comes from the Spirit and power of God (Lk 1:35). (We will explore this in chapter 6.) Second, the question itself tells us something about Mary and the extraordinary commitment to virginity she must have had, which we will consider next.

Chapter Five

The Mystery of Mary's Question
(Luke 1:34)

"How will this be, since I do not know man?" (Lk 1:34).

Most scholars admit that Mary's question is quite surprising. In response to Gabriel's message that she will conceive a child, Mary raises the concern that she does not "know" man. To appreciate the perplexing nature of her question, two points must be noted.

First, in the Old Testament, "to know" is a euphemism for sexual relations, as when Genesis says, "Adam knew Eve his wife" (Gn 4:1). Second, Mary is a betrothed woman. As we saw in chapter 1, Mary at this point would be bound to Joseph in marriage but still on her way toward the second stage known as the "taking home," which is when a couple starts living together and engaging in sexual relations.[1]

It is for this reason that Mary's question—"How will this be, since I do not know man?" (1:34)—is so puzzling. Why would a betrothed woman object to being told that sometime in the future she will conceive a child?[2] After all, bearing children is usually what happened when betrothed couples reached the "taking home" stage and started engaging in marital intercourse! If Mary were an ordinary Jewish betrothed woman, this message about having a baby in the future should not cause such bewilderment. It's true that she may not at the present moment "know" man, but once she is living with Joseph, it generally would be expected that she would "know" her husband sexually at that time. So if Mary was intending eventually to consummate her marriage, as any ordinary betrothed woman in her day would, why would she ask this question?

Various solutions have been offered, but there are two that have gained more widespread support in recent scholarship. One interpretation views Mary's question as merely a *literary device*. In this view, Luke the storyteller invents Mary's question and inserts it into his narrative in order to give Gabriel the natural opportunity to talk about how the Virgin Mary will conceive her child by the power of the Holy Spirit.[3]

A second interpretation holds that Mary understood the angel's message to imply *an immediate conception*. She thinks the angel is telling her that she will conceive the child right away—before her period of betrothal ends—and she questions how that could happen since she has not yet reached the "taking home" stage of her marriage to Joseph.[4] Since Mary, as a betrothed woman, does not yet "know" man, she wonders how becoming pregnant is possible at this moment.

We will weigh these two interpretations, which are common among scholars today. Then we will consider a third approach, held by numerous Church Fathers, saints, and Doctors of the Church, which may help us better understand the meaning of Mary's question.

Just a Literary Device?

First, let's look at the *literary device view*. At the foundation of this approach is a resistance to what some scholars call "psychological" explanations—interpretations of 1:34 that assume Luke's account is interested in presenting what Mary was thinking "as if it were meant to explain how she gained a knowledge of the way in which her child was conceived."[5] Brown, for example, argues that Luke's main concern is not to get into the mind of the historical Mary (what she was thinking about at this moment), but to inform "*the reader* about how the child was conceived and hence to explain his identity."[6] In this perspective, Mary's question is simply a literary device invented by the evangelist to help make some theological points that are important for his readers to know. We are not meant to ponder what the question meant for Mary herself, but how the question Luke places on her lips helps communicate the theological messages he wants to pass on through his story.

It's argued that one purpose of Mary's question is to draw attention to her virginity again and thus emphasize the amazing miracle that will soon take place: the child will not be conceived in the normal human way through marital intercourse but by the Holy Spirit while Mary remains a virgin. From a literary standpoint, Mary's question helps break up the angel's message and gives Gabriel a narrative prompt, an "opening," to explain how the child will be conceived through the power of God (1:35).[7] Together, Mary's question in 1:34 and the angel's answer in 1:35 underscore the divine origins of the child: the child is not just the royal son of David; he is the divine Son of God, conceived in the Virgin Mary's womb by the power of the Holy Spirit. As Brown explains:

> Mary is a spokeswoman for Luke's christological message even as Gabriel is a spokesman; and between them they fill in the picture of the Messiah's conception as God's Son, a conception not through marital intercourse (Mary's contribution) but through the Holy Spirit (Gabriel's contribution).[8]

A second reason some say Luke inserts Mary's question into his account is to show how this scene fits the birth announcement pattern found throughout the Bible. When an angel or the Lord himself appears to someone to announce a birth, the person responds by either raising an objection or requesting a sign.[9] This is what Abraham, Samson's parents, and Zechariah did when they received a heavenly announcement that they would miraculously be blessed with a child playing a key role in God's plan of salvation. Luke is aware of this typical scriptural pattern and wants to frame Gabriel's birth announcement around it. So he creates Mary's question and inserts it into his account of the Annunciation in order to place the scene within this framework. Her question is not meant to be part of a "biographical account" of Mary, but is simply an added literary element to show how this scene should be read in light of the basic birth announcement pattern in Scripture.[10]

The supposed benefit of this line of interpretation is that it avoids all "psychological" explanations in favor of a literary one. Once we see Mary's question merely as a literary device created by Luke, the bewildering aspects of why a betrothed woman like Mary would raise concerns about someday conceiving a child evaporate. What Mary's question meant for her personally is not something that should concern the reader. The question is simply a literary tool that helps underscore how the child will not be conceived through sexual relations and gives the angel the opportunity to explain the child's divine origins in 1:35.[11]

But the Question Must Still Make Sense

There are, however, significant challenges with this approach, as New Testament scholar Jane Schaberg notes. Though her own interpretation of this passage is problematic,[12] Schaberg's critique of the so-called "literary" interpretation is particularly insightful. She argues that it actually fails to be a *literary* explanation in the end because it fails to make sense of the narrative itself.

Here's a brief summary of her argument. First, Schaberg critiques the opposition to *all* "psychological" solutions. She notes that a crucial part of interpreting any narrative is reconstructing the psychology of the characters in it. Readers naturally wonder why they do what they do and why they say what they say.

Thus, in Luke 1:34, it is important to consider "the psychology of Mary, a character in the narrative." Why would Mary—as a key person in Luke's drama—ask the question she asks? When a character in a story asks another character a question, readers should expect that the question makes some sense within the logical flow of the narrative. Scholars who say Mary's question in 1:34 is a mere literary device still need to explain how her question makes sense within the unfolding storyline. "To read Mary's question as only a 'literary necessity' in the way that has been suggested is to read it . . . as literary nonsense."[13] Therefore, it simply will not do to say that Luke inserted an unintelligible question into his account in order to serve his Christological message. Mary's question in Luke 1:34—no matter what other theological purposes it might have—should still make sense within the flow of the story.

Nor is it sufficient to say that Luke inserted Mary's question in order to fit the birth announcement pattern found in the Jewish Scriptures. Mary's words certainly bring to mind the objections people in the Old Testament made when a birth was announced to them. But this does not mean her question can be just a random one that doesn't make any logical sense in Luke's account. After all, the question is not only a part of a biblical annunciation pattern; when found in Luke's narrative, it is also an essential part of Luke's own storyline and must be intelligible there as well.[14] David Landry, commenting on this point of Schaberg's argument, explains further:

> [E]ven though it is true that Luke is following a formal pattern here, it is simply not true that the use of formal patterns allowed or obliged authors to include material in their narratives that disrupts the narrative logic of the story. Luke seldom "ruins" the harmony of his narrative out of deference to the requirements of a "form." In other words, even where formal patterns can be detected, the story should make sense as a story to the reader, and readers should attempt to make sense of the story insofar as this is possible.[15]

Imminent Conception View

This leads us to consider a second mainstream explanation of 1:34 that has gained much support in modern scholarship—an interpretation that takes more seriously how Mary's question fits into the logical flow of Luke's account. According to the *imminent conception view*, Mary understood the angel's message as referring to a conception that will take place in the immediate future and she wonders how this can be since she is still in the betrothal period when she did not know Joseph yet.

New Testament scholar David Landry makes a strong case for this position, first by giving evidence from Luke's narrative that shows that the conception did indeed take place quickly. Though the text does not give an explicit timetable, Mary's pregnancy began sometime between Gabriel's appearance to her and her visiting Elizabeth, when Elizabeth describes Mary as "the mother of my Lord" and says to her "blessed is the fruit of your womb" (Lk 1:42–43).

How long was that interval between the conception of Mary's child and her visit to Elizabeth? The Bible doesn't say exactly, but Luke reports Mary went "with haste" to visit Elizabeth, suggesting it was a short period of time. Moreover, Elizabeth is already six months pregnant at Mary's Annunciation (1:37) and Mary stays with her for "about three months" before the birth of John the Baptist is narrated (1:56–57). Since a pregnancy is typically about nine months, that seems to leave little time between the Annunciation and Visitation scenes. Landry concludes: "Readers would likely have thought of the onset of Mary's pregnancy as immediate, seemingly not long enough for the home-taking to have taken place."[16]

This, however, is Landry's first interpretive misstep. It is true that the reader would conclude that Mary's pregnancy began either at or just after the angel's announcement to her. But this conclusion would only be made after one had read the rest of the Annunciation and Visitation scenes. At the reader's *first* encounter with Mary's question in 1:34, however, one most likely would *not* have reached this conclusion. All that the angel has revealed up to this point is that Mary *sometime in the future* will conceive the promised child (1:31–33). No timetable is given as to when this will take place. Thus, the meaning of Mary's question would not yet be apparent. It would be natural for the reader, at least at this point in the narrative, to wonder why Mary, as a betrothed woman, would object to becoming pregnant sometime in the future. Presumably such a conception could easily take place after the "taking home" stage of their marriage began.

Even more problematic for Landry's position is the fact that, even if the *reader* would eventually see that Mary would conceive by the power of the Holy Spirit and that this conception would, in fact, take place in the imminent future, *Mary as a character in the narrative does not know this yet.*

·Here, Landry fails to consider adequately the psychology of Mary as a character precisely at this point of the story unfolding. At this moment in the account, Mary would not have known *when* she was to conceive of the promised child. Nothing in the angel's announcement thus far indicates to her that the conception would be a miraculous virginal conception. And nothing in the angel's message thus far suggests to her that the conception would be immediate. The angel's message so far has been about her becoming the Mother of the Messiah—not about the supernatural way in which this would occur, nor about the *timing* in which this would take place.[17]

In his commentary on Luke's Gospel, New Testament scholar John Nolland notes that the immediate conception view still fails to explain the logic of the text, and he raises an important question: If Mary did interpret the angel as pointing to an immediate conception and did view this as problematic merely because she was not yet at the stage when relations with her husband would begin, why does Mary not say, "I do not *yet* (*outo*) know man"? Instead, she simply states, "I do not know man." Moreover, if Mary were focused on an immediate conception, one might have expected the angel to have said to her, "You will *now* (*arti*) conceive…" in 1:31.[18] But that's not the case. All of the verbs in the angel's message about the child are in the future tense: "You *will* conceive . . . you *shall* call his name Jesus. He *will* be great, and *will* be called . . . the Lord God *will* give to him . . . he *will* reign . . ." After hearing the angel's message in 1:31–33, an ordinary betrothed woman would assume the conception would take place at the "taking home." There is no reason at this point in the story for her to think that the pregnancy will necessarily begin in the imminent future.[19]

Not So Fast

Landry offers a second significant argument to support the imminent conception view. He asserts that the birth annunciations in the Old Testament all proclaim pregnancies that either have already taken place or will take place in the immediate future. Landry concludes that Mary realizes there are no delays between birth announcements and conceptions in the Old Testament—that "annunciations occur after or shortly before the beginning of the pregnancy they announce."[20] Therefore, "Mary clearly sees that, if she was to conceive by Joseph, then the angel would have waited until after the home-taking to present her with this annunciation."[21]

But this is not necessarily the case. While it is true that one Old Testament birth announcement story involves a pregnancy that already had begun (Gn 16:11—Ishmael), it is not clear at all that an immediate conception is an essential part of Old Testament birth announcement scenes. The account of the angel's announcement to Samson's parents is ambiguous on this point (Jgs 13:3, 5, 7, 24). And other birth announcements in the Bible typically describe a future event—with no emphasis on an immediate conception.

Take, for example, the announcement about Isaac's birth. Abraham is first told of his promised descendants in Genesis 12:1–3 and more specifically of the son who would be his heir in Genesis 15:3–6—at least thirteen years before the birth of Isaac. More specifically, Isaac's actual birth is announced to Abraham in Genesis 17:21 as something that will take place "at this season next year." Indeed, there is no indication in this timetable that the conception was to take place right away or in the next few days. It seems that a few weeks or months might pass before the child was conceived.

Furthermore, the Genesis narrative does not indicate that it is trying to emphasize an immediate conception. The narrative allows many episodes to pass before it reports that the Lord visited Sarah and that she conceived Isaac in 21:1–3. This takes place three chapters (and many scenes) after the initial announcement in 17:21. Readers would not walk away with the impression that the conception took place immediately, right after the Lord's message to Abraham, and this certainly is not the kind of account that would create an expectation for readers that all other birth announcements must involve an immediate conception.

We find a similar situation in the Immanuel prophecy of Isaiah 7:14, a text that is directly alluded to by Mary's question in Luke 1:34, where the language is almost identical ("you will conceive . . ."). No immediate conception is emphasized in this announcement of the coming Immanuel child. In fact, the only time frame given in this passage is about when the foreign threat of the Syrian-Samarian alliance will pass—a period described as taking place "before the child knows how to refuse evil and choose the good" (Is 7:14–16). In other words, this is many years down the road, long *after* the child is born.[22]

Therefore, not all birth announcements involve an immediate conception. The evidence from the various texts would not clearly create an expectation for readers (or for Mary) that an essential element of all birth announcements is the conception of the child in the imminent future. So the basic puzzle about Mary's question, "How will this be, since I do not know man?" still remains unsolved: Why would a betrothed woman object to the prospect of someday in the future conceiving a child? That's typically what happened when couples reached the second stage of marriage and began sexual relations.

Another Possibility?

We have seen so far that the two most popular interpretive options for Luke 1:34 in recent scholarship—the so-called literary explanation and the view that Mary is questioning how she could become pregnant as a betrothed woman—do not work. They both fail to explain how Mary's question makes sense within the narrative logic of Luke's account. Let us now turn to a third possibility, which considers insights from a traditional view that Mary had some desire or commitment to remain a virgin.

If Mary were just an ordinary Jewish betrothed woman—planning on consummating her marriage once she reached the "coming together" stage—when would she expect such a pregnancy to take place? In other words, if a betrothed woman in the first century had a prophet inform her that she was going to have a child sometime in the future, when would that woman think it would occur? Presumably, sometime after betrothal—after the coming together, when sexual intercourse was permitted. Spoken to an ordinary betrothed woman, such an announcement about conceiving a child would naturally point to her future married life after consummation.

Thus, Mary's question seems rather peculiar: "How will this be, since I do not know man?" If Mary is planning on consummating her marriage with Joseph in the near future, the answer to her question should be obvious. While she does not *right now* have the power to conceive a child (since she doesn't know man sexually yet), if Mary intends to "know" Joseph after the "coming together," then she evidently *will have the possibility of conceiving a child at that point*. Therefore, *if* Mary is planning on consummating her marriage with Joseph, her question—"How will this be, since I do not know man?"—simply does not make sense.

This is what Denis Farkasfalvy, a theologian serving on the Pontifical Biblical Commission, concludes:

> If Mary is espoused with the intention of entering into sexual relations with Joseph, her objection makes no sense: she would naturally have thought the Angel was speaking of a Child to be born of her relation with Joseph. The text must be allowed to suggest beyond what it directly states. In other words it is unavoidable to perceive the suggestion by Mary's reply to the Angel that she has no intention to consummate her marriage and live with Joseph as his wife.[23]

This is why some Church Fathers and Doctors of the Church have seen in Mary's question an indication that she was *not* intending to consummate her marriage. According to this perspective, Mary raises her question because she has made a decision to remain a virgin throughout her life. This view, advanced in various forms by theologians such as St. Augustine, St. Thomas Aquinas, and St. Bonaventure (and even Martin Luther), explains Mary's question not as one of doubt, but one that seeks clarification as to how she can conceive a child if she has committed herself or desires to commit herself to the Lord in virginity.

One of the earliest proponents of this position, St. Gregory of Nyssa, points out how Mary's question makes no sense on the lips of a betrothed woman—unless she had made some prior commitment to lifelong virginity. After all, why would she ask this question if she was intending to have sexual relations with Joseph?

> For if Joseph had taken her to be his wife, for the purpose of having children, why would she have wondered at the announcement of maternity, since she herself would have accepted becoming a mother according to the law of nature?
>
> But just as it was necessary to guard the body consecrated to God as an untouched and holy offering, for this same reason, she states,

even if you are an angel come down from heaven and even if this phenomenon is beyond man's abilities, yet it is impossible for me to know man. How shall I become a mother without [knowing] man? For though I consider Joseph to be my husband, still I do not know man.[24]

More recently, Pope St. John Paul II drew a similar conclusion, teaching that before the Annunciation, Mary's heart was inclined toward virginity as the Holy Spirit inspired in her a desire for full communion with God as his faithful bride.

Neither the Gospels nor any other New Testament writings tell us when Mary decided to remain a virgin. However, it is clearly apparent from her question to the angel at the time of the annunciation that she had come to a very firm decision. Mary did not hesitate to express her desire to preserve her virginity even in view of the proposed motherhood, showing that her intention had matured over a long period.[25]

"I Do Not Know Man"

According to John McHugh, when Mary's question is seen in this light, her statement about not knowing man further indicates her intention to remain a virgin. He notes how Mary's expression about not "knowing" man is in the present tense, which "reveals the permanence and continuity" of her virginal state. Mary says she does not know man in the sense that she does not *intend* to know man.[26]

To use an analogy: If someone said to me, "You will die of lung cancer in the future" and I replied, "How can this be, since I do not smoke?" my response would not simply describe a present circumstance ("I don't happen to be smoking right now"). Rather, it would indicate a long-term intention on my part to avoid smoking ("Smoking is not something I ever intend to do"). Somewhat analogously, Mary's expression "I do not know man"—when seen in the wider context of the Annunciation account—further suggests her commitment to remain a virgin for the rest of her life.

Why Would Mary Marry?

While Mary's commitment to virginity makes the most sense out of her question, two objections commonly arise. First, some argue that Jews in the first century did not hold up virginity as a religious ideal and that there is no historical evidence for ancient Jewish women taking vows of sexual abstinence. It is also pointed out that the Old Testament highlights being fruitful and multiplying as a blessing; dying a virgin is perceived as something to be bewailed. However, while a commitment to virginity was not mainstream in ancient Judaism, it was not unheard of. The prophet Jeremiah was called by God to remain celibate (cf. Jer 16:1). John the Baptist, Paul, and Jesus himself remained celibate. A Jewish sect known as the Essenes had many members who practiced celibacy and even some married members who practiced sexual abstinence up to three years at a time and refrained from marital intimacy during pregnancy.[27] The first-century Jewish writer Philo of Alexandria tells of another group called the Therapeutae, consisting of some Jewish women who remained virgins by their own choice.[28] Therefore, while virginity may not have been a widespread religious ideal, remaining a virgin in order to dedicate oneself to God was not completely unknown in the first-century Jewish world in which Mary lived. If these others willingly lived lifelong virginity, there's no reason to exclude the possibility of Mary doing so, too.

A second question often raised is "Why would Mary accept betrothal to Joseph if she intended to remain a virgin?" Diverse explanations have been given for this unique marriage. Perhaps, since remaining a single woman was not as socially feasible in the ancient world of Judaism as it is today, marriage would have provided economic stability and social protection for Mary. Perhaps the marriage was arranged. Perhaps marriage would free Mary from other men seeking her hand in marriage and thus protect her vow. Perhaps God led Mary to marriage because in his providence he wanted to protect her reputation for the future, when she would conceive by the Holy Spirit.

Ancient Jewish Vows

One passage from the Jewish Scriptures, however, may shed much light on Mary's commitment to virginity. It comes from the book of Numbers, chapter 30, which is entirely devoted to vows taken by women. In his work *Jesus and the Jewish Roots of Mary*, Brant Pitre argues that this chapter offers historical evidence from the ancient Jewish tradition for vows of sexual abstinence being made by widowed or divorced women, unmarried women, and married women.

Here are the verses that pertain to vows taken by married women:

> "If she is married to a husband, while under her vows or any thoughtless utterance of her lips by which she has bound herself, and her husband hears of it, and says nothing to her on the day that he hears; then her vows shall stand, and her pledges by which she has bound herself shall stand. But if, on the day that her husband comes to hear of it, he expresses disapproval, then he shall make void her vow which was on her, and the thoughtless utterance of her lips, by which she bound herself; and the Lord will forgive her.

> . . . Any vow and any binding oath to afflict herself, her husband
> may establish, or her husband may make void. But if her husband
> says nothing to her from day to day, then he establishes all her
> vows, or all her pledges, that are upon her; he has established them,
> because he said nothing to her on the day that he heard of them.
> But if he makes them null and void after he has heard of them,
> then he shall bear her iniquity." These are the statues which the
> Lord commanded Moses, as between a man and his wife . . . (Nm
> 30:6–8, 13–16)

Pitre makes three key observations about this passage.
First, he notes how this particular law is centered on a
woman's vow to "afflict herself" (Nm 30:13). The particular
expression in Hebrew (*le-annoth nephesh*) can be translated
"deny herself" (NRSV), and it often describes fasting from
food or drink but also includes abstaining from sexual
relations. Indeed, that's what we find in the most ancient
Jewish interpretation that we have of this expression, which
appears also in the laws in the book of Leviticus regarding
fasting and abstaining from sexual relations on the Jewish
Day of Atonement: "You shall deny yourselves" (Lv 16:29
NRSV).[29]

Second, if a woman "denying" or "afflicting" herself points
to sexual abstinence, then Numbers 30 as a whole can be seen
as offering legislation regarding vows of sexual abstinence
made by three types of women: unmarried women (Nm
30:3–5), married women (30:6–8, 13–15), and widowed or
divorced women (30:9–12). Pitre notes how there is one key
that determines whether these vows are binding: the consent
of the father or husband. If a woman makes a vow of sexual
abstinence and the father or husband, upon hearing of it,
rejects it, then the vow is not binding. But if a woman makes
such a vow and the father or husband hears of it and says
nothing against it, the vow stands. In this case, the man's
silence implies consent.

Third, Pitre notes how the various vows in Numbers 30 are *perpetually* binding if the husband or father hears of the woman's vow and accepts it:

> Although the teaching in Numbers 30 could conceivably be applied to temporary vows, the context suggests the primary meaning is permanent vows. After all, what meaning would a temporary vow of sexual abstinence have for an unmarried virgin in her father's house? The text only makes sense if it refers to a permanent vow of abstinence, of which the girl's father approves. Likewise, what meaning would a temporary vow of abstinence have for a widow? If she had taken a vow of temporary abstinence from relations with her husband, she would (obviously) be automatically released from the vow by his death! If a permanent vow of sexual abstinence is in view in both of these cases, then it makes sense to suggest a *permanent* vow of sexual abstinence for a married woman is also in view.[30]

This insight sheds light on why the law in Numbers 30:13 addresses a husband's right, upon hearing of his wife's vow to "deny herself," to "make void" his wife's vow. After all, what other kind of vow would merit giving a law in the book of Numbers protecting the husband's right to void it? Concerns about a wife merely fasting from food doesn't seem to warrant such legal attention. But something involving sexual relations between husband and wife most likely would.[31]

In summary, Pitre demonstrates that there is, indeed, historical evidence for ancient Jewish women taking vows of sexual abstinence, and it's found right in the Jewish Scriptures. The fact that later Jewish writings tell of groups like the Therapeutae in Egypt and some Essene married women making commitments to abstain from sexual relations confirms this point found in Numbers 30 regarding married women living out vows of sexual abstinence. This background, therefore, can help support the traditional interpretation of Luke 1:34 that Mary had made a vow of virginity and why she still accepted betrothal with Joseph. We can imagine an ancient Jewish woman like Mary taking a vow to abstain from sexual relations. If her husband Joseph hears of the vow and says nothing against it, then, according to Numbers 30:13–14, the vow is binding. But if Joseph changes his mind "and makes them null and void after he has heard of them," then he will be responsible for the sin of the vow being broken: "[H]e shall bear her iniquity" (Nm 30:15). Pitre notes, however, that Matthew's Gospel emphasizes how Joseph is a righteous man, obedient to the Law (Mt 1:19). He writes, "If Mary took a vow of sexual abstinence—and her words 'How can this be, since I do not know man?' (Lk 1:34) constitute evidence that *she did*—and if Joseph accepted this vow at the time of their betrothal, then he would have been bound by Mosaic Law to honor her vow of sexual abstinence under the penalty of sin."[32]

Why Joseph chose to go along with Mary's vow of abstinence remains a mystery. While there are some traditions about Joseph being an elderly man at the time of his betrothal to Mary, the Bible itself does not say. Pope St. John Paul II pondered this question, too, and offered his own suggestion—one that merits our consideration:

> We can wonder why she would accept betrothal, since she had the intention of remaining a virgin forever.... It may be presumed that at the time of their betrothal there was an understanding between Joseph and Mary about the plan to live as a virgin. Moreover, the Holy Spirit, who had inspired Mary to choose virginity in view of the mystery of the Incarnation and who wanted the latter to come about in a family setting suited to the child's growth, was quite able to instill in Joseph the ideal of virginity as well.[33]

Chapter Six

Mary's Fiat
(Luke 1:35–38)

What was Mary thinking after Gabriel finished his breathtaking announcement to her?

Feel the weight of all that has been revealed to her in this brief conversation with the angel. Gabriel tells her "the Lord is with you" and "you have found favor with God"—two expressions that immediately signal God is entrusting her with some important mission.[1] Then, Gabriel reveals the nature of her vocation: She will become a mother, but not the mother of just any Jewish baby. She will carry in her womb the hopes of all Israel as she bears the long-awaited prophesied one: the royal Son of David, the Messiah. This alone would be a lot to take in during one short conversation with an angel.

But it doesn't stop there. Gabriel is about to give her the most extraordinary part of his message: Mary will conceive this child not through natural means, but as a virgin by the power of the Holy Spirit. Think about receiving *that* news: there's never been a conception like that before! And to top it off, Gabriel goes on to inform her that the child she will bear is no ordinary child, but the holy Son of God.

What was Mary pondering at this moment? What was she going through? Luke does not explicitly say. But there's one verse at the end of the scene that gives us at least a glimpse into her soul at this pivotal moment. She says, "Behold, I am the handmaid of the Lord; let it be to me according to your word" (Lk 1:38).

Let's take a closer look at this last part of the Annunciation to Mary: Gabriel's breathtaking revelation about the virginal conception (Lk 1:35–37) and Mary's full-hearted response with her *fiat* (Lk 1:38).

"The Holy Spirit Will Come Upon You" (Lk 1:35a)

Here, Gabriel reveals more the unique divine intervention about to take place in Mary's life. In response to her question, "How will this be, since I do not know man?" Gabriel answers, "The Holy Spirit will come upon you, and the power of the Most High will overshadow you" (1:35).

Three beautiful points about Mary can be unpacked from this sentence.

First, the words point to the Spirit acting in Mary in an extraordinary way that takes us back to the very beginning of the Scriptures. Luke's description of the Holy Spirit coming upon Mary recalls the creative activity of God's Spirit at the creation of the cosmos (Gn 1:2; Ps 33:6)[2] and in the creation of individuals (Jb 33:4; Ps 104:30; Jdt 16:14). Luke is underscoring how what's happening in Mary with the conception of her child is completely the work of God—a new creation. As Brown notes, the Spirit that comes upon Mary brings to mind "the Spirit of God that hovered over the waters before creation in Gen 1:2. The earth was void and without form when that Spirit appeared; just so Mary's womb was a void until the Spirit of God filled it with a child who was His Son."[3]

More broadly, the image also recalls how the Spirit empowers people to carry out a mission from God. Various judges, for example, such as Othniel (Jgs 3:10), Gideon (Jgs 6:34), Jephthath (Jgs 11:29), and Samson (Jgs 13:25) had the Spirit descend upon them to help them achieve their task. Similarly, Saul (1 Sm 10:6) and David (1 Sm 16:13) had the Spirit come upon them at their anointing as king, and then each began to prophesy. And the future Davidic king was depicted as having the Spirit come upon him (Is 11:1–2). Just as the Spirit came upon these men to equip them to carry out their mission, so the Holy Spirit will come upon Mary to enable her to fulfill her vocation and become the mother of Christ. Indeed, it is the Holy Spirit who will accomplish this conception in her womb.

Second, the particular verb Luke employs for the Spirit *coming upon* Mary (*eperchesthai epi*) is linked with God's Spirit in Isaiah 32:15 (LXX)—a passage that foretells the eschatological coming of the Spirit that causes the wilderness to become a fruitful field and is associated with the coming of a righteous king.

> Behold, a king will reign in righteousness, and princes will rule in justice. . . . For the palace will be forsaken, the populous city deserted; the hill and the watchtower will become dens for ever, a joy of wild donkeys, a pasture of flocks; until the Spirit is poured upon us from on high, and the wilderness becomes a fruitful field, and the fruitful field is deemed a forest (Is 32:1, 14–15).[4]

This was a prophecy about what God would do for Israel in the messianic age. But now Luke 1:35 is announcing that this anticipated day is finally dawning and Mary is the initial recipient of the blessing promised in Isaiah 32. Notice the similar themes in both passages. Just as the *Spirit* would *come upon* desolate Israel and make her fruitful when the righteous *King* arrives, so that same *Spirit* is *coming upon*

Mary to cause her to bear fruit in her womb. Indeed, Mary will give birth to that righteous *King* foretold in Isaiah 32.

Third, Gabriel's statement about how the Spirit will "come upon" Mary anticipates the Spirit coming upon the disciples at Pentecost. Although the verb "come upon" (*eperchesthai*) occurs seven times in Luke-Acts, it's only in the account of Jesus's Ascension in Acts 1:8 that it is used in association with the coming of the *Spirit*, where Jesus foretells the Spirit coming upon his disciples. Moreover, in both passages, the Holy Spirit is identified as God's *power*. Hence, we have in both scenes these three key terms—"Spirit," "power," and "come upon"—that link the gift of the Spirit coming upon Mary with the gift of the Spirit to the disciples at Pentecost. In this way, Luke is making an important point about Mary. She is the first disciple to receive the gift of the Spirit, anticipating what other faithful disciples will receive. She goes before the other disciples who will receive this gift after Jesus's Death, Resurrection, and Ascension.[5]

"The Power of the Most High Will Overshadow You" (Lk 1:35b)

Gabriel goes on to describe how God's power will overshadow (*episkiazein*) Mary. This recalls God's presence in the glory cloud overshadowing the Tabernacle at Mount Sinai (Ex 40:35).[6] In fact, the only other passage in which Luke employs this verb is in the Transfiguration scene, where it describes the divine glory present in the cloud overshadowing the disciples (Lk 9:34).[7] As Nolland observes, Luke's use of *episkiazein* in 1:35 "has probably been influenced by the LXX [Septuagint] text of Exod 40:35 perhaps via the transfiguration account (Luke 9:34): Mary's experience is to be compared to the dramatic way in which God's glory and the cloud marking his presence came down upon the completed tabernacle."[8] In this way, Luke invites readers to view Mary as a new Tabernacle, a new vessel of God's presence, the new dwelling place of God.

As we will see in chapter 10, this is a theme that will be developed even more in the Visitation scene, where Luke will associate Mary more directly with the Ark of the Covenant, over which the divine presence rested in the Tabernacle. But at this stage of Luke's narrative, Mary is primarily being portrayed as a recipient of God's overshadowing presence in ways that recall the divine presence coming upon the Tabernacle in the Old Testament. Just as the glory cloud of the divine presence overshadowed the Tabernacle at Sinai, so does the Holy Spirit now overshadow Mary, who is becoming the Mother of God's Son.

The Holy Son of God (Lk 1:35c)

Next, Gabriel elaborates on the meaning of Jesus's divine sonship, now seen in connection with the virginal conception that takes place by the power of God's Spirit. "Therefore, the child to be born will be called holy, the Son of God" (1:35). In 1:32, Gabriel tells Mary that her child will have a special father-son relationship with God. He will be the "Son of the Most High" by virtue of his Davidic kingly role. But now, in 1:35, that divine sonship is expanded as Luke links it with Jesus's conception by the Spirit, which, according to Strauss, is "connecting this sonship to his divine origin rather than merely to his *role* as king."[9]

> Luke grounds this sonship not in Jesus's role but in his *origin*. Luke seems to be consciously opposing the view that Jesus's divine sonship is merely "functional"—a special relationship with God by virtue of his role as king. He is rather the Son of God from the point of conception, before he has taken on any of the functions of kingship.[10]

Whereas 1:32–33 associated Jesus's divine sonship with the special filial relationship the Davidic King had with God, Luke 1:35 shows that Jesus's divine sonship is the result of divine intervention in his conception. Mary will conceive Jesus through God's intervention—"*therefore* the child to be born will be called . . . the Son of God" (Lk 1:35).[11]

The Sign

Finally, Gabriel gives Mary a sign, even though she did not ask for one. He informs her of Elizabeth's remarkable pregnancy. Since Elizabeth has just come out of her five-month seclusion (see Lk 1:24, 26, 36), Mary would not have known of her pregnancy. Now she learns that her elder and previously barren kinswoman is already in her sixth month of carrying a child.

Gabriel tells her this in order to underscore that Elizabeth is able to conceive a child for the same reason Mary will be able to conceive as a virgin: God is at work. "For with God nothing will be impossible" (1:37). The language recalls what God said to the barren Sarah: "Is anything impossible with God?" (Gn 18:14, LXX). The same God who accomplished in the barren Sarah what seemed humanly impossible has been at work in Elizabeth to give her a child in her old age. The implication is that this same God can do the impossible in Mary, as well. But while there is precedent for God intervening in miraculous pregnancies, the magnitude of what is being asked of Mary is much greater than what Sarah and Elizabeth were asked to believe. There are instances of barren women unexpectedly becoming pregnant. But never in the history of the world has a virgin conceived a child. Mary, therefore, is being asked to believe in something that has never before happened in all of biblical history.[12]

Mary's *Fiat* (Lk 1:38)

Now we arrive at the climactic moment of the Annunciation scene: How will Mary respond? Put yourself in Mary's shoes and consider all that has just been revealed to her. An angel suddenly appears, greeting her with the words "the Lord is with you"—signaling that something significant is about to be asked of her by God. Gabriel informs her that she will conceive and will carry in her womb Israel's long-awaited Son of David, the Messiah. She will conceive this child not through natural means, but by the power of the Holy Spirit. And to top it all off, she's told that her child will be the holy Son of God. That's enough to make most people faint. What was going on inside Mary at this moment?

Mary's response to all this is exemplary: "Behold, I am the handmaid of the Lord; let it be to me according to your word" (1:38). These words give us a glimpse into the soul of this magnificent woman of Nazareth. In other birth announcement and commissioning scenes like this, God or his heavenly messenger typically speaks last before departing. Abraham, Sarah, Zechariah, and Samson's parents do not give a grand statement of consent—a *fiat*—in the biblical narratives of the birth announcements made to them. Neither does Moses or Gideon when God commissions them. But here, Mary remarkably stands out for getting the last word in the dialogue with the angel.[13] And these words of consent reveal much about Mary's desire to serve God.

First, note how Mary refers to herself as a "handmaiden." The word in Greek (*doulē*) literally refers to a female *slave* or servant. The term in its masculine and feminine forms describes someone in a humble position addressing a superior, and often portrays righteous people when speaking to God (1 Sm 1:11, 25:41; 2 Sm 9:6; 2 Kgs 4:16; Ps 86:16).

In referring to herself as a *slave of the Lord*, Mary places herself completely at God's disposal. God can do with her whatever he wants. The title "servant of the Lord" was applied to some of Israel's great leaders, such as Moses (Jos 14:7), Joshua (Jos 24:29, Jgs 2:8), David (1 Kgs 8:26, 11:13; Ps 36), and Solomon (1 Kgs 8:28, 30). Even the whole nation of Israel was described as the Lord's servant (Neh 1:6). Mary's self-description as a female *slave* of the Lord (*doulē*) perhaps echoes most particularly that of Hannah, who when expressing her humble condition before God, referred to herself as a "handmaid" (*doulē*) of the Lord (1 Sm 1:11). In narrating this title of Mary, Luke underscores how Mary stands in a group of some of Israel's greatest servants called by the Lord.[14]

Second, Mary's concluding words "Let it be to me" (*genoito moi*) express a wish or a longing on her part. These are not words of mere submission or resignation. In this particular grammatical form in ancient Greek (known as the optative), Mary's "let it be" (*genoito*) communicates a wish or longing. As de la Potterie explains,

> The resonance of Mary's "fiat" at the moment of the Annunciation is not that of the *"fiat voluntas tua"* of Jesus in Gethsemane, nor that of a formula corresponding to the Our Father. Here there is a remarkable detail, which has only been noticed in recent years, and which even today is frequently lost from sight. The "fiat" of Mary is not just a simple acceptance or even less, a resignation. It is rather a joyous desire to collaborate with what God foresees for her. It is the joy of total abandonment to the good will of God. Thus the joy of this ending responds to the invitation to joy at the beginning.[15]

As such, Mary's *fiat* stands as a model for all of us who strive to be faithful disciples. Her example inspires us to be true servants of the Lord, seeking to use our lives not for our own purposes but for the Lord, who is our good and loving Master. Her *fiat* also encourages us to view obedient discipleship not as mere submission or acceptance of God's will, but as a joyful longing to run after God's will in our lives, like a lover wanting to fulfill the desires of the beloved.

Chapter Seven

The Visitation—Why the Haste?
(Luke 1:39)

Mary travels to visit her kinswoman Elizabeth. But do you know about the interior *spiritual* journey she makes in this scene?

Luke introduces Mary's visit to Elizabeth with three small details that may suggest a profound movement taking place in her soul in the Visitation scene:

1. Mary *arose.*

2. She *went.*

3. She went *in haste.*

At first glance, these might seem to be insignificant details. But we will see that each of these expressions tells us something about what is happening within Mary's interior life as she sets off to visit her kinswoman Elizabeth.

Arise

First, Mary "*arose*" to go visit Elizabeth. In Luke's Gospel, the Greek verb here for *arose* (*anistanai*) can imply more than simply standing up. Luke uses the word in a figurative way to depict a kind of spiritual endeavor beginning, an action involving great spiritual effort. For example, the Prodigal Son came to his senses and "arose" to return to his father (Lk 15:18, 20). Similarly, when Jesus called Levi the tax collector to become a disciple, Levi left everything behind and "rose" (*anastas*) to follow Jesus (Lk 5:27–28). Mary, too, received a call in her life, and she "arose" to visit Elizabeth. Like the son in the parable and Levi the tax collector, Mary is setting off on a new journey with the Lord as she embraces her mission as the Mother of the Messiah. As Pope St. John Paul II once explained, "Considering that this verb is used in the Gospels to indicate Jesus's resurrection (Mk 8:31; 9:9, 31; Lk 24:7, 46) or physical actions that imply a spiritual effort (Lk 5:27–28; 15:18, 20), we can suppose that Luke wished to stress with this expression the vigorous zeal which led Mary, under the inspiration of the Holy Spirit, to give the world its Savior."[1]

A Spiritual Journey

Second, Mary "went." The account of the Visitation is framed with a travel theme. Luke introduces the story by noting how Mary went from Nazareth to the hill country of Judea (1:39–40), and then concludes it by noting that she returns to her home (1:56). This travel motif in the Visitation scene isn't the only one in the opening chapters of Luke's Gospel, for he marks his entire infancy narrative with various sojourns: Mary and Joseph travel to Bethlehem (2:1–7); the shepherds journey from the fields to find the Christ Child in the manger (2:8–20); Mary and Joseph travel to the Jerusalem Temple for Mary's purification (2:22–39), and twelve years later they journey there for the Passover (2:41–51).[2] Each of these sojourns anticipates the climax of Luke's Gospel, Christ's own journey to Jerusalem at the culmination of his public ministry.[3]

But Mary is not merely going on a physical journey, moving from one geographic location to another. Luke hints that she is embarking on a *spiritual* journey, moving with purpose, participating in God's plan. For when Luke narrates that Mary "went" to visit Elizabeth, he uses a word that will have important theological meaning in his narrative: *poreusthai*.[4] Though the word itself means "to go" or "to walk," Luke uses it elsewhere to describe a journey with a divine purpose, particularly Jesus's own journey from Galilee to Judea as he progresses to the ultimate destination of his public ministry, Jerusalem (Lk 9:51; 13:22). As New Testament scholar François Bovon explains, the word "has theological significance in the Gospel of Luke: Jesus, and here Mary, 'walk' according to God's will and plan of salvation."[5]

Why the Haste?

Luke draws further attention to the nature of Mary's journey by employing three phrases beginning with the word "into" (*eis*). Nolland notes that each "into" phrase defines Mary's destination "with increasing degrees of precision": *into* the hill country, *into* a city of Judea, *into* the house of Zechariah.[6] As Bovon explains, "Everything is directed toward arrival, as the thrice-repeated, almost exaggerated [*eis*] ('to, into') makes clear."[7]

Moreover, Luke reports that Mary went "with haste." Why does she go with haste (*meta spoudēs*), and what is the meaning of this phrase? It is sometimes suggested that she departed for the house of Zechariah in haste to cover up her pregnancy; she did not want people in Nazareth to know about it. However, as Bock notes, if this were the case, why would she return three months later when she would have been even further along in her pregnancy?[8]

A more common explanation is that Luke mentions Mary going in haste to highlight her prompt obedience to the angel's message.[9] In this view, Luke's description denotes the quickness in which she departed and reflects her immediate obedience to the angel's announcement, "an instant response to God's leading."[10]

Mary going in haste may point to her trust in the angel's words, but the phrase *meta spoudēs* also can be translated "with eagerness," as it is used in the non-canonical Jewish work known as 3 Maccabees 5:2 (LXX) and other texts.[11] Since Mary was not commanded by the angel to visit Elizabeth, it is likely that Luke employs the phrase in this way to point to Mary's joy and wonder over what God is accomplishing for Israel at the dawn of the messianic era—a divine plan in which she and her kinswoman Elizabeth are now intimately bound.[12] Mary enthusiastically seeks to observe the sign that the angel revealed to her about Elizabeth's miraculous pregnancy (1:36).[13] The related verb *speusantes* is used in Luke 2:16 to express the joy of the shepherds who go in haste to verify the Good News of salvation announced to them by the angel. Mary's haste should be viewed in a similar light. Her urgency reflects a desire to be strengthened in the hope of the message received from the angel. It also can be seen as a joyful response to the redemptive work already begun (cf. 19:5–6).[14] As Culpepper explains, Luke's narration of Mary's haste is "an indication of joy and wonder. . . . The verbs convey the movement, the urgency, and the joy of her journey: Mary set out, went with haste, entered the house and greeted Elizabeth."[15]

In conclusion, Luke's mention of Mary going in haste does not seem to point simply to her obedience. After all, she was not commanded by the angel to visit Elizabeth. Rather, Mary goes *meta spoudēs*—with eagerness—to see Elizabeth, with whom she now realizes she shares a common destiny and common experience of a miraculous pregnancy.[16] Like the shepherds who long to see the Good News announced to them by the angel, Mary eagerly goes to visit Elizabeth to witness firsthand the great things God is doing in Elizabeth's life. Mary's barren kinswoman has, in her old age, miraculously conceived a child who will play a crucial role in God's redemptive plan. In the process, she will encounter the impossible—an older barren woman pregnant—and thus be confirmed in the message that "with God nothing will be impossible" (1:37). This will give her encouragement moving forward in her own even more miraculous and utterly unique pregnancy, having conceived the holy Son of God as a virgin by the power of the Holy Spirit.

Chapter Eight

The Queen Mother
(Luke 1:40–43)

Mary greeting Elizabeth in Luke 1:40 is just what we would expect, for it was customary for the younger to greet the elder in first-century Judaism. But what is remarkable is the way Elizabeth in turn greets Mary. Elizabeth showers on Mary words of praise that stand out in the biblical tradition. She calls Mary "blessed among women" and "mother of my Lord"—two accolades that in Scripture had not been used in many centuries and point to Mary's unique roles in God's plan of salvation (Lk 1:42–43).

"Blessed Among Women" (Lk 1:42)

In Luke 1:42, Elizabeth says Mary is "blessed among women." Only two other women in all of Scripture have been given such praise. Jael in Judges 5:24–26 is called "most blessed of women" because she crushed the head of the Canaanite general Sisera with a tent peg. Judith is called "blessed by the Most High God above all women on earth" because she cut off the head of the Assyrian general Holofernes (Jdt 13:18).

But what does the young Blessed Virgin Mary have in common with these warrior-like women of the Old Testament? Like Jael and Judith, she plays a critical role in God's plan for rescuing Israel from her enemies. But there are two big differences. First, unlike Jael and Judith, Mary's battle is not a physical one. She does not take up a sword or a tent peg. Rather, she plays her part in God's plan of salvation by carrying the Messiah in her womb. And that's what Elizabeth goes on to praise her for. Mary is "blessed among women" because, as she is told, "blessed is the fruit of [her] womb" (Lk 1:42).

Second, the enemy is different. Jael and Judith helped liberate the people from pagan armies. Mary's child will save Israel from a much more dangerous enemy than the Canaanites or Assyrians or any military in this world. As Luke's Gospel makes clear, Mary's child will save the people from their sins (see Lk 1:77).

One other important point of connection between Mary and Jael and Judith is the association with Genesis 3:15. Jael and Judith are blessed among women because they struck the heads of their enemies—an image that recalls the first prophetic foreshadowing of the Messiah in Genesis 3:15 (see *CCC*, 410). In Genesis 3:15, God announces that the first woman, Eve, will have a son, a descendant, who will crush the head of the serpent (the devil). Jael and Judith striking Israel's military enemies can be seen as an anticipation of the one who will crush the head of Israel's greatest enemy, the devil. Elizabeth calling Mary "blessed among women" associates Mary with the ultimate fulfillment of Genesis 3:15. She is the "woman" whose son will defeat the devil as Genesis 3:15 foretold (see Rev 12:1–9; cf. Jn 2:4; 19:25–27).

"Mother of My Lord" (Lk 1:43)

Elizabeth addressing Mary as "mother of my Lord" (1:43) is also significant, for it evokes the royal court language in the Old Testament and recalls the important role of the queen mother.[1]

The mother of the reigning king held an important office in many ancient Near Eastern kingdoms. She influenced political, military, economic, and cultic affairs in the royal court and played an important role in the process of dynastic succession. In fact, it was generally the king's *mother* who ruled as queen, not the king's wife. We see this in Hittite, Ugaritic, Egyptian, and Assyrian kingdoms, as well as in ancient Israel.[2]

At first glance, the importance of the king's mother may seem unusual to modern ears—why wouldn't the king's *wife* serve as queen? But when we recall that most ancient Near Eastern kings practiced polygamy and had large harems, the role of the queen mother begins to make more sense. Though kings may have had many wives, they each had only one mother, and the queenship was given to her. Ancient Israel had a similar practice. In the kingdom of Judah, the king's mother had a special supremacy over all other women in the kingdom, even over the king's wives. She was called the *gebirah*—or "great lady"—and reigned as queen in her son's kingdom.

We can see the queen mother's importance in the Jewish Scriptures in various ways. First, in the succession narratives of 1 and 2 Kings, the king's mother is presented as having such significance that almost every time a new Davidic king is introduced in the kingdom of Judah, the *mother's* name is also mentioned, but the wife's name is not. Therefore, at the key turning points of dynastic succession, 1 and 2 Kings time after time underscores the queen mother's place alongside the new king. As Montague explains, "On the throne the queen mother represented the king's continuity with the past, the visible affirmation of God's ongoing plan for his people, the channel through which the Lord's dynastic promise to David was fulfilled."[3]

Second, the queen mother had a royal office in the kingdom of Judah. She is depicted with royal symbols, wearing a crown (Jer 13:18) and having a throne (1 Kgs 2:19, cf. Jer 13:18). And she is listed among the members of the royal court in 2 Kings 24:12–15. In this passage, the queen mother is the first person listed among the members of the king's royal court. According to Miguens, this little detail underscores the special place the queen mother held in the kingdom:

> She is mentioned *before* the "wives of the king" (2 Kings 24:15) and before the ministers, dignitaries and officers (2 Kings 24:12, 15; Jer. 29:2). Significantly these biblical passages say that the [*gebirah*] is the second, only to the king, in the list of prominent official persons brought into captivity. This detail speaks very highly of the political significance of "the mother of the king."[4]

Third, the queen mother exercised real royal authority, truly sharing in her son's reign. Hers was not merely a figurehead position. For example, consider what the prophet Jeremiah says to both the king and the queen mother in Jeremiah 13.

> Say to the king and the queen mother: "Take a lowly seat, for your beautiful crown has come down from your head. . . . Lift up your eyes and see those who come from the north. Where is the flock that was given you, your beautiful flock?" (Jer 13:18, 20)

Notice how the prophecy is addressed both to the king *and* to the queen mother. As such, it recognizes the important royal office the king's mother possessed. In a foreboding oracle about God's coming judgment, both the king and queen mother are told to "take a lowly seat"—expressing how both had thrones but would lose them soon. Similarly, both the king and queen mother are told they will lose their crowns—another image foretelling their coming downfall. Most significant is how they both are portrayed as shepherding the flock of the people of Judah, a flock they will soon lose. God says to both the king and the queen mother, "Where is the flock that was given you, your beautiful flock?"

In sum, we can see how this prophecy portrays the queen mother as participating in the king's reign: she has a throne and a crown with the king, and she shares in the king's royal responsibilities of shepherding the people.

At the King's Right Hand

The two passages that best illustrate the queen mother's significance are found in 1 Kings 1–2. Here, we can compare Bathsheba's role in the kingdom when she was just the *wife* of the king with how she is treated once she becomes the *mother* of the king. In 1 Kings 1, her husband King David is still alive, so she is not the queen mother. She is just a wife of the king. When she goes to meet him, she bows before her husband and pays him homage (1 Kgs 1:16). She leaves the room, honoring him by saying, "May my lord King David live for ever!" (1 Kgs 1:31).

Things dramatically change, however, in the next chapter. David has died and Bathsheba's son Solomon now sits on the throne. This makes her the queen mother. This time, when she meets the king, she is treated differently. Instead of Bathsheba giving a reverential bow before the king, it's the other way around. King Solomon stands up and bows before *her*, honoring her in her role as mother of the king. Next, Solomon brings in a throne for her—a symbol of her royal position in the kingdom. Moreover, her throne is placed at the king's right hand, which in Scripture is a position of honor and authority. Consider all the honor given to the queen mother: the bow, the throne, the place at the king's right hand. As Timothy Gray notes, "Nowhere else in the Bible does the king honor someone as Solomon does the gebirah."[5]

Fourth, the queen mother served as a counselor to her royal son.[6] The Old Testament gives some evidence for this. Proverbs 31, for example, is about a queen mother giving wise advice to her son about how to care for the poor, rule his kingdom with justice, avoid too much alcohol, and select a good wife. The queen mother's counsel seems to have had the ability to influence greatly affairs in the kingdom, though not always this positively. Second Chronicles 22:3, for example, tells how King Ahaziah "walked in the ways of the house of Ahab [an evil king], for his mother was his counselor in doing wickedly."

Advocate

A fifth way we see the queen mother's influence is in her role as intercessor for the people.[7] In ancient Israel, the queen mother was an advocate who took petitions from the people and presented them to her royal son. An example of this is found in the passage from 1 Kings 2 that we just considered about Bathsheba's meeting her royal son, Solomon. As soon as Solomon is crowned king, making her queen mother, her new intercessory role is recognized by Adonijah, who asks Bathsheba to bring a petition to the king.

Notice the confidence Adonijah has in her intercessory power: he says to her, "Please ask King Solomon—*he will not refuse you*" (1 Kgs 2:17).[8] Also notice how seriously the king receives the petitions of his queen mother. After Bathsheba tells the king she has a small petition to present, Solomon responds by saying, "Make your request, my mother; for I will not refuse you" (1 Kgs 2:20). Indeed, Solomon's words reveal the king's ordinary commitment to the queen mother's petitions.[9]

In conclusion, we have seen how the queen mother held an official position in the royal court, sharing in the shepherding responsibilities of the king and serving as a counselor for the king and as an advocate for the people.

Mary, Mother of the King

All this serves as important background for considering Elizabeth's words to Mary in the Visitation. She calls Mary "the mother of my Lord" (Lk 1:43), an expression charged with royal significance. While "Lord" was used often in the Old Testament as a title for God, it also could refer to the royal son of David (2 Sm 24:21; 1 Kgs 1:13–47) and the future anointed king (Ps 110:1). Luke's Gospel uses "Lord" in this twofold way. On one hand, it can refer to Jesus's total authority and place him on par with Yahweh (Acts 2 and 10).[10] On the other hand, it can have Christ's kingship more in focus. The latter seems to be the case at this point in the narrative, where Elizabeth's use of "Lord" is "a prophetic foreshadowing" of Jesus's full identity to be revealed later in the Gospel, but in this first use "could be seen to signify simply the Lordship of the Messiah (Luke 20.41–44)."[11]

Furthermore, Elizabeth's words to Mary, "And why is this granted me, that the mother of my Lord should come to me?" (Lk 1:43), echo 2 Samuel 24:21, where the phrase "my lord" is used as a royal title honoring the king. In that text,

Araunah greets King David, saying: "Why has my lord the king come to his servant?" (2 Sm 24:21). With this in the background, Elizabeth's words here in 1:43 would have regal connotations that further present Jesus as a Davidic king.

It is also significant that the title in 1:43 is not used in an absolute sense ("the Lord"), but stands alongside the first person possessive, "*my* Lord." This may further signify its royal messianic meaning, since this expression was used in the Old Testament to denote the king and the future Messiah. As Brown has observed, "Both in the Gospel (20:41–44) and in Acts (2:34) Luke uses Ps 110:1, 'the Lord said to *my Lord*,' to show that Jesus is the Messiah and Son of God; and Elizabeth is recognizing Mary as the mother of 'my Lord,' i.e., of the Messiah."[12]

Thus, when Elizabeth calls Mary "the mother of my Lord," these words not only point to Jesus as the Messiah, but they also tell us something important about Mary. While recognizing the messianic lordship of Mary's child, Elizabeth, at the same time, acknowledges Mary as the mother of her king.

Here it should be pointed out that in the New Testament Mary is often referred to as the "mother of Jesus" or "his mother," but nowhere is she called the "mother of my Lord" except here in 1:43.[13] Thus, this unique title for Mary seems to draw attention to her position not just as mother of Jesus in a general sense but as mother of Jesus specifically in his role as messianic Lord. From this, we can conclude that Elizabeth, in greeting Mary as "the mother of my Lord," refers to her as *mother of the Messiah-King*—which would point to Mary's role as the queen mother in Christ's Kingdom.

Moreover, it has been noted that in royal court language of the ancient Near East, the title "Mother of my Lord" would have been used to address the queen mother of the reigning king (who himself was addressed as "my lord" [cf.

2 Sm 24:21]).[14] Thus, within the strong Davidic context of Luke's infancy narrative, Elizabeth addressing Mary with this royal title provides a basis for viewing her in light of the queen-mother tradition of the Old Testament. Other New Testament passages, especially Revelation 12, will further demonstrate this point.

Treat Her Like a Queen

This queen-mother theme in Scripture tells us much about Mary, for it's the mother of the king who reigned as queen in the Davidic kingdom of old. Consider this from the ancient Jewish perspective: if Jesus is the new Son of David, the Messiah-King, and Mary is his mother, then Mary would be the queen mother in Christ's kingdom. That's what the biblical tradition of the queen mother would lead us to conclude. New Testament passages such as Luke 1:43 and Revelation 12 present Mary in light of this queen-mother background and add further support for this conclusion. No wonder an early Christian tradition developed of viewing Mary as a royal figure worthy of our honor.[15] No wonder Christians throughout the centuries have turned to her for her intercession. In Scripture, the queen mother served as an advocate for the people. They would bring their petitions to her, and the queen mother would present them to her son. From a biblical perspective, Christians seeking Mary's intercession makes perfect sense. If she is our queen mother as the New Testament reveals she is, then it is most fitting that we would lovingly turn to her with our needs, trusting that she will present them to her royal Son, Jesus.

Chapter Nine

Ark of the Covenant
(Luke 1:39–56)

I remember when I was a child, people at my local parish would say the Rosary before Mass and then recite a series of prayers known as the Litany of Mary. In this traditional Catholic devotion, the parishioners would ask Mary to pray for them under various titles:

Holy Mary…Pray for us.

Holy Mother of God…Pray for us.

Holy Virgin of Virgins…Pray for us.

The litany went on and on with the people addressing Mary under fifty different titles—honorable names ranging from "Mother of our Creator" to "Queen of the Apostles"—and after each title, the people would say, "Pray for us."

But there was one title that always stood out among all the others, which woke me up and grabbed my attention:

"Ark of the Covenant…Pray for us."

That title was so fascinating! The famous movie *Raiders of the Lost Ark* had recently come out, so every time I heard this title of Mary, I had images of Harrison Ford closing his eyes and German Nazis melting before the power of God that was unleashed when they opened up that ancient Israelite sacred treasure known as the Ark of the Covenant.

I eventually came to realize, however, that the primary background for understanding this mysterious title "Mary, Ark of the Covenant" was not Hollywood's adventuresome presentation, but the Bible, and that God's Word, especially in Luke's Gospel, is clearly revealing Mary to be the new Ark of the Lord.[1]

The New Ark

To appreciate Mary's connections to the Ark, we first need to step back and consider how the Ark of the Covenant was the most sacred vessel in all of Israel. According to Hebrews 9:4, it housed three items of great importance for God's people:

(1) A jar holding *the manna* (the heavenly bread that fell in the desert to feed the Israelites in the time of Moses);

(2) The remains of the stone tablets upon which God had written the *Ten Commandments*; and

(3) The *staff of Aaron*, the first high priest of Israel.

The most significant aspect of the Ark, however, was that it was associated with *the holy presence of God*, which was visibly manifested in the cloud of glory that overshadowed the Ark (Ex 40:34). It was this connection with God's presence that made the Ark the most sacred vessel in all of Israel and explains why it was kept in the holiest spot on the face of the earth, the innermost chamber of the Temple called the Holy of Holies. Indeed, God's presence over the Ark is what made the Holy of Holies so holy!

But the Ark did not remain in the Temple forever. About six centuries before the time of Jesus, the glory of the Lord departed from the Temple shortly before Babylon captured Jerusalem and destroyed the house of the Lord in 586 BC (Ez 10). Noteworthy is the fact that the Ark was not listed among the many sacred items the Babylonians took from the Temple (see 2 Kgs 25:13–17; Jer 52:17–23). Moreover, there are no accounts of the Ark of the Covenant or the glory cloud returning to Jerusalem when the Jews later rebuilt the Temple in Jerusalem. Indeed, in Jesus's day, the Holy of Holies in the Temple stood empty.[2] No Ark of the Covenant, no cloud of glory.

What happened to the lost Ark? Various traditions, theories, and even Hollywood movies have attempted to answer that question. But according to the oldest Jewish tradition we have regarding the lost Ark, it was hidden in a mountain by the prophet Jeremiah. That's what the second book of Maccabees tells us:

> It was also in the writing that the prophet [Jeremiah], having received an oracle, ordered that the tent and the ark should follow with him, and that he went out to the mountain where Moses had gone up and had seen the inheritance of God. And Jeremiah came and found a cave, and he brought there the tent and the ark and the altar of incense, and he sealed up the entrance. Some of those who followed him came up to mark the way, but could not find it. When Jeremiah learned of it, he rebuked them and declared: "The place shall be unknown until God gathers his people together again and shows his mercy. And then the Lord will disclose these things, and the glory of the Lord and the cloud will appear, as they were shown in the case of Moses, and as Solomon asked that the place should be specially consecrated." (2 Mc 2:4–8)

Not only does this passage tell us about what happened to the Ark of the Covenant when Babylon destroyed the Temple in the sixth century BC, but it also gives us a foreshadowing of when it will appear again. As Brant Pitre points out, in this last reference to the Ark of the Covenant in the Old Testament, Jeremiah foretells that, although the Ark had been hidden, its location will be revealed in the future. And on that day, the glory of the Lord and the cloud will appear again.[3]

The Return of Glory

Now we can begin to see how Mary might be caught up in the story of the lost Ark. Think about it: When is the next time in the Bible we have an allusion to the glory of God's presence returning to his people? This is an important question, for according to Jeremiah's prophecy, when the glory cloud of God's presence returns, the location of the Ark will be revealed. So when does that cloud of glory that overshadowed the Tabernacle on Mount Sinai and filled the Jerusalem Temple come back? It's at the Annunciation to Mary.

We saw in chapter 6 how Luke 1:35 makes a subtle connection between the cloud of glory covering the tent of meeting and the Holy Spirit coming upon Mary when Gabriel tells her:

> The Holy Spirit will come upon you,
>> and the power of the Most High will overshadow (*episkiazein*)
>> you;
>> therefore the child to be born will be called holy,
>> the Son of God.

Here, Luke uses the same language depicting the cloud of glory *overshadowing* the Tabernacle (which housed the Ark of the Covenant at Sinai) to describe how the Holy Spirit *overshadowed* Mary. Just as the cloud of glory overshadowed (*episkiazein*) the tent of meeting on Mount Sinai (Ex 40:35), so Mary is told that the Holy Spirit, "the power of the Most High," will overshadow (*episkiazein*) her when she conceives the Son of God (Lk 1:35). In other words, the glory of the Lord has returned! The same cloud of glory that covered the tent of meeting will cover Mary. This is the first allusion to God's holy presence returning to his people since Jeremiah's prophecy about the Ark was revealed in the second book of the Maccabees. The glory cloud that used to overshadow the Ark is now overshadowing Mary. She is the new resting place of God. The location of the new Ark of the Covenant has been revealed!

The New Ark

In this way, Luke's account of the Annunciation to Mary subtly reveals her to be the new dwelling place for the holy presence of God, like the Ark of old. But this subtle connection is made crystal clear in Luke's Visitation scene. For Luke portrays Mary's visit to Elizabeth in ways that have numerous parallels with an important journey the Ark of the Covenant made in the Old Testament (2 Sm 6). Let's bring to mind some specific points from this story in order to see how they parallel Mary's journey to Elizabeth.

After David was made king of the Twelve Tribes of Israel, he decided to bring the Ark to the city of Jerusalem. The passage in 2 Samuel 6 notes how David went up from Baale-judah (*the hill country of Judea*) to bring the Ark of the Covenant to Jerusalem (2 Sm 6:2). On the way, David was in awe of God's presence and power in the Ark, saying, "*How can the ark of the LORD come to me?*" (2 Sm 6:9). The Ark stayed in the *house of Obed-edom* for *three months* (2 Sm 6:10–11), after which it was brought to Jerusalem in a grand procession with people rejoicing and *shouting* in praise of

God (2 Sm 6:15) and with king David *leaping* and dancing before the Ark of the Lord (2 Sm 6:16).

With this background in mind, we can see how Luke presents Mary's visit to Elizabeth in ways that clearly recall the Ark's journey to Jerusalem. Like the Ark of old, Mary travels to the *hill country of Judah* (Lk 1:39). Just as the Ark stayed at "the house of Obed-edom" for three months, so Mary stays in "*the house of Zechariah*" (Lk 1:40) for *three months* (Lk 1:56). Just as the people welcomed the Ark into the city with shouting and rejoicing, so Elizabeth "*exclaimed* with a loud cry" when she greeted Mary (Lk 1:42).

Moreover, just as David *leaped* and danced before the Ark of the Lord, so John the Baptist leaps in Elizabeth's womb when Elizabeth hears Mary's greeting (Lk 1:41). Finally, both the Ark and Mary provoke similar questions. David greeted the Ark, saying, "How can the ark of the LORD come to me?" Elizabeth welcomes Mary, saying, "*And why is this granted to me, that the mother of my Lord should come to me?*" (Lk 1:43).[4]

Shout to the Lord

Perhaps the strongest parallel between Mary and the Ark of the Covenant comes in Luke 1:42, which tells us that Elizabeth "exclaimed" when she greeted Mary. That may seem like a small, insignificant detail, until we realize that the Greek verb for "exclaim" (*anaphonein*) that Luke chose for this verse is used almost everywhere else in the Greek Old Testament to depict the Levites making sounds of praise before God's holy presence in the Ark of the Covenant.[5] Like those Levites of old, Elizabeth (who herself comes from the tribe of Levi!), shouts (*anaphonein*) praises before the Lord whom Mary carries in her womb.

The Ark in 2 Samuel 6	Mary in Luke 1:39–56
"Baale-judah" (hill country of Judah) (v. 2)	"Hill country ... of Judah" (v. 39)
"How can the ark of the LORD come to me?" (v. 9)	"And why is this granted to me, that the mother of my Lord should come to me?" (v. 43)
"House of Obed-edom" (v.10)	"House of Zechariah" (v. 40)
"Three months" (v. 11)	"Three months" (v. 56)
"King David leaping and dancing before the LORD" (v. 16)	"The child leaped in her womb" (v. 41)
"David and [the people] brought up the ark ... with shouting" (v. 15)	"[Elizabeth] exclaimed" (v. 42)

This biblical connection between Mary and the Ark of the Covenant makes sense. Like the Ark of old, Mary bears the presence of God in her womb. Just as the Ark held the manna, so Mary carries in her womb the one who will call himself the true Bread of Life (cf. Jn 6:48–51). Just as the Ark contained the Ten Commandments, so Mary bears the one who is the fulfillment of the Law (cf. Mt 5:17). And just as the Ark carried the staff of the high priest Aaron, so does Mary carry in her womb the true High Priest, who will offer his life on the Cross for our sins (cf. Heb 8:1–7).

The biblical revelation of Mary as the Ark of the Covenant can also point to her importance in the Christian life. Two spiritual reflections could be drawn from this image. First, drawing near to the Ark of the Covenant meant drawing near to the holy presence of God. The Israelites drew near the sanctuary where the Ark resided, camping around the Tabernacle that housed the Ark during their journey through the wilderness and coming to the Jerusalem Temple where the Ark later resided to worship God. The

Ark was not God, of course, but played an important role when people wanted to draw near to the Lord's presence. Similarly, if Mary is the new Ark of the Covenant, then she, too, plays an important role in helping people draw near to God's presence today.

Second, the Ark of old was used in some of Israel's greatest battles. The Levites carried the Ark seven times around the city of Jericho before the trumpets were blown and the city walls miraculously fell down. As the new Ark of the Covenant, Mary can be seen as going before us in our spiritual battles today— our struggles with our own weaknesses and sins—helping us gain victory through her powerful intercession for us.

◆

So far, we have seen how the Visitation reveals Mary as playing an important role in God's plan of salvation. Elizabeth calls her "blessed among women," putting her on par with the heroines Jael and Judith and associating her with the woman of Genesis whose offspring would one day crush the head of the serpent (Gn 3:15) (see chapter 8). Elizabeth also addresses Mary as "the mother of my Lord," revealing her to be the queen mother in the Kingdom of her Son (see chapter 8). Moreover, Luke's account of the Visitation presents Mary as the new Ark of the Covenant, the holy dwelling place of God. How does Mary respond to all that is happening in her life? That's what we'll look at next, as we consider the Magnificat—Mary's beautiful words of praise and thanksgiving for the great things the Lord has done in her (Lk 1:46–55).

Chapter Ten

Magnificat
(Luke 1:46–55)

Do you desire to praise God from the depths of your soul? If so, Mary models how to do that in her hymnlike praise of God for all he is doing in her life and in his people (Lk 1:46–55).

These verses are known as the Magnificat, a title based on the Latin translation of Mary's first words: *Magnificat anima mea Dominum* (My soul *magnifies* the Lord). It is the first of four canticles that appear in Luke's narrative of Christ's birth and serves as a "narrative pause" by which Luke brings the rush of action to a halt and gives us as readers a chance to reflect on the *meaning* of these many dramatic events surrounding the birth of the Messiah.[1]

Take a moment now and consider all that has happened so far in Luke's Gospel. In the opening scene, readers are thrust to the edge of their seats as they learn about Zechariah the priest being chosen by lot to perform the honorable duty of offering incense in the Temple on behalf of all the people of Israel—something that may have been a once-in-a-lifetime opportunity for an ordinary Levitical priest like Zechariah.

The drama heats up when Zechariah enters the inner courts of the sanctuary and discovers something no priest has ever seen there before: an angel of the Lord! And this angel gives him a most remarkable message: Zechariah's elderly and infertile wife will miraculously conceive a son. Even more astonishing for Zechariah is the news that this coming son of his will be the new Elijah, the prophet whom the Old Testament foretold would prepare the way for the Messiah (Mal 4:1–5).

After Zechariah is reduced to silence for his unbelief, we see the same angel next appearing to Mary in Galilee to announce something even more amazing: Mary will conceive a child as a virgin by the power of the Holy Spirit. And this child will be Israel's long-awaited Messiah-King, the one who will bring all of Israel's prophecies to fulfillment. To top it all off, this child will not be any ordinary child, but the holy Son of God himself.

Without any time to take all this in, the reader is suddenly carried off into the next scene, in which Mary travels "in haste" to Judea to visit her kinswoman Elizabeth, the pregnant wife of the priest Zechariah. There, Elizabeth showers on Mary many words of praise that have not been used in the Bible for many centuries, calling her "blessed among women" and "mother of my Lord."

All that is a lot for us to take in from these three opening scenes of Luke's Gospel. Readers need to take a moment to ponder the meaning of all these dramatic events that have been rapidly unfolding before us. Mary's Magnificat gives us that opportunity, serving as a "narrative pause" to slow down and, like Mary, "keep and ponder" these profound mysteries at the dawn of the messianic age.

That's the narrative context for understanding the Magnificat. Think of it as an invitation to join Mary in prayerfully reflecting on the meaning of these dramatic events and in praising God for all that he is already accomplishing in her life and in the world.

Mary and Hannah

Consider Mary's words in the Magnificat:

> And Mary said,
> "My soul magnifies the Lord,
> and my spirit rejoices in God my Savior
> for he has regarded the low estate (*tapeinosin*) of his
> handmaiden.
> For behold, henceforth all generations will call
> me blessed;
> for he who is mighty has done great things for me,
> and holy is his name.
> And his mercy is on those who fear him
> from generation to generation.
> He has shown strength with his arm,
> he has scattered the proud in the imagination
> of their hearts,
> he has put down the mighty from their thrones,
> and exalted those of low degree (*tapeinous*);
> he has filled the hungry with good things,
> and the rich he has sent empty away.
> He has helped his servant Israel,
> in remembrance of his mercy,
> as he spoke to our fathers,
> to Abraham and to his posterity forever."
> And Mary remained with her about three months,
> and returned to her home. (Lk 1:46–56)

Many of these words and images from the Magnificat recall another hymnlike song of praise from the Old Testament: Hannah's song in 1 Samuel 2:1–10. Hannah was a godly Israelite woman but was scorned for being childless. After begging God for a child, she was blessed with a son, Samuel, whom God called to lead the people of Israel back to himself. In thanksgiving for this child, Hannah brought Samuel to the Temple and dedicated him to the Lord's service. There, she offered this famous canticle of praise, thanking God for looking kindly upon her in her affliction and blessing her with a child.

Hannah also prayed and said,
"My heart exults in the LORD;
        my strength is exalted in the LORD.
My mouth derides my enemies,
        because I rejoice in your salvation.

"There is none holy like the LORD,
    there is none besides you;
    there is no rock like our God.
Talk no more so very proudly,
    let not arrogance come from your mouth;
for the LORD is a God of knowledge,
    and by him actions are weighed.
The bows of the mighty are broken,
    but the feeble gird on strength.
Those who were full have hired themselves out for bread,
    but those who were hungry have ceased to hunger.
The barren have borne seven,
    but she who has many children is forlorn.
The LORD kills and brings to life;
    he brings down to Sheol and raises up.
The LORD makes poor and makes rich;
    he brings low, he also exalts.
He raises up the poor from the dust;
    he lifts up the needy from the dung heap,
to make them sit with princes
    and inherit a seat of honor.
For the pillars of the earth are the LORD's,
    and on them he has set the world.

He will guard the feet of his faithful ones;
    but the wicked shall be cut off in darkness;
    for not by might shall a man prevail.
The adversaries of the LORD shall be broken to pieces;
    against them he will thunder in heaven.
The LORD will judge the ends of the earth;
    he will give strength to his king,
    and exalt the power of his anointed."

Notice how Mary's Magnificat recalls various themes from Hannah's song. Both praise the Lord as their Savior and recognize him as holy. Both women proclaim dramatic reversals God is bringing about in the world: the rich and mighty will be cast down while the poor and lowly will be exalted. Those who have their fill now will walk away empty, whereas the hungry will be satisfied.

The women themselves have several similarities. Like Hannah, Mary has a child because of a miraculous conception. As did Hannah, so will Mary dedicate her son in the Temple (Lk 2:22–24). Like Hannah, Mary responds to God's favor in her life with a song of praise and thanksgiving for the child God has given her. Finally, just as Hannah's song concludes with the hope of a future king (1 Sm 2:10), Mary's song praises God for the arrival of the long-awaited Messiah, whom she now carries in her womb.

Hannah's Song (1 Sm 2:1–10)	Mary's Song (Lk 1:46–55)
"My heart exults in the LORD; my strength is exulted in the LORD" (v.1)	"My soul magnifies the Lord" (v. 46)
"My mouth derides my enemies because I rejoice in your salvation" (v. 1)	"and my spirit rejoices in God my Savior" (v. 47)
"There is none holy like the LORD" (v. 2)	"and holy is his name" (v. 49)
"The bows of the mighty are broken, but the feeble gird on strength" (v. 4)	"He has shown strength with his arm, he has scattered the proud in the imagination of their hearts" (v. 51)
"Those who were full have hired themselves out for bread, but those who were hungry have ceased to hunger ... The LORD makes poor and makes rich; he brings low, he also exults. He raises up the poor from the dust; he lifts the needy from the dung heap, to make them sit with princes and inherit a seat of honor." (v. 5, 8)	"He has put down the mighty from their thrones, and exalted those of low degree; he has filled the hungry with good things, and the rich he has sent empty away." (v. 52–53)

From Lowliness to Exaltation

Another important aspect of Mary's Magnificat involves the relationship between the first and second halves of her canticle. The first half of the canticle focuses on how the Lord has looked upon *Mary's own lowliness* and done great things for her (1:46–50). The second half of the song tells how God has looked mercifully upon *all the lowly* and has raised them up from their afflictions (1:51–55). Notice how God moves both Mary as an individual and the people as a whole from lowliness to exaltation. This reversal of fortunes—the exaltation of the lowly—is an important key to unlocking the meaning of the Magnificat.

Let's look at the first half, where the focus is on Mary herself. Mary mentions her own "low estate" and uses a particular word (*teipeinōsin*) in 1:48, which describes not simply a general spiritual humility but some intense situation of suffering. Indeed, the Old Testament often used this word to portray the affliction God's people suffered when they were oppressed and about to be rescued by God's saving hand (Dt 26:7; 1 Sm 9:16; 2 Kgs 14:26; Ps 136:23). For example, Psalm 136 recalls how God freed Israel from slavery in Egypt, and then says: "It is he who remembered us in our *low estate* . . . and *rescued* us from our foes" (Ps 136:23–24; emphasis added).

Now we can begin to see how Mary views herself as in some sense being lifted up by God in the midst of her own suffering (*teipeinōsin*). Yet we are left wondering, "What is the nature of Mary's affliction?" Considered within the social context of Roman and Herodian oppression in first-century Galilee, Mary's "low estate" would bring to mind the pains experienced by many Jews who were suffering under foreign domination at that time. As Nolland has explained, "It is not that Mary has some personal and individual affliction;

her affliction is simply that of God's people awaiting his saving intervention on their behalf."[2] Mary thanks the Lord for looking upon her lowliness with mercy (1:50) and doing "great things" for her (1:49). Even though she was a young Jewish virgin suffering under Roman oppression while living in the insignificant town of Nazareth, God has chosen her to become the Mother of Israel's Messiah.

Mary's People

With this background, we can better understand the second half of the Magnificat. In this part of the canticle, we are no longer zoomed in on Mary and the particular blessings bestowed just on her. It's as if the camera lens is pulled back so that we can see God's people as a whole—the people for whom Mary stands as a faithful representative.[3] Mary proclaims that what God has done for her in her own "low estate" (1:48), he is about to do for the many in Israel who also are of "low degree" (1:52). "The proud," "the mighty," and "the rich" will be cast down, while "those of low degree" (*tapeinous*) will be exalted and "the hungry" will be filled.

To fully appreciate Mary's words here, it is important to note that in Luke's Gospel, the terms "rich" and "poor" are not merely about finances and economics. "The poor," for example, points not just to people experiencing material want, but more broadly to all the suffering and outcasts, including the blind, the lame, the deaf and the lepers, and people impacted by various social-political injustices, such as "the hungry," "the oppressed," "the persecuted," and "the captives."[4]

Similarly, "the rich" does not simply refer to the wealthy. It's a social term describing those who ignore, marginalize, or exploit the various "poor" outcasts of society. Thus, when Mary speaks of how "the lowly" will be exalted, she is prophetically announcing dramatic reversals in society. God has remembered the suffering and oppressed in Israel and will gather them into the Kingdom of his Son, while "the proud," "the mighty," and "the rich" who oppose God's people are about to be cast down. In this way, the bond between the two halves of the Magnificat makes an important point about the relationship between Mary and God's people. God exalting Mary in her lowliness (first half) foreshadows how God will look with mercy upon the afflictions of *all* the lowly in Israel (second half). In other words, what God has done for Mary, he is going to do for the rest of his people. The Magnificat is thus not just about blessings for Mary. It's about the blessings starting to fall on all the faithful.

The Song of the Church

What can we take away from our reflections on the Magnificat? First, Mary's canticle foreshadows the key areas of her Son's mission. Indeed, Jesus's public ministry brings about these dramatic reversals proclaimed by Mary's song, whether it be in his feeding the hungry, forgiving sinners, and extending fellowship to the estranged or in his confronting the social, political, and religious leaders of the day. Jesus's core teachings about the Kingdom also sum up the same news of salvation announced in Mary's song. Like Mary, Jesus announces blessing upon "the poor"—the hungry, the persecuted, and the excluded—while he announces woe to those who are "rich"—comfortable, socially accepted, and having their fill (Lk 6:20–26). In this way, the theme of reversal first proclaimed in Mary's Magnificat is carried out in Christ's public ministry.

Second, the Magnificat also anticipates the prayer of the Church, which perpetually "proclaims the greatness of the Lord." The first half of the Magnificat invites us to join Mary in praising the Lord for mercifully looking on her lowliness and raising her up to become the Mother of Israel's Messiah. The second half invites us to ponder the profound relationship between Mary and the rest of God's people. What God has done for this lowly woman of Galilee he will do for all of us through her Son: meet us in our own lowliness, poverty, weakness, and suffering and do "great things" for us. As such, Mary is a representative of all the faithful, going before us as the first and model disciple and the one who receives in a singular way what God wants to give to all his people: his merciful love. Indeed, at the dawn of the new covenant era, Mary stands as the first Christian disciple to receive the amazing mercy of God in Jesus.

Chapter Eleven

Mary at the Nativity:
Keep and Ponder (Luke 2:1–20)

Consider how Mary is often depicted in the Christmas cards we receive each December. There in the stable, she bears a serene smile, leaning over the manger, gazing at her newborn son. Her hands are piously folded in prayer, and her clothes are spotless—pure white and blue—perfectly draped as if they just came back from the dry cleaner.

These images from sacred art magnificently point to the truth of Mary's interior beauty—her purity, holiness, and ardent devotion to her Son. They inspire us to contemplate her love of God and the mystery of the Christ Child she bore. But this is only one angle into her life in those days; it doesn't capture the whole picture. The Gospel of Luke, in fact, suggests that there was much stress, turmoil, and suffering in the period leading up to her giving birth to the baby Jesus. Let's step back and consider what Luke's Gospel tells us about the trials Mary faced in the Nativity.

The Bethlehem Prophecy

"In those days a decree went out from Caesar Augustus that all the world should be enrolled" (Lk 2:1).

The fact that Mary gives birth to Jesus in the context of Caesar Augustus's census is no minor detail. While it's true that enrollments were carried out from time to time in the Roman Empire with the purpose of listing people and property for military conscription and tax assessment, Luke goes out of his way to draw our attention to this census, mentioning it four times in the opening six verses of chapter 2. Indeed, Luke provides more details about the enrollment than about the actual birth of Jesus. Why? At least in part to underscore the oppressive conditions in which Jesus was born. The Romans inflicted heavy taxes on people they conquered as a way of demeaning them and gathering funds to help enforce their dominance over them. As one Roman general explained to the Gauls after suppressing their revolt in AD 70: "We, though so often provoked, have used the right of conquest to burden you only with the cost of maintaining peace. For the tranquility of peoples cannot be had without armies, nor armies without pay, nor pay without tribute."[1]

Being forced to submit to a Roman enrollment and to pay the taxes would have been a painful reminder of the Jewish people's oppression. In Luke's Gospel, therefore, the census serves as a symbol of Rome's control over Israel and the rest of the world. In a single decree, Augustus makes his presence felt by families throughout the empire who are uprooted and forced to travel to their ancestral towns to participate in the emperor's census.

One of those families on the move is Mary and Joseph's. Being from "the house and lineage of David" (Lk 2:4), Joseph must go to Bethlehem, the city of his family's origins, and Mary goes with him. On another level, however, Luke is showing that there is someone else who is *really* in control of the world's affairs. For Luke, Caesar's powerful decree providentially serves God's larger plan for the Messiah-King to be born in his proper city, Bethlehem. For, as the prophet Micah foretold, God one day would send a new king to Israel, a king who "shall be great to the ends of the earth" (Mi 5:4). And that future king would come from Bethlehem.

> But you, O Bethlehem Ephrathah,
> who are little to be among the clans of Judah,
> from you shall come forth for me one who is to be ruler in Israel,
> whose origin is from of old, from ancient days. (Mi 5:2)

Caesar, in his own show of might with the worldwide census, unwittingly serves the purposes of God. As a result of Caesar's decree, Mary and Joseph are brought to Bethlehem, and the prophecy is fulfilled as a new king is born in "the city of David" (Lk 2:4).

Still Betrothed?

Luke's account of the Nativity describes Mary in two ways that might be surprising to modern readers. First, Mary is described as being "betrothed" to Joseph (Lk 2:5). We have seen how in first-century Judaism a "betrothed" woman was legally married to her husband but not yet living with him (see chapter 1). Mary being called betrothed at the Annunciation scene makes perfect sense, but it seems surprising here in the Nativity, since she is traveling with Joseph and living with him now. Luke calls Mary Joseph's "betrothed" to highlight her continued virginity at the time of Christ's birth (cf. Mt 1:25). She is traveling and living with Joseph, but the marriage has not been consummated. This would imply not just a virginal conception but a virgin birth and remind us that the Christ Child came into the world not through natural means, but through the power of the Holy Spirit (1:35).[2]

The First-Born Son

Second, Luke describes Mary as giving birth to her "first-born son" (Lk 2:7). This was a legal title associated with the special status given to the oldest son in ancient Israel and does not suggest that Mary had other children after him. The term can be used without implying any other children to follow. It simply points to Jesus's holding the revered role of the firstborn in his family. The firstborn was to be consecrated to the Lord (Ex 13:2), held an important role of leadership in the family, and received the rights of inheritance (Dt 21:15–17).

But what kind of inheritance would Jesus receive from his father Joseph? Surely, something much more valuable than the carpentry shop. While Luke's Gospel does not tell us about Joseph's property, possessions, or wealth, the one thing it does emphasize is his Davidic descent. In fact, here in the account of Jesus's birth we read that Joseph travels to Bethlehem, "the city of *David*," because he is "*of the house and lineage of David*" (2:4). Luke goes out of his way to stress Joseph's connection with the house of David. Thus when we read that Jesus is Joseph's "first-born son," we understand that he would be seen as inheriting Joseph's most valuable possession: his royal Davidic lineage.

This sheds light on a common question about Christ's claim to kingship: How can Jesus be a true descendant of David if he is not the physical son of Joseph? After all, since Jesus is only the adopted son of Joseph, he does not have the same blood as Joseph has. For ancient Jews, adoption was much more than a contractual arrangement forming legal ties between the man and the child. Adoption was covenantal, forming real family bonds between the two. Adoption would make them father and son. The adopted child would be considered a true son and thus an heir. This is why ancient Jews would have no difficulty seeing Jesus as a true son of David even though he does not have the Davidic blood line of Joseph. As the adopted son of Joseph, Jesus would inherit all that his father had to pass on—most especially his Davidic ancestry.

No Room in the Inn?

"And she gave birth to her first-born son and wrapped him in swaddling clothes, and laid him in a manger, because there was no place for them in the inn" (Lk 2:7).

Where exactly did Mary gave birth to Jesus? Did she deliver the child in a stable? A cave? Or some other dwelling? Luke's Gospel does not say. The only clue Luke offers is that Mary "laid him in a manger, because there was no place for them in the inn."

The reference to a manger suggests Jesus was born in a setting where animals dwelt. The mention of the "inn" is harder to unpack. Often translated "inn," the Greek word *katalyma* actually has a broader meaning, denoting any kind of lodging place. In the Bible, it can refer to a guest room in a home (Lk 22:11), a primitive inn (Ex 4:24; 1 Sm 1:18), or simply "a place to stay" (Sir 14:25; cf. Ex 15:13).

One interpretation views *katalyma* as referring to a traveler's inn believed to be located near Bethlehem (cf. Jer 41:17). Such a dwelling place would have been different from a modern hotel setting with private living quarters and comfortable accommodations. A primitive inn from this area would have housed large groups of travelers under one roof where guests would sleep in cots alongside the animals. In this interpretation, Mary and Joseph could not find room in the traveler's inn, so they went somewhere closer to the animals or to the stable to deliver the child.[3]

A second interpretation holds that *katalyma* refers to some type of guest room. After all, Joseph is visiting his family's ancestral town. One might expect him to stay not at an inn for travelers, but at the home of one of his relatives. In many peasant homes in ancient Palestine, family and animals slept in one enclosed space, with the family sleeping on a raised platform while the animals resided on a slightly lower level. In this view, since there was no place to lay the baby in the presumably crowded sleeping quarters (*katalyma*), Mary put him in the manger that would have been kept inside the home.

A third view is based on an early tradition going back to the second century, which holds that Jesus was born in a particular cave on the outskirts of Bethlehem.[4] St. Jerome suggests that the Romans may have unwittingly helped preserve the memory of this place by building a pagan shrine over the spot of Jesus's birth: "In the cave where the Christ-child once cried, they wept for Venus' lover."[5] As Ratzinger explains, "The fact that after the expulsion of the Jews from the Holy Land in the second century, Rome turned the cave into a shrine of Tammuz-Adonis, thereby evidently intending to suppress the Christian memorial cult, confirms the age of this shrine and also shows how important it was thought to be by the Romans."[6] By AD 325, the tradition was so strong that Constantine erected a basilica over a series of Bethlehem caves to commemorate the place where Jesus was believed to have been born. According to this view, there was no lodging within Bethlehem, so Joseph brought Mary to a cave near the village. This seems plausible since caves sometimes served as housing for peasants and their animals.[7]

Wherever the precise location of Jesus's birth in Bethlehem was, the one thing Luke makes clear is that Israel's Messiah-King was born of humble origins, in a crowded living space, where the only place to lay him was in an animal's feeding trough. This would have been difficult for any mother, but one can imagine how puzzling this would have been for Mary. Nine months earlier, she was told by the angel that this child would be the great Messiah-King, the holy Son of God. But the way he enters the world seems to be unfitting for such a royal child. If he really is the Messiah, why does he enter the world like this, in such conditions of poverty, humility, and rejection? Pope St. John Paul II considered the anguish this apparent contradiction would have caused Mary. "Mary experienced childbirth in a condition of extreme poverty. She could not give the Son of God even what mothers usually offer a newborn baby. Instead, she had to lay him 'in a manger,' an improvised cradle which contrasts with the dignity of the 'Son of the Most High.'"[8]

"Keep and Ponder"

How does Mary respond to all this? Here we come to what is perhaps the most important point Luke makes about Mary in his account of the Nativity—her response to all that takes place at the birth of her Son: Mary "kept all these things, pondering them in her heart" (Lk 2:19). Let's take a closer look at three key words in this statement: heart, keep, and ponder.

First, in Scripture, the "heart" is not just a vital organ. It refers to the center of one's desires, thoughts, and attentions. All actions flow from the heart. Mary is described as keeping and pondering in her heart the profound events surrounding Jesus's birth.

Second, the mention of Mary "pondering" these things in her heart means a lot more than her simply bringing to mind or remembering something. The word "to ponder" (*symballein*) can be translated literally as "to throw side by side." It describes someone comparing ideas, reflecting, and organizing various thoughts together in order to see the whole.

Third, "kept" also tells us something important about Mary. In the Old Testament, this particular Greek verb (*synterein*) refers to someone reflecting on the significance of mysterious events, especially when God is revealing something to the person. When the patriarch Joseph, for example, told his father and brothers about the strange dreams he was having about the sun, moon, and eleven stars bowing down before him, his father, Jacob, "kept the saying in mind" (Gn 37:9–11). In a similar way, when the prophet Daniel explained King Nebuchadnezzar's dream, the king "kept" Daniel's interpretation in his heart. Daniel himself received a vision from God and "kept" the meaning of the vision that was revealed to him (Dn 7:28). From these passages, we can see that "to keep" refers to someone wanting to understand the meaning of a dream or vision accurately.

The expression has even greater significance in the Wisdom books of the Old Testament. There, "to keep" describes someone striving not only to understand a message correctly, but also to live it out, to put it into practice. Psalm 119:11 is a good example: "I have laid up your word in my heart, that I might not sin against you." Here we see that the Psalmist doesn't just want to comprehend God's Word in his head. He seeks understanding in his heart, so that he will observe God's law in his life. In a similar way, a father says to his son in Proverbs 3:1, "Let your heart keep my commandments." The statement focuses not merely on the son's knowing his father's commands but on him living them out—"keeping" his father's wise counsels in the sense of observing them. A similar point is made in the book of Sirach, which relates how the wise man keeps with concern the parables and prophecies of God that have been handed down to him (Sir 39:1–3).

When Luke states at the end of the Nativity story that Mary "kept all these things, pondering them in her heart," he portrays her as a woman seeking to understand the deeper significance of the mysterious circumstances surrounding her Son's birth. She is striving to grasp the depths of what God is showing her through these various puzzling and surprising events. Why did she have to move just before the child was to be born? Why did her Son enter the world under the oppressive Roman census? Why was there no proper place in which he could be born? Why the manger and such humility and poverty? Mary does not have all the answers. She keeps and ponders, which means she strives to grasp God's purposes in these challenging events so that she can conform her life to whatever the Lord may be trying to teach her.

As Mary does this, she will eventually come to see even more clearly a crucial point that Luke subtly makes when he narrates Jesus's birth in 2:7. Of all the details Luke could report, he chooses to focus on how the child was "wrapped" in swaddling clothes and "laid" in a manger. Luke uses these two verbs back-to-back only one other time in his entire Gospel: at the end of Jesus's life when he was taken down from the Cross. Just as Jesus at the start of his life was *wrapped* in bands of cloth and *laid* in a manger (Lk 2:7), so too at the end of his life he was *wrapped* in a linen cloth and *laid* in a tomb after being crucified on Calvary (Lk 23:53). In this way, Luke underscores the connection between Bethlehem and Calvary, between Christmas and Good Friday. Jesus enters the world in conditions of poverty, humility, and rejection, pointing to how he will leave this world. He is indeed the king, as Gabriel announced, but he will establish his Kingship not through worldly power and might but through his sacrifice on the Cross. To express this connection between the two scenes, some Christian iconography later depicted Christ's birthplace as looking like a sepulcher.[9]

Mary Shares in Jesus's Sufferings: "For Them" (Lk 2:7)

But there may be one other profound point Luke subtly makes about Mary in this verse, one that sheds light on the mystery of her participation in Christ's sufferings. Luke seems to be linking Mary with the theme of Christ's rejection in this passage when he says, "There was no place *for them* in the inn" (Lk 2:7).

Who is the "them" for whom there is no place? Readers typically assume it refers to Mary and Joseph (or Mary, Joseph, and the baby Jesus in the womb), who are unable able to find a good place for the child to be born. But if we take a closer look at this verse, we will see how everything is centered on Mary and the child Jesus. Joseph is not even mentioned.

> And *she* gave birth to *her first-born son*
> and wrapped him in swaddling clothes,
> and laid him in a manger,
> because there was no place for *them* in the inn. (Lk 2:7)

As New Testament scholar Beverly Gaventa has noted, Mary is the subject of all the verbs in this sentence and the child is the one who receives all the actions in this verse. Mary gave birth to her firstborn son. Mary wrapped the child in swaddling clothes. Mary laid the child in a manger. Gaventa explains: "Three active verbs describe the events, each of which has Mary as its subject and the babe as its object. Here Mary acts alone. . . . Even Joseph remains hidden from the narrator's vision."[10]

Thus, at the end of this verse, when Luke says there was no room "for them," this most naturally refers to Mary and the child. In this way, Luke subtly reveals how Mary at the Nativity already participates in the suffering and rejection of her Son: there is no room "for them." While this theme becomes more explicit at the Presentation with Simeon's prophecy about the sword piercing her own soul also (Lk 2:35), Mary is already participating in her Son's affliction here at the Nativity. Pope St. John Paul II understood Luke 2:7 in this way as well:

> The Gospel notes that "there was no place for them in the inn" (Lk 2:7). This statement, recalling the text in John's Prologue: "His own people received him not" (Jn 1:11), foretells as it were the many refusals Jesus will meet with during his earthly life. The phrase "for them" joins the Son and the Mother in this rejection and shows how Mary is already associated with her Son's destiny of suffering and shares in his redeeming mission.[11]

Therefore, at the birth of Jesus, Mary gets a taste of the suffering her Son will experience. The message of the Nativity foreshadows the message of the Cross. It is this message that Mary keeps and ponders and will come to understand more fully over time.

Interior Reflection

The beauty of Mary keeping and pondering can be even better appreciated when set alongside the response of the people who hear the shepherds' report about the angels and their message. Those people "wonder" without pausing to keep and ponder the meaning of these events. There is a crucial difference between their superficial reaction and Mary's response. Consider how Luke himself notes the contrast: "All who heard it wondered at what the shepherds told them. *But (de)* Mary kept all these things, pondering them in her heart" (Lk 2:18–19).

In Scripture, wonder is a common, human response to supernatural events. The word itself does not carry negative overtones, but in Luke's Gospel mere "wonder" does not imply faith and does not always translate into true understanding. When Jesus preaches in his hometown of Nazareth, for example, the people there initially *wondered* at his teaching. But, at the end of that scene, those same people tried to kill him (Lk 4:22, 28–29). The initial excitement did not translate into faithfulness and obedience.

Mary's response at the Nativity, however, is much greater than this kind of simple amazement. She, unlike the hearers of the shepherds' report, is a person who reflects interiorly on the meaning of the events in her life to discern what the Lord is trying to show her. She is not someone who is amazed and then rushes off to the next stimulating event. Rather, she is the one who "kept all these things, pondering them in her heart"—a biblical expression that we have seen portrays people who have received a revelation that goes beyond what they can grasp on their own and so turn to God to show them the meaning. As Francis Moloney explains,

> There is a mystery about the revelation whose significance he or she cannot fully grasp. In such a situation one can simply marvel, and then go one's way (see, for example, Lk 2:18), or one can "treasure in the heart." The mystery can be taken into the deepest recesses of one's being, guarded and pondered over in one's heart. The faithful ones simply await God's time and plan for the full revelation of the mysteries entrusted to them.[12]

This certainly applies to Mary. The Mother of Jesus is given a unique grace and more revelation than anyone else in Luke's Gospel, but that does not mean she has all the answers. She still must walk by faith and not by sight.

Her faith continues to seek understanding as she keeps and ponders these things in her heart, patiently awaiting further insight from the Lord.

But her wait will not be long. Just forty days after this scene, Mary will receive a troubling revelation from the prophet Simeon that further reveals what God was starting to show her at the Nativity: the mystery of her Son's Suffering and Death.

Chapter Twelve

Mary at the Presentation
(Luke 2:21–24)

And at the end of eight days, when he was circumcised, he was called Jesus, the name given by the angel before he was conceived in the womb. And when the time came for their purification according to the law of Moses, they brought him up to Jerusalem to present him to the Lord (as it is written in the law of the Lord, "Every male that opens the womb shall be called holy to the Lord") and to offer a sacrifice according to what is said in the law of the Lord, "a pair of turtledoves, or two young pigeons." (Lk 2:21–24)

It's just forty days after Jesus's birth in Bethlehem. The Christ Child is brought to the Jerusalem Temple. We must remember that this is *his* Temple, the house of the Lord. In the scene commonly known as the Presentation, the Lord returns to his Holy Temple as a forty-day-old child.

Nevertheless, Jesus's entry into this most sacred building escapes the notice of most people that day. He comes not in royal splendor but humbly as a child. And his family proceeds like everyone else, as obedient Jews who follow God's Law. Notice how much Luke emphasizes this point in 2:21–24. Even before introducing the Presentation scene, Luke goes out of his way to tell us three facts in 2:21 that emphasize that Mary and Joseph are faithful, obedient, law-abiding Jews.

1.   Jesus was *circumcised*;

2.   He was circumcised *at the proper time*—"at the end of eight days"; and

3.   He was *given the name the angel had instructed Mary to give him*—Jesus (1:31).

Next, Luke bends over backward to make sure we view the Presentation scene in a similar light. He not only alludes to Mary and Joseph fulfilling a particular ritual prescribed by the Law (the purification of the mother), he also specifically tells us that their actions in the Temple that day were performed "as it is written in the law" and "according to what is said in the law of the Lord." Luke even quotes part of the Law to demonstrate the point: "Every male that opens the womb shall be called holy to the Lord" (2:23) and "a pair of turtledoves or two young pigeons" (2:24).

What an awkward way to relay a simple story! Why all the emphasis on them acting "according to the law" and giving citations from legal texts? Luke's approach doesn't make sense unless he is trying to drive home a point about the Holy Family's faithful compliance with the Law.[1] Luke clearly wants us to see the Holy Family as obedient, law-abiding Jews.

Two Turtledoves

Now let's take a closer look at the two Jewish customs in the background of this scene—the purification of the mother and the redemption of the firstborn son—and what they would tell us about Mary and Jesus.

After giving birth to a male child, a Jewish mother was considered ritually impure for the seven days before his circumcision and then remained confined for thirty-three days, during which time she could not enter the Temple. When her forty days of purification were completed, she was to offer a lamb and a young pigeon to the priests at the sanctuary. If a woman could not afford a lamb, she could present two young pigeons or doves instead (Lv 12:1–8).

This background tells us something important about Mary and Joseph. The fact that they offer "a pair of turtledoves or two young pigeons" (2:24) indicates that they are poor—they cannot afford a lamb for the sacrifice. Nevertheless, they have something much more valuable to present to the Lord. As Pope St. John Paul II has pointed out, they bring to the Temple "the true Lamb," the child Jesus, who will redeem humanity through his sacrifice on the Cross.[2]

Redemption of the Firstborn

The second tradition in the background of this scene is the redemption of the firstborn son. In the previous chapter we saw how firstborn sons possessed the right of inheritance. Originally, their position in the family held even greater importance, as they were meant to be consecrated to God, set apart for special service to the Lord (cf. Ex 13:1–2). However, after Israel's act of idolatry in worshipping the golden calf on Mount Sinai, this role was stripped from the firstborn sons and given to the only tribe who remained faithful to Yahweh that day, the Levites (cf. Ex 32:29; Nm 3:11; 8:14–19). Since the firstborn were originally meant to be consecrated, Jewish Law required them to be "bought back" so that they could be released from their special service to the Lord. The price of five shekels was paid to the Temple to support the ones who replaced them, the Levites (Nm 18:15–16).[3] As a firstborn son from a non-Levitical tribe (see Lk 1:27), Jesus would be expected to be "bought back" from service to the Lord.

What is unusual about this scene, however, is that Luke does not mention the five shekels being paid to "buy back" the Christ Child, and there is no mention of the redemption of the firstborn. Instead, Luke describes how Mary and Joseph "present him to the Lord." In doing so, Luke turns the act of redemption into "a *presentation* of the child in the Jerusalem Temple,"[4] reminiscent of how the prophet Samuel, as a child, was dedicated to the service of the Lord (1 Sm 1:28).

We should not think of this as a presentation in the modern sense of merely introducing someone or displaying something for all to see. The word in Luke 2:22 for "present" (*paristanai*) is *sacrificial* language in the Bible. It means "to offer" in the sense of sacrifices being offered in the Temple. Paul's letters, for example, use this word with a particularly sacrificial overtone (Rom 6:13–19; 12:1; 1 Cor 8:8; 2 Cor 4:14; 11:2; Eph 5:27; Col 1:28).[5] The Holy Family is presenting the child Jesus like a lamb would be presented for sacrifice in the Temple. The scene is, therefore, a subtle prelude to the Passion. As Ratzinger explains,

> Evidently Luke intends to say that instead of being "redeemed" and restored to his parents [as was normal custom], this child was personally handed over to God in the Temple, given over completely to God. . . . The language of sacrificial offering and priesthood is evoked here. Luke has nothing to say regarding the act of "redemption" prescribed by the law. In its place we find the exact opposite: the child is handed over to God, and from now on belongs to him completely. None of the aforementioned acts prescribed by the law required an appearance in the Temple. Yet for Luke, Jesus's first entry into the Temple as the locus of the event is essential. Here, in the place of encounter between God and his people, instead of the reclamation of the first-born, what happens is that Jesus is publicly handed over to God, his Father.[6]

All this sets the stage for Mary's dramatic encounter that day with a prophet named Simeon. Simeon offers two oracles at the Temple. One encourages Mary, confirming for her that her child is indeed the promised Messiah, who will be a light of revelation for the Gentiles and glory for the people of Israel (see chapter 13). The other prophecy, however, reveals what will happen when her Son carries out this mission: he will be opposed, plotted against, and eventually killed. The infant in her arms will grow up, begin his ministry, and eventually be pierced by a sword (see chapter 14).

Chapter Thirteen

Mary and the Return of Glory
(Luke 2:25–32)

After entering the Temple, Mary and Joseph encounter a mysterious man named Simeon. He is "righteous and devout" and a prophet who has the Holy Spirit upon him (Lk 2:25). Most remarkable is that the Spirit told Simeon that he would not die before seeing the Lord's Messiah (2:26).

That day comes in the Presentation scene. He holds the Christ Child in the air and blesses God, saying:

> Lord, now let your servant depart in peace,
> according to your word;
> for my eyes have seen your salvation
> which you have prepared in the presence of all peoples,
> a light for revelation to the Gentiles,
> and for glory to your people Israel. (Lk 2:29–32)

Think about what these words mean for Mary. Simeon describes her child as God's "salvation" and as "a light of revelation to the Gentiles"—images from the book of Isaiah about the redemptive work God would accomplish in the future. Isaiah foretold that one day "all the ends of the earth shall see the salvation of our God" (Is 52:10; cf. Is 40:5) and that God would send his servant to be "a light to the nations."

Drawing on these images from Isaiah, Simeon's words are another encouraging confirmation for Mary that her Son is indeed the Christ, just as Gabriel, the shepherds, and the angels over Bethlehem said. Her child is the one who will fulfill these prophecies from Isaiah.

The Glory of the Lord

Simeon also proclaims the Christ Child to be "glory" for the people of Israel. We already have seen how "glory" is often used in the Bible to describe the visible manifestation of God's holy presence, especially over the Ark of the Covenant, in the Tabernacle, and in the Temple. At Mount Sinai, the *glory* of the Lord in the form of a cloud overshadowed the Tabernacle where the Ark resided (Ex 40:34). When Solomon dedicated the Temple in Jerusalem, "the *glory* of the Lord filled the house of the Lord" (1 Kgs 8:11). When the prophet Ezekiel received a vision of the Temple, he saw it filled with "the *glory* of the Lord" and fell on his face in worship (Ez 44:4).

As we saw in chapter 9, however, God's glory did not remain in the Temple always. Shortly before Babylon conquered Jerusalem and destroyed it in 586 BC, Ezekiel received a vision of God's glory leaving the Temple and departing from the city—an ominous sign of the impending judgment upon Jerusalem (Ez 10–11). The second book of Maccabees tells how in this period Jeremiah hid the Ark of the Covenant in a cave to protect it from being desecrated by the Babylonian invaders. He said it would not be found until the day God gathers his people together again (2 Mc 2:4–8).

Even though many Jews returned to Jerusalem in 515 BC and rebuilt their city and their Temple, things were not the same. The new house of the Lord did not contain God's presence as it had done before the exile. The Temple still stood on sacred ground and served as the center of Jewish worship, but there is no account of the Ark of the Covenant or "the glory of the Lord" returning to the sanctuary. For hundreds of years, the Jews longed for God's glory-presence to be with them again in the Temple.[1] Some prophets even foretold how the cloud of God's glory would one day return to Israel (Bar 5:8–9; Is 4:5; 35:2; 40:5; 60:1–3). Most notable is Ezekiel's oracle, which specifies the Temple as the place where the Lord's glory will return: "And behold, the glory of the God of Israel came from the east. . . . As the glory of the LORD entered the temple by the gate facing the east, the Spirit lifted me up, and brought me into the inner court; and behold, the glory of the LORD filled the temple" (Ez 43:2–5; 44:4).

With this background in mind, we can see that when Simeon stands within the barren Temple of the Lord and calls the infant Jesus "*glory* to your people Israel" (Lk 2:32), he is saying a lot. God's glory-presence, which has not been with the people for over 500 years, has finally returned to the Temple with the arrival of the infant Jesus. At the Nativity, the glory of the Lord was made manifest to the shepherds in the fields at night (2:11). Now, forty days later, it has returned to the Temple in the Christ Child. As Raymond Brown explains, "It was the proudest boast of the Temple theologians that the glory of God dwelt in the sanctuary (1 Kgs 8:10–11; Ezek 44:4); and now as Simeon stands before that barren sanctuary, he proclaims Jesus to be a glory for God's people Israel."[2] René Laurentin similarly notes, "The whole Infancy Narrative is polarized by this entry of Jesus into the holy place. As a climax of a series of converging hints, the manifestation of Jesus in the Temple is identified with the eschatological manifestation of the Glory (that is, of Yahweh) in the midst of the people of Israel."[3]

All this has significant implications for understanding Mary in this scene. Fittingly, it is Mary who has brought Jesus to the Temple. We already have seen how Luke's Gospel portrays Mary as the new Ark of the Covenant, bearing God's presence (see chapter 9). Like the Ark of old, Mary now carries the God-Man to Jerusalem and restores the glory of the Lord to the Temple.

Seventy Weeks of Years

We can go a step further with this theme of God's presence returning to the Temple if we consider how a prophecy given in the book of Daniel, chapter nine, relates to this scene.

First, let's consider the background of the prophecy. Daniel was a Jewish man who grew up in Babylon during the Exile. Seventy years had passed since the Babylonians destroyed the Jerusalem Temple and carried the people off into captivity. It's at this point that Daniel pleads with God to free the Jews from their pagan oppressors. For all these seventy years, the Jerusalem Temple has been deserted, lying in ruins, while the people have been enslaved hundreds of miles from home. In the midst of his prayer, Daniel asked God to restore the Temple and return his presence there: "O Lord, *cause your face to shine on your sanctuary* which is desolate" (Dn 9:17). Since in the Bible "the face of God" is an expression describing God's presence, Daniel is asking God to return to his house, the Temple, which has been desolate since 586 BC.

In response to this plea, God sends the angel Gabriel to Daniel to give him a prophecy that would give hope to the Jews for centuries to come. At the hour of the evening sacrifice, Gabriel appears to Daniel and announces that God will answer his prayer, but only after a long period of time—a period described as "seventy weeks of years" (Dn 9:24). At the end of that time, God would send "an anointed one" (*messiah*) who would bring an end to sin, atone for iniquity, usher in everlasting righteousness, fulfill all prophecy, and anoint a most holy place (Dn 9:24–27).

While the "seventy weeks of years" symbolizes 490 years (since "a week" of years would symbolize 7 years, and 70 x 7 years = 490 years), the central takeaway of Gabriel's message signals that it will be several centuries before God sends his "anointed one" to restore the Jewish people and shine his face again on the holy Temple. This prophecy is important for Luke's Gospel, because after the book of Daniel, the next time the angel Gabriel appears in the Bible is about five centuries later (reminiscent of the 490 years!) in Luke's opening scene, the Annunciation to Zechariah. Remarkably, there are many parallels between Gabriel's announcement to Zechariah and his message to Daniel. Just as *Gabriel* appeared to Daniel *in response to his prayer at the hour of Temple sacrifice* to announce the "seventy weeks of years," so the same angel *Gabriel* visited *Zechariah in response to his prayer at the hour of the Temple sacrifice* to announce the dawn of the new covenant. Gabriel's return in such a similar manner after several centuries of silence signals the end of Israel's "seventy weeks of years" of suffering under Gentile rule. It also marks the beginning of the new era that would finally answer Daniel's prayer for *God's face to shine again in the sanctuary*—the age when sin would be atoned for, prophecy would be fulfilled, and *the Holy of Holies would be anointed.*[4]

490 Days

This background helps us see Daniel chapter 9's significance for the Presentation scene. The chronology of Luke's infancy narrative subtly expresses the fulfillment of Daniel's "seventy weeks of years" by narrating a 490-day period that begins and ends in the Temple. Luke begins his Gospel with Gabriel's announcement to Zechariah in the Temple, and he brings his narrative to a significant climax 490 days later when Jesus is presented in the Temple.[5]

We will see how Luke's infancy narrative offers various chronological signposts, hinting that he wants us to be noting the time frame between scenes. Walk with me, now, as I map out the chronology of these amazing 490 days at the opening of Luke's Gospel.

Day 1: Annunciation to Zechariah

On the first day in Luke's narrative, the angel announces to Zechariah that his wife Elizabeth will bear a child. At the end of this scene, we are told that Elizabeth kept her pregnancy hidden for "five months" (1:24).

Day 180: Annunciation to Mary

The next scene—the Annunciation to Mary—comes one month later, in "the sixth month" of Elizabeth's pregnancy (1:26). Since a month was considered thirty days, Mary's conception of Jesus "in the sixth month" suggests that Jesus was conceived on the 180th day in Luke's Gospel—about 180 days after the annunciation to Zechariah (6 months x 30 days = 180 days).

Day 450: Birth of Jesus

The next significant chronological marker is the birth of Jesus. Mary would have been pregnant for nine months, which in the biblical perspective would be 270 days (9 months x 30 days = 270 days). That means Jesus would have been born 270 days after the Annunciation to Mary. Since the Annunciation to Mary occurred in the sixth month (or 180th day), that means Jesus's birth, coming nine months (270 days) later, took place on the 450th day in Luke's Gospel (180 + 270 = 450).

Day 490: The Presentation of Jesus in the Temple

Finally, the climactic point in Luke's infancy narrative is the Presentation scene. Since the purification of the mother took place forty days after the birth of a male child, Mary would have presented Jesus to the Temple forty days after the Nativity—which would make it the 490th day in Luke's Gospel. Thus, we can see that 490 days after the start of Luke's Gospel, when Gabriel appeared to Zechariah to signal the end of Daniel's "seventy weeks of years," *God's glory-presence returns to the Temple in the infant Jesus.*

In other words, on this climactic 490th day in Luke's narrative, Daniel's plea for God's face to shine in the sanctuary is finally answered in the Presentation scene as Mary brings the Christ Child to the Temple. The 490-year wait is finally over on the 490th day in Luke's Gospel. Indeed, the glory-presence of God is now made manifest in the child she carries. How appropriate that it is Mary, the new Ark of the Covenant (see chapter 9), who helped make this possible. Like the Ark of old, Mary bears the glory of the Lord to the Temple, and God's face shines once again on his sanctuary through the anointed child in her arms.

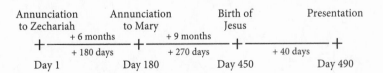

Annunciation to Zechariah	Annunciation to Mary	Birth of Jesus	Presentation
+ 6 months	+ 9 months		
+ 180 days	+ 270 days	+ 40 days	
Day 1	Day 180	Day 450	Day 490

Chapter Fourteen

Pierced by a Sword
(Luke 2:33–35)

And his father and his mother marveled at what was said about him; and Simeon blessed them and said to Mary his mother, "Behold, this child is set for the fall and rising of many in Israel, and for a sign that is spoken against (and a sword will pierce through your own soul also), that thoughts out of many hearts may be revealed." *(Lk 2:33–35)*

There is much to rejoice over in Simeon's first oracle: Mary's child is "God's salvation," "light to the nations," and "glory" for Israel. It is no wonder that Mary and Joseph "marveled at what was said" about their Son (2:33).

But the joy of Simeon's first oracle stands in stark contrast with the ominous words that come next. In his second oracle, which is addressed specifically to Mary (2:34), Simeon warns Mary about the difficult road that lies ahead. Her child will endure many painful trials when he enters his adult years: Jesus will be at the center of much conflict. People will oppose him and plot against him. He will be killed. And this hostile opposition will cause her much pain.

Ratzinger calls these words "a kind of Passion prophecy" foreshadowing how this hostility will lead to Christ's Death.[1]

But before we examine the line most directly related to Mary—the image of a sword piercing her soul (2:35)—let's consider the other statements Simeon makes in this second oracle, and we will see how the message as a whole comes together to foretell the persecution and suffering her son Jesus will face.

"Set for the Fall and Rising of Many in Israel" (Lk 2:34)

First, Mary is told that her Son is "set for the fall and rising of many in Israel" (2:34). The imagery recalls the theme of reversal that Mary herself expressed in the Magnificat: in this dawning messianic age, some (like the mighty) will be cast down, while others (like the lowly) will be exalted.[2] Simeon's words here also foreshadow how Jesus will be a source of division, causing the fall and rise of many in Israel. Through his public ministry, many of the social, religious, and political leaders will be cast down as they reject Christ's message, while many of the lowly, the poor, and the Gentiles will be raised up in Christ's Kingdom.

"A Sign That Is Spoken Against" (Lk 2:34)

Next, Simeon says the child will be "for a sign that is spoken against" (2:34). New Testament scholar Scott Cunningham notes how in Luke-Acts this particular verb for "spoken against" (*antilego*) always comes in the context of specifically Jewish religious opposition to Christ (Lk 2:34; 20:27; 21:15) and his disciples (Acts 4:14; 13:45; 28:22). In fact, the entirety of Luke-Acts can be seen as framed by this theme of Jewish leaders opposing Christ's work: the first use of this word is found near the start of Luke's Gospel in Simeon's prophecy about the Christ Child being a sign that is spoken against (*antilegomenon*) (2:34), and the final use of this word comes at the end of Acts and involves the Jewish leaders in Rome telling Paul that the Christians are spoken against (*antilegetai*) everywhere (Acts 28:22). As Cunningham explains, "The link shows Luke intends his reader to see Lk. 2:34 as encompassing the whole of Luke-Acts. Here the last words spoken concerning Jesus in the infancy material contain a note of rejection, and this is verbally and conceptually connected to the last scene of Acts, where that rejection continues. Thus, from the beginning of Luke to the end of Acts, Jesus, both personally and through his disciples, will encounter rejection especially from the Jews."[3]

"That Thoughts out of Many Hearts May Be Revealed" (Lk 2:35)

Simeon goes on to say that Jesus's ministry will cause division so that the "thoughts out of many hearts may be revealed" (2:35b). The heart (*kardia*) points to the deepest seat of human thought, desire, and action. The words *kardiōn dialogismoi*, therefore, refer to one's deepest, inmost thoughts. But for Luke, *dialogismoi* always denotes negative thoughts that Jesus exposes. Sometimes it refers to the Pharisees reasoning against Jesus (5:22; 6:8; 20:14) that Jesus makes known. Other times it describes the disciples misunderstanding Christ (9:46–47; 24:38). Simeon's mention of these hostile or misunderstanding thoughts being revealed (*apokalyphthōsin*) anticipates what Jesus will say in Luke 12:1–2: "Nothing is covered up that will not be revealed (*apokalupsthēsetai*), or hidden that will not be known."[4]

"And a Sword Will Pierce through Your Own Soul Also" (Lk 2:35)

Now we are prepared to examine Simeon's cryptic words to Mary, "And a sword will pierce through your own soul also" (2:35a). As Ratzinger explains, here "Simeon's Passion prophecy becomes quite specific."[5] These words about the sword would tell Mary two important things.

First, a sword will pierce her Son. The fact that she is told about a sword piercing "through [her] soul also" implies that this sword will pass through Jesus first. But what is the meaning of the sword? In the Old Testament, the sword symbolized bloodshed, death, and war (e.g., Gn 27:40; Lv 26:6; Dt 32:25; Jos 5:13; Is 1:20). Thus, the image of a sword piercing Jesus points to the violent hostility he will eventually face. Simeon's words subtly foreshadow how Jesus's ministry will culminate in his bloody Death on the Cross—where, in fact, a Roman soldier will pierce his side with a sword (Jn 19:34).

The second thing these words tell Mary is that this intense opposition to Jesus will affect *her* as well: "A sword will pierce through *your soul also*" (Lk 2:35). The sentence draws attention to Mary in numerous ways.

First, it puts emphasis on Mary as an individual by having her addressed directly by Simeon in the second person singular. Nowhere else in Simeon's oracle is anyone else addressed personally this way.[6]

Second, the sentence structure itself uses intensifying words and pronouns that put Mary at the center.[7] In fact, the opening of the sentence could be translated as "and of you yourself also."[8] As Evans notes, "With the utmost emphasis it directs attention to Mary and to her personal experience as a result of what is being prophesied."[9] This emphatic opening underscores how the sword passing through Mary's soul is linked with what Simeon already underscored in this second oracle: the rejection of the child who will bring the falling and rising of many in Israel (Lk 2:34).[10]

Third, Luke may be linking Mary with her Son's sufferings as both Mary and the child are *recipients* of hostile acts in back-to-back sentences. As Nolland observes, the passive construction of the previous sentence about how the child is a sign that is spoken against and this sentence about how Mary will have a sword pass through her soul "favors a comparison between the fate of the sign and the fate of Mary: Mary stands with her son as one opposed."[11] Nolland thus concludes that "we must find mirrored in the words concerning Mary the full degree to which her son will be opposed . . . a sword will pass through her soul (she will suffer the loss of her son in death) because the opposition to her son will reach such a pitch that by the hands of his opponents a sword will pass through his soul (he will be put to death)."[12]

The Sword

Now let's consider the full image itself as it relates to Mary—the sword passing through her soul. The word Luke uses for "sword" in 2:35 is a graphic one: *rhomphaiai* denotes a very large, broad, two-edged sword. This is no small dagger. The picture of such a large weapon passing through Mary's soul underscores the intense suffering she will endure because of her Son's rejection. The image draws heavily from Psalm 22, a psalm to which Luke alludes in his Passion narrative.[13] Psalm 22 describes the persecution of the righteous man being pierced in his hands and his feet and having his garments divided among his enemies, who cast lots for them (Ps 22:16–18). Luke clearly has this psalm in mind when he reports that those who crucified Jesus "cast lots to divide his garments" (Lk 23:34).

It is important to note that the righteous man in Psalm 22, in the midst of his various afflictions, cries out to the Lord, "Deliver my soul (*psychēn*) from the sword (*rhomphaias*)"

(Ps 22:20 [21:21 LXX]). This seems to be the primary backdrop to Simeon's words to Mary in Luke 2:35: "A *sword* (*rhomphaiai*) will pierce your *soul* (*psychēn*)."[14] Both texts use the same two key words (*rhomphaia* = large sword, and *psychēn* = soul) and both involve the context of hostile opposition. With these verbal and thematic similarities between Psalm 22:20 and Luke 2:35, Luke links Mary with his narrative of Jesus's rejection and Passion, a narrative that alludes to Psalm 22. As Goulder notes, "[Luke's] thought is of her son's coming rejection by his people, and he thinks what this will mean to her too, especially in the crucifixion; he has taken the image from Ps. 22 because that is where the Passion prophecies come, and the sword that will pass through Mary's soul can have no other meaning than this. . . ."[15] He sums up his point, stating, "[Mary] is to suffer the pain of the sign that is spoken against also, and Luke, thinking especially of the Cross, applies to her a text from Ps 22 (LXX 21.21), 'Save my soul from the sword (*rouphaias*.)'"[16]

Here we have a foreshadowing of the suffering Mary will endure when her son dies on the Cross. Pope St. John Paul II once described Simeon's words as "a second annunciation to Mary." These words "tell her of the actual historical situation in which the Son is to accomplish his mission, namely, in misunderstanding and sorrow . . . it also reveals to her that she will have to live her obedience of faith in suffering, at the side of the suffering Savior, and that her motherhood will be mysterious and sorrowful."[17]

Indeed, here at the Presentation, Mary receives a fuller picture of what she signed up for when she first consented to serve as the Mother of the Messiah at the Annunciation. Now, nine months and forty days later, she gains a deeper understanding of just how demanding this vocation will be. Her *fiat* in Galilee where she first accepted the life of the Christ Child in her womb will ultimately lead her to Calvary, where she will sorrowfully witness him offer his life on the Cross.

Mary's Soul

One last reflection: Simeon describes how a sword will pass through Mary's soul (*psychēn*), which in Scripture refers to the vital principle of a human person, the source of consciousness and freedom. Simeon tells Mary that at the core of her being something devastating will happen to her: a sword will pierce her soul.

This is particularly interesting because the only person in Luke's Gospel whose soul is mentioned and described is Mary's.[18] Luke mentions Mary's soul not just once, but twice. First, in the Magnificat, Mary says, "My soul [*psyche*] magnifies the Lord" (Lk 1:46). Second, here in the Presentation, Simeon says, "a sword will pierce your soul [*psychēn*] also" (Lk 2:35).

If we were to view these two references to Mary's soul together, perhaps we could draw out the following spiritual lesson: Mary's soul magnifies God the most by sharing in the sword of Christ's sufferings. In the Magnificat, Mary's soul magnifies the Lord. In the Presentation, we learn more about *how* Mary's soul does that best. Mary makes God great in her soul the most when she participates in the sacrificial love of her Son—when her soul is pierced by the sword.

Chapter Fifteen

Finding Her Son in the Temple
(Luke 2:41–52)

Now his parents went to Jerusalem every year at the feast of the Passover. And when he was twelve years old, they went up according to custom; and when the feast was ended, as they were returning, the boy Jesus stayed behind in Jerusalem. His parents did not know it, but supposing him to be in the company they went a day's journey, and they sought him among their kinsfolk and acquaintances; and when they did not find him they returned to Jerusalem, seeking him. (Lk.2:41–45)

The fact that Mary each year made the pilgrimage to Jerusalem for Passover is significant. According to the Old Testament Law, Jewish men were required to make a pilgrimage to the Jerusalem Temple for three of Israel's main feasts: Passover, Pentecost, and Tabernacles (cf. Ex 23:17; 34:23; Dt 16:16). But the Torah did not require women to go. For Mary to make the trek to Jerusalem year after year for the Passover feast is a sign of her special devotion to the Lord.[1]

Mary and Joseph would have taken the eighty-mile journey from Nazareth to Jerusalem in a large caravan, which was typical at the time. Journeying in large travel groups offered protection from bandits along the roadways while relatives and friends could share resources and offer each other assistance during the three- to four-day trip.[2]

Such a caravan of families would have been chaotic with people traveling at different paces, some faster than others. But at the end of each day, the whole group would meet together to rest for the night. The twelve-year-old Jesus was free to spend time with other friends and relatives his age, and since extended family often shared responsibility to watch over the children, it would be common for parents to assume that their fellow kinsmen in the caravan were looking after their child. That seems to be what happened with Mary and Joseph in this scene: "Supposing him to be in the company [i.e., the caravan] they went a day's journey, and they sought him among their kinsfolk and acquaintances" (Lk 2:44). Not finding him among their friends and family, Mary and Joseph immediately returned to Jerusalem to search for their lost son.

Searching Anxiously

After a full day of traveling out of Jerusalem, and probably a day retracing their steps back to the city, Mary and Joseph finally find Jesus in the Temple "after three days" (2:46). Part of what they see would have been quite common at the time: a Jewish boy sitting with his elders, listening to them, and asking them questions (2:46).

What is remarkable, however, is what Luke reports in the following verse: "And all who heard him were amazed at his understanding and his answers" (2:47). For a Jewish child to astonish his elder teachers in the Temple with his own insights would have been extraordinary. Since Jesus was only twelve years old, he would not yet have been viewed by Jewish Law as fully responsible before the Lord. That wouldn't occur until he turned thirteen. Nevertheless, the young Jesus impresses the elders of the Temple, who are "amazed at his understanding and his answers" (2:47). The particular word here for "amazed" (*existanto*) is employed elsewhere by Luke to express the wonder a person experiences when he witnesses a miraculous act and senses that he is in the presence of God (Lk 8:56; Acts 2:7, 12; 8:13; 9:21). With this word, Luke portrays the elders in the Temple as being in awe over such a young boy so gifted by God. They recognize God's hand upon him, endowing this twelve-year-old with a unique gift of wisdom.

Luke notes that Mary and Joseph also are filled with awe, but he uses a different word (*explagēsan*) to depict their wonder. This change in wording might suggest that their amazement was different from that of the elders. Perhaps they were amazed not over their child's wisdom, but over finding him completely immersed in his discussions with the teachers, seemingly unaware of the pain this three-day separation from his parents has caused them.[3]

Mary addresses her shock with Jesus: "Son, why have you treated us so? Behold, your father and I have been looking for you anxiously" (Lk 2:48). That last word—anxiously (*odynōmenoi*)—helps us catch a glimpse of the trauma Mary and Joseph underwent in those three days of searching. The word describes a deep spiritual or mental torment. Luke uses it to describe the torment someone experiences in Hades (Lk 16:24–25) and the Ephesian Christians' anguish in saying goodbye to Paul, realizing they will never see him again (Acts 20:38). The Greek Old Testament (the Septuagint) uses the word twice to depict the terror parents experience when losing a child. In one instance, Tobias tells his new father-in-law that he must return home right away because his father will worry if he is not back in time. Tobias says, "And if I delay long, he will be greatly distressed" (Tb 9:4). The story goes on to show how Tobias's delay does, in fact, cause his parents great anguish. His mother even worries she will never see her son again. Similarly, the mother in the book of Maccabees who witnesses the martyrdoms of her seven sons is described in the non-canonical Jewish work known as 4 Maccabees as being thankful that her deceased husband did not have to experience the same anguish (*odynoun*) she did in watching them all be killed (4 Mc 18:9).[4]

We can view Mary and Joseph's anguish in a similar way. Like the mother in Maccabees and Tobias's parents, Mary and Joseph experience great torment when they lose their son for three days in Jerusalem.

My Father's House

Jesus replies to Mary, saying, "How is it that you sought me? Did you not know that I must be in my Father's house?" (Lk 2:49).

Think about how perplexing these words would have been for Mary. Mary asks Jesus why he has treated his parents this way. But Jesus responds by asking challenging questions of his own. Luke notes how these questions from Jesus leave Mary and Joseph in the dark: "And they did not understand the saying which he spoke to them" (2:50).

What do Jesus's cryptic words mean? First, note the contrast between "your father" and "my father" in this dialogue. Mary says, "*Your* father and I have been looking for you anxiously." But Jesus replies speaking of "*my* father" in reference to his Heavenly Father: "Did you not know that I must be in my Father's house?" This is not a rejection of Joseph's fatherhood. Luke goes on to emphasize how Jesus returns home with his parents to Nazareth and remains obedient to them. But Jesus does draw a contrast between his earthly father and his Heavenly Father. His primary allegiance is to his Father in Heaven.

Second, let's ponder the meaning of "my Father's house." On a basic level, these words refer to the Temple, the house of the Lord. But the expression could also be translated as "in my Father's affairs"[5] or "in the things of the Father."[6] In the ancient Greco-Roman world, the idea of a "household" could refer not only to a place, but also to a family authority.[7] Both these meanings may come into play here. Jesus needed to be in the house of the Lord, the Jerusalem Temple, because he needed to be about his Father's affairs, doing the work of his Heavenly Father there. And this commitment to pursue his Father's will sometimes causes his human parents great sorrow, as it does during these three days.[8]

Mary's "Renewed *Fiat*"

Mary is being personally challenged by Jesus's words. Even though she had received more insight into Jesus than anyone else, she does not fully understand the meaning of all that is occurring in this scene, especially Jesus's words about needing to be in his Father's house. All she can do is surrender to the mystery of this event, keeping all these things and pondering them in her heart (2:51). As Ratzinger explains, "Even Mary's faith is a 'journeying' faith that is repeatedly shrouded in darkness and has to mature by persevering through the darkness. Mary does not understand Jesus's saying, but she keeps it in her heart and allows it gradually to come to maturity there."[9]

Pope St. John Paul II describes this surrender as Mary's "renewed *fiat*"—a profound moment in her growth as a disciple. Before this scene, Mary has related to Jesus primarily in a familial way as his mother. She bore him in her womb, gave birth to him in Bethlehem, and presented him to God in the Temple as a forty-day-old infant.

In the child's infancy, Mary's motherly heart experienced anguish at the way her Son was treated by others (as with Caesar's oppressive census, the lack of room for the child, and the humble, austere conditions of Jesus's birth). She would also have grieved over the way she knew he would be treated in the future (Simeon's prophecy about the rejection of her Son). But now, in this incident with the twelve-year-old Jesus lost in the Temple, it is not some other person or circumstance that inflicts grief on Mary. It is something Jesus himself does that is at the root of her sorrow and uncertainty. In pursuing his Father's will, Jesus does some things that cause Mary pain, and she does not understand. Mary is being challenged to relate to her Son in a new way as she is confronted more directly with his mission to do his Heavenly Father's will. As Pope St. John Paul II explains, Mary kept and pondered these events, "offering her cooperation in the spirit of a renewed 'fiat.' In this way the first link was forged in a chain of events that would gradually lead Mary beyond the natural role deriving from her motherhood, to put herself at the service of her divine Son's mission."[10]

He "Must" Be in His Father's House

One small word in Jesus's response can tell us something that Mary will ever more deeply come to understand: how this event is related to her Son's future sufferings. Jesus says he "must" (*dei*) be in his Father's house. This is a key term that Luke employs at strategic points in his narrative to emphasize an important aspect of Jesus's ministry being set forth.

The word itself means "it is necessary," but Luke uses it most especially to describe the urgent necessity of Jesus to give up his life for our sins: he *must* go to Jerusalem (13:33); he *must* be rejected by this generation (17:25); he *must* fulfill Scripture and be reckoned with criminals (22:37); he *must* suffer many things, be rejected, be killed, and be raised on the third day (9:22); and he *must* suffer and come into his glory (24:26) because the Law and the Prophets *must* be fulfilled (24:44). Right at the outset, Luke's Gospel narrates Jesus using this key word. Therefore, as Ratzinger points out, the twelve-year-old Jesus "is already bound by the 'must' at this early hour: he *must* be with the Father. . . . He is in the Temple . . . as the obedient one, acting out of the same obedience that leads to the Cross and resurrection."[11]

And this is at the core of what Mary must keep and ponder in her heart (2:51). The whole event is a foretaste of the suffering she will experience in her Son's Passion. "Something of the sword of sorrow of which Simeon had spoken (cf. Lk 2:35) becomes palpable for Mary at this hour. The closer one comes to Jesus, the more one is drawn into the mystery of his Passion."[12]

Indeed, this seems to be a point Luke is subtly making as this scene prefigures what will happen when Jesus follows his Heavenly Father's will all the way to the Cross. As a twelve-year-old, Jesus journeys with his family on *pilgrimage* from *Galilee to Jerusalem* for the feast of *Passover*. He enters the *Temple* and amazes the elders with his wisdom. He must be *doing the will of his Father*, but in the process is *separated from his mother*, causing her much pain. But *on the third day*, the child Jesus is found again.

All this pre-enacts what will take place at the climax of Jesus's public ministry. He will make another pilgrimage from Galilee to Jerusalem and for the same feast of Passover.

As in his youth, Jesus will enter the Temple and display his wisdom in the Holy City. Mary will lose her Son again, but this time in an even more profound way as he is crucified on Calvary, causing her much pain. However, just as in his youth, Jesus will be found on the third day when he rises from the dead (Lk 24:7).

The *Catechism of the Catholic Church* notes how Mary pondered this experience from her Son's childhood in her heart. "The *finding of Jesus in the temple* is the only event that breaks the silence of the Gospels about the hidden years of Jesus. Here Jesus lets us catch a glimpse of the mystery of his total consecration to a mission that flows from his divine sonship: 'Did you not know that I must be about my Father's work?' Mary and Joseph did not understand these words, but they accepted them in faith. Mary 'kept all these things in her heart' during the years Jesus remained hidden in the silence of an ordinary life" (*CCC*, 534).

◆

So far, we have focused our attention on Luke's Gospel and his presentation of Mary in those early years of Christ's life, from the Annunciation in Nazareth to the finding of her twelve-year-old Son in the Temple. Now we turn our attention to the Gospel of John to consider Mary's role in the scene that marks the beginning of Jesus's public ministry: the Wedding at Cana.

Chapter Sixteen

Mary at Cana
(John 2:1–3)

On the third day there was a marriage at Cana in Galilee, and the
mother of Jesus was there; Jesus also was invited to the marriage,
with his disciples. When the wine failed, the mother of Jesus said to
him, "They have no wine." (Jn 2:1–3)

Some people think Mary is not an important figure in the
Gospel of John. Her personal name is never mentioned.[1] She
only appears in two scenes: the Wedding at Cana and the
Crucifixion. And she only has two lines in the entire Gospel:
"They have no wine" (Jn 2:3) and "Do whatever he tells you"
(Jn 2:5).

Admittedly, this doesn't seem to be a lot to work with. But
that doesn't mean she's insignificant in the Fourth Gospel.
As we will see in the next four chapters, though Mary is given
limited space in John, her appearances come at two of the
most pivotal moments in the narrative: at the launching of
Christ's public ministry at the Wedding at Cana (Jn 2:1–11)
and at the climax of his mission at the Cross (Jn 19:25–27).
And she plays an important role in both these scenes.

Zooming in on the wedding feast, we can appreciate
her prominence right at the start: she is the first character

mentioned in the story. As Francis Moloney points out, "The fact that she is the first person introduced to the account, even preceding Jesus, is a sign that what she says and does is crucial to the story."[2] Moreover, she is mentioned three times in the opening five verses. As John sets up this story, he gives more attention to her than to anyone else, including the bride, the groom, the servants, the disciples, and even Jesus himself. In fact, after John tells us that "the mother of Jesus was there," he goes on to say, "Jesus also was invited to the marriage, with his disciples." As Moloney describes: "The scene has been set as a group of people headed by the mother of Jesus has gathered … for the celebration of a wedding 'on the third day.'"[3]

"They Have No Wine" (Jn 2:3)

To run out of wine at a first-century Jewish wedding feast was not just embarrassing or inconvenient. It would have been a social disaster. The groom's family had the responsibility to provide enough food and drink for the people in attendance. The success of the feast expressed to the community the family's level of social status and honor. That's why running out of wine would have been no small humiliation. It would have inflicted shame on the family for a long time to come.

Who is the first person to notice this impending disaster? Mary. And to whom does she turn? To the only person there who can solve the problem immediately: Jesus. The Catholic Tradition has often seen in Mary's intervention at Cana a sign of her compassion and attentiveness to others' needs. Vatican II, for example, described Mary at Cana as being "moved with pity."[4] Pope St. John Paul II said Mary was "prompted by her merciful heart" to help this family by bringing her concern for them to Jesus. "Having sensed the eventual disappointment of the newly married couple and guests because of the lack of wine, the Blessed Virgin compassionately suggested to Jesus that he intervene with his messianic power."[5]

This account can also be seen as offering a pattern for Marian intercession. Just as Mary at Cana noticed the family's needs, so Mary in Heaven continues to notice our needs before we do and better than we do. And just as Mary at Cana brought those needs to Christ, so does she continue to bring our needs to her Son through her intercession for us. Pope St. John Paul II once said this scene at Cana exemplifies *"Mary's solicitude for human beings,* her coming to them in the wide variety of their wants and needs." He continues:

> At Cana in Galilee there is shown only one concrete aspect of human need, apparently a small one of little importance ("They have no wine"). But it has a symbolic value: this coming to the aid of human needs means, at the same time, bringing those needs within the radius of Christ's messianic mission and salvific power. . . . Mary places herself between her Son and mankind in the reality of their wants, needs and sufferings.[6]

Asking for a Miracle?

But what exactly is Mary hoping for when she says to Jesus, "They have no wine" (Jn 2:3)?

Some say Mary wants Jesus to use his supernatural power and miraculously provide some wine. Others, however, argue that such a request would not be possible because Jesus had not performed any miracles yet at this point in the Fourth Gospel. How would Mary know that Jesus could perform a miracle to provide wine for the feast? Ignace de la Potterie expresses this perspective when he says, "It is more in conformity with the text to say that Mary states simply that there is no more wine. . . . It is practically impossible that

Mary is asking for a miracle, since Jesus has yet to perform any miracle. We are still at the outset of his public ministry."[7]

But is this the case? Would it be impossible for Mary to perceive the supernatural at work in Jesus just because he had not performed any public miracles yet? First, other characters in John's Gospel already have recognized something extraordinary about Jesus without seeing him perform supernatural works. Andrew believes Jesus is the Messiah (1:41); Philip says Jesus is the one of whom "Moses in the law and also the prophets wrote" (1:45); Nathanael acknowledges Jesus as "Son of God" and "King of Israel" (1:49); and John the Baptist calls Jesus "the Lamb of God who takes away the sin of the world" and gives testimony to seeing the Spirit descend upon him (1:29, 32).[8] As the authors of the ecumenical work *Mary in the New Testament* explain, if other people in John's Gospel recognize something supernatural in Jesus even before the first public display of his divine power, so could Mary.

> The Johannine Jesus has an air of mystery about him which causes some people to react with at least a glimmering of the heavenly reality they are encountering. . . . [Mary's] inaugural recognition is not to be negated by the practical question, "How could Mary have known that Jesus would be able to do anything about such a problem?" Such a question does not do justice to the literary genre or to the atmosphere of the Johannine narrative.[9]

Second, a canonical reading of John 2:3 within the context of the rest of Scripture sheds additional light on Mary's statement. When we read this verse, for example, in light of Luke's accounts of the Annunciation, Visitation, Nativity, and Presentation, then it's quite reasonable to conclude that Mary could have believed in Jesus's ability to perform miracles at this early stage of his life. After all, the same woman who had an angel appear to her, who witnessed the elderly Elizabeth's miraculous pregnancy, who encountered the shepherds reporting all that the angels told them about her Son, who heard Simeon's words about the child fulfilling prophecies from Isaiah, and most of all, who personally experienced the greatest miracle up to that point in history—the conception of her child as a virgin by the power of the Holy Spirit!—that same woman could surely have faith that her Son could perform a miracle at the Wedding Feast at Cana. In fact, it would be unreasonable to automatically rule out such faith. As Leon Morris explains,

> She knew that angels had spoken about Jesus before his birth and that she had conceived him while still a virgin. She knew that his whole manner of life stamped him different. She knew, in short, that Jesus was the Messiah, and it is not unlikely that she now tried to make him take such action as would show him to all as the Messiah she knew him to be.[10]

Third, Mary's statement doesn't make sense if she's *not* asking for a miracle. On one hand, it's clear that her words imply some kind of request. She is asking something of Jesus. She's not simply passing on information or stating a fact, such as "The food is good.... The bride is beautiful.... They have no wine." As the authors of *Mary in the New Testament* note, Jesus's strong response to Mary's words "indicates clearly that she has placed some burden on him, and so we should recognize on Mary's part some expectation that Jesus can meet the need."[11]

And if Mary is asking something of Jesus, what would that be if it's not about him doing something supernatural? In other words, if Mary is making a request of Jesus, her request doesn't make any sense if she is *not* asking for a miracle. It's not as if Jesus is known for being a resource for quick, easy access to large quantities of wine. As Jean Galot explains, "There is no natural means by which Jesus can furnish the wine, and if Mary had hoped for some natural help to save the situation she would not have turned to her Son but to someone who would have had the provision of wine at his disposal and from whom she could expect an act of generosity."[12]

We can reach a similar conclusion if we compare Mary's words "they have no wine" with the formula used by the sisters of Lazarus who say, "He whom you love is ill" (Jn 11:3). André Feuillet points out that in both cases, "the discretion of language should not prevent our recognition of the fact that a request is being made."[13] Since Jesus was not a doctor, it does not seem likely that Lazarus's sisters were asking Jesus for some medicine or for an ordinary cure. Similarly, since Jesus is not a wine salesman, it does not seem likely Mary is asking for an ordinary response.

Mary's Great Faith

Finally, Mary's words "they have no wine" point to the exemplary faith she has in her Son. Think about it. From a practical human perspective, Jesus is just a guest there, not one of the people in charge. The servants, the steward in charge of the feast, or the family would have been the more natural people to turn to for help with this problem.

So why would Mary turn to Jesus when this dilemma unfolds? Why does she seek him out and say, "They have no wine" (Jn 2:3)? Her surprising move here suggests that she believes Jesus can do something about the problem. And the help she's looking for is more than human assistance. Since Jesus is not one of the people running the feast or someone who carries a large amount of wine with him, Mary must be hoping Jesus will perform some supernatural work to solve the problem.

Mary's faith stands out all the more when we recall that up to this point in the Gospel story Jesus has yet to perform the miracles of his public ministry. Though she encountered much divine intervention in the child's conception, birth, and infancy (as discussed above), she had yet to witness the mighty deeds of his public ministry. Nevertheless, Mary exhibits trust in Jesus's supernatural power and believes he can help with the wine shortage at the wedding. In this way, Mary anticipates the great faith Jesus spoke about to doubting Thomas: "Blessed are those who have not seen and yet believe" (Jn 20:29). As Galot expresses it, "Our Lord's words to Thomas apply exactly to Mary's attitude at the wedding feast of Cana; she had never seen a miracle, but she believed."[14] Pope St. John Paul II made a similar point: Mary at Cana anticipates the faith of the disciples who will come to believe in Jesus only *after* they have witnessed the miracle of water being changed into wine (Jn 2:11). But her faith is greater, for she believed in Jesus's supernatural power *before* it was made manifest that day.[15]

With this background, we are now prepared to examine the meaning of Jesus's response to Mary's request—mysterious words which, though some interpret as Jesus rebuking his mother, actually reveal something beautiful about her role in God's plan of salvation.

Chapter Seventeen

The Woman, the Hour, and the Wine
(John 2:4)

The following may be the most perplexing verse about Mary in all of Scripture:

> O woman, what have you to do with me? My hour has not yet come. (Jn 2:4)

To our modern ears, Jesus's words to Mary at Cana seem rough, as if he is rebuking his mother or distancing himself from her. Imagine a mother calling her son to the dinner table, and him responding, "O woman, what have you to do with me? My hour has not yet come!" Such words sound like something you might expect from a rebellious teenager, not the holy Son of God!

But let's consider Jesus's words in light of his first-century Jewish culture and within the wider context of John's Gospel. We will see that, far from implying any hostility between Jesus and Mary, these words reveal something beautiful about their relationship and the role Mary plays in God's plan of salvation.

Not a Rebuke

A simple read of the next two verses at least makes clear that, whatever Jesus's cryptic words may mean, they were not taken as a harsh rebuke. Consider how Mary responds. Does she interpret Jesus's words as a rejection of her request? Just the opposite. When she hears these words, she immediately says to the servants, "Do whatever he tells you" (Jn 2:5). Mary seems to interpret Christ's words so positively that she confidently believes he is going to fulfill her request and tells the servants to be ready to carry out her Son's commands. So whatever Jesus's mysterious words mean, Mary doesn't seem to interpret them in a negative light. She assumes that Jesus will grant her wish.

Moreover, Jesus's own actions indicate that he looks with favor on Mary's appeal for more wine for the feast. He not only fulfills her request, but he supplies more wine than Mary or anyone at the feast would have imagined. The six stone jars used for ritual purification would have each held about twenty gallons of water. That means Jesus's miracle would have produced some 120 gallons of wine for the party. It's hard to interpret such a prodigious amount as a *rejection* of Mary's request for wine.

So, at a most basic level, we can at least conclude that Jesus's words—"O woman, what have you to do with me? My hour has not yet come"—are not about rebuking his mother or pushing her away. But let's go a step further and consider what these mysterious words actually mean. Here, we will unpack, step-by-step, the three key things Jesus says to Mary in John 2:4:

1.   "Woman"

2.   "What have you to do with me?"

3.   "My hour has not yet come"

"Woman"

First, why does Jesus address Mary as "woman"? To modern ears, this seems to be a strange way to talk to one's mother. But in the Gospel of John, this is not a disrespectful address. Jesus talks to other women this way, and he does so in contexts that imply a warm, positive relationship. He calls Mary Magdalene "woman" when he tenderly appears to her on Easter Sunday (Jn 20:15). He addresses the woman who committed adultery in this way when he forgives her sins (Jn 8:10). And he uses this address with the Samaritan woman as he draws her to faith in him as the Messiah (Jn 4:21). Since Jesus uses "woman" in an encouraging way to speak to other women in the Fourth Gospel, his calling Mary "woman" also should be interpreted as something positive and not as indicating a reproach or a lack of affection.

But we can go a step further. According to one traditional interpretation going all the way back to the early Church, Jesus calls his mother "woman" in order to associate her with the first "woman," Eve. In this view, when Jesus calls Mary "woman"—both here at Cana and in John's account of the Crucifixion (Jn 19:26)—he is associating her with the "woman" of Genesis who played an important part in the first prophecy about the coming Messiah.

After Adam and Eve's sin in the Garden, God confronts the serpent and announces his eventual defeat, saying:

> I will put enmity between you and the woman,
> and between your seed and her seed;
> he shall bruise your head,
> and you shall bruise his heel. (Gn 3:15)

These words, known as the protoevangelium ("first Gospel"), foretell how the woman will one day have a seed, a son, who will crush the head of the serpent (*CCC*, 410).

According to this traditional view, Jesus calling Mary "woman" at Cana is revealing her to be the woman of this first prophecy—a "new Eve"—the woman whose Son, Jesus, will defeat the serpent.

New Eve?

But some scholars say that this New Eve interpretation is reading too much into the text. It is argued that while the Mary-Eve motif is found in symbolic interpretations in the early Church, it is not something John's Gospel is itself presenting. They claim that there are no indications that John intends for us to be thinking of the woman of Eden and the prophecy of Genesis 3:15 in the background of this passage. De la Potterie, for example, asserts that the Mary-Eve theme is traditional, "[b]ut neither at Cana nor at the Cross is there the slightest hint of the Genesis account."[1]

It is also argued that Mary should not be singled out for association with Eve. After all, if Jesus addresses other women in the Fourth Gospel with the title "woman," why aren't *they* considered New Eve figures as well? Gaventa pointedly asks this good question: "If we are to think that its use in 2:4 makes Jesus's mother a symbolic figure, then why not draw the same conclusion concerning Jesus's address to the Samaritan woman and to Mary Magdalene? Are they also symbols of Eve or of the church?"[2] To draw out the Eve connection only with Mary seems to be an arbitrary interpretation, for Jesus addresses these other women with this title as well.

These are fair questions. But we can respond to them in two ways. First, while it is true that in John's Gospel Jesus addresses multiple females with the title "woman," the fact that he calls his *mother* "woman" is remarkable—something that seems to be completely unheard of in Jesus's world and sets Mary apart from the other women he addresses in this way. While a man in Jesus's day might address a female as "woman," we have no known evidence in ancient Israel or the ancient Greco-Roman world of a son addressing his mother this way. Jesus calling his own mother "woman" seems to be unique in all of antiquity. This suggests that Jesus had some particular reason for calling his mother "woman"—some purpose that goes beyond the ordinary, friendly way he addresses other women in the Fourth Gospel.[3]

Second, the way John sets up the Wedding at Cana account makes clear that he is directing readers to think of Jesus's dialogue with Mary in light of the story of Genesis. Though de la Potterie asserts there is "not the slightest hint of the Genesis account," some of his own insights into the way John opens his Gospel make clear that Genesis is very much in the background of this scene.

A New Creation Week

First, notice how John's Gospel opens up with an outpouring of key words and images from the Genesis account of creation.

> In the beginning was the Word,
> and the Word was with God,
> and the Word was God.
> He was in the beginning with God;
> all things were made through him,
> and without him was not anything made that was made.
> In him was life, and the life was the light of men.
> The light shines in the darkness,
> And the darkness has not overcome it. (Jn 1:1–5)

The first phrase in the Gospel—"In the beginning"—harkens back to the very first verse in the book of Genesis:

"In the beginning God created the heavens and the earth" (Gn 1:1). John then goes on to tell of *light, life, creation, and light shining in darkness*—images taken right out of the creation story in Genesis 1. By drawing on so many themes from Genesis 1, John sets up the story of Jesus against the backdrop of the story of creation, highlighting how Jesus comes to bring about a renewal of all creation.

Second, John continues the Genesis allusions in his opening sequence of events by setting up a series of seven days, which establishes a kind of new creation week. De la Potterie beautifully demonstrates how in the first chapter John lays out a succession of four days. After telling of John the Baptist's discussions with the priests and Levites on the first day in the Gospel narrative (1:19–28), John demarcates a second day in 1:29 with the words "The next day" and uses the same phrase to note a third day in 1:35 ("The next day") and a fourth day in 1:43 ("The next day").

Finally, after the sequence of these first four days in the Gospel, the story of the Wedding Feast at Cana is introduced as taking place three days after the fourth day: "*On the third day* there was a marriage at Cana. . . ." (2:1). The third day after the fourth day would be the seventh day in the Gospel of John.[4]

The New Creation Week in John:

1:19–28	John the Baptist's Testimony (Day 1)	
1:29	"The next day ..."	– Jesus's Baptism (Day 2)
1:35	"The next day ..."	– Andrew, Peter, and a disciple of John encounter Jesus (Day 3)
1:43	"The next day ..."	– Philip and Nathanael encounter Jesus (Day 4)
2:1	"On the third day ..."	– Marriage at Cana (Day 7)

De la Potterie thus argues that the story of the Wedding at Cana in John 2 is meant to be seen as the climax of the new week of days that started in John 1. He concludes, "Thus the days are enumerated exactly; in reality we have here the account of a week of days . . . where the wedding feast of Cana would take place on the seventh day, the last day of that week."[5] Therefore, with the opening images of creation ("in the beginning," light, life, light shining in darkness) and the series of seven days, the Wedding at Cana takes place on the seventh day, the climax of the new creation week in John's Gospel.

The New Eve

Now we are ready to understand the profound meaning of Jesus calling his mother "woman" at the Wedding Feast at Cana. Think about how John's use of the Genesis-Creation theme sheds light on this. It's as if John is preparing his readers for the Cana scene by decorating the stage with props from Genesis 1: "*In the beginning . . .* " All things created through him. Light. Life. Light shining in darkness. A series of seven days. John clearly wants us to view the story of Cana in light of the story of creation. Then coming onto the stage are the two main characters, Jesus and Mary. Against all this Genesis-Creation imagery on stage, Jesus calls his mother "woman." What woman should we be thinking of? Clearly, the woman of Genesis, Eve.

So we conclude that Jesus calling his mother "woman" does indeed portray her in association with the first woman, Eve. At the Wedding Feast at Cana, Jesus calls his mother "woman" and in doing so honors her in a way no woman has ever been honored before. Indeed, the connection with Eve makes sense for Jesus's mother at Cana, but is not as strong with the

Samaritan woman, the woman caught in adultery, or Mary Magdalene. Jesus might call them "woman" as well, but not in scenes that have this much Genesis imagery in the background.

But at Cana, a scene filled with such rich allusions to Genesis, Jesus calling Mary "woman" is not merely the polite address it is for Mary Magdalene or the Samaritan woman. Rather, the title reveals Mary to be the woman of Genesis 3:15. She is the New Eve, the woman whose long-awaited Son will defeat the devil and fulfill the prophecy of Genesis.

"My Hour Has Not Yet Come" (Jn 2:4)

Next, let's consider the meaning of Jesus's words "my hour has not yet come." This is the first reference to Jesus's "hour" in the Fourth Gospel—a motif that points to the Father's appointed time for Jesus to accomplish his mission. It ultimately refers to the hour of Jesus's Passion and Death, when Jesus's glory will be revealed as he is lifted up on the Cross, defeats the devil, and gathers all humanity to himself (Jn 12:23–33; 13:1; 17:1).[6]

For some reason, Jesus associates Mary's request for wine with the hour of his Passion, and he wonders why Mary has made her request since his Passion has not yet come. He has not yet even begun his public ministry.

"What Is It to You and to Me?" (Jn 2:4)

An important key to understanding John 2:4 is found in the idiomatic expression *ti emoi kai soi*, which can be translated "What is it to you and to me?" In the Old Testament, the expression sometimes implied hostility or opposition between two parties (Jgs 11:12; 2 Chr 35:21; 1 Kgs 17:18). In other cases, it simply describes a difference of understanding or lack of agreement but without the adversarial tone (2 Kgs 3:13; Hos 14:8). Whether there is an antagonistic connotation or not can only be discerned by considering the context.

Since the Gospel of John does not present an adversarial relationship, but rather a positive one between Jesus and his mother (both here at Cana and at the Cross), most scholars interpret 2:4 in the second way: Jesus and Mary looking at something differently, but without the hostile overtones. Mary wants Jesus to do something about the lack of wine. Jesus, however, sees her request for wine differently than she does. For Jesus, there is a lot more meaning to the wine he will provide than simply offering more drink for the wedding feast.

The Good Wine

In the Jewish tradition, wine was associated not just with the union of husband and wife (Sg 1:2–4; 4:10; 5:1), but also with wisdom (Prv 9:2–5; Sir 24:17–21) and the Torah.[7] Most importantly for our understanding of Jesus's words at Cana, the abundance of wine was associated with the arrival of the messianic age. The prophet Amos, for example, envisions that when God restores the Davidic kingdom, "the mountains shall drip sweet wine, and all the hills shall flow with it" (Am 9:13). Isaiah foretold that all peoples would one day come together on the Lord's mountain for a feast of wine when God comes to save them (Is 25:6–9). By the late first century, Jewish tradition linked the coming of the Messiah with an abundance of wine. A late first-century/early second-century Jewish text known as Second Baruch, for example, depicts the advent of the Messiah as coinciding with grape vines producing an unimaginable amount of wine: "[O]n one vine will be a thousand branches, and one branch will produce a thousand clusters, and one cluster will produce a thousand grapes, and one grape will produce a cor of wine."[8] Along different lines, Jewish tradition also associated festive drinking of wine with the law the Messiah would teach. "In this very time the King-Messiah will reveal himself to the assembly of Israel, and the children of Israel will say to him: 'Come, be our brother, let us go up to Jerusalem; and with you we will imbibe the words of the law, with you we will drink old wine.'"[9]

So when Jesus hears Mary say, "There is no wine," he may immediately think of this tradition about the *messianic* wine. So he says to her, "What is this to you and to me?" as if to say, "What is *this wine* to you and to me?" In other words, Mary is asking Jesus to provide wine for the wedding feast. But Jesus sees that he will need to perform a miracle to do so. And if he does that—if he miraculously changes the water into wine—his glory will be revealed for the first time, people will start to believe in him (Jn 2:11), and the public ministry of the Messiah will begin. Performing the miracle, therefore, will mark the beginning of his public ministry and the march toward his hour—the hour of his Passion and Death. That's why Jesus associates Mary's request for wine with his hour: "My hour has not yet come." Is Mary ready for that hour to arrive?

A Higher Level

In John's Gospel, people often approach Jesus with an understanding or need on the natural, physical plane. But Jesus challenges them to raise their understanding to the supernatural or spiritual level.[10] For example, when Jesus says to Nicodemus, "Unless one is born anew, he cannot see the kingdom of God," Nicodemus thinks Jesus is speaking about entering back into the mother's womb. He interprets

Jesus's words on the physical level. But Jesus is speaking about spiritual realities—about being born from above through water and spirit in Baptism (cf. Jn 3:3–6). Similarly, when Jesus speaks about giving the Samaritan woman "living water," she thinks he is talking about a source of running water so she doesn't have to return to the well anymore, but Jesus is talking about the living water of the Spirit (Jn 4:11–15; cf. 7:37–39).

The same can be seen between Mary and Jesus at Cana. Mary approaches Jesus with a concern about the material wine at the wedding feast, but Jesus sees in this request something more. He sees how it relates to the messianic wine as he is about to launch his public ministry. As Aristide Sera explains,

> While Mary noted the shortage of the *material wine*, Jesus takes the discussion to the level of *spiritual realities*, those concerning his hour. It's as if to say: the Virgin speaks of the *material wine* that was exhausted during the banquet; Jesus, however, alludes to wine as a symbol of his *revealing Word*, his Gospel, which is manifested in full precisely when the Hour of Jesus comes for him to pass from this world to the Father.[11]

This sheds much light on the meaning of "What is this to you and to me?" It's as if Jesus is saying, "For me and for you, the wine has different meanings." Mary comes with a request about natural wine, but Jesus sees deeper symbolism in this. If he grants her request, he will perform his first public miracle and his public ministry will be launched. He recognizes that her simple request for the wedding feast is bound up with God's plan of salvation! De la Potterie explains it this way: "Scarcely having heard the word 'wine' Jesus thinks of the symbolism of wine in the biblical tradition. Without refusing to interest himself in the present situation, since he will perform the miracle, Jesus, at once, wishes to make it understood what this *signifies*, by raising the conversation to the level of his mission to the world . . . this wine which he will give in profusion is the 'sign,' the symbol of his mission."[12]

In conclusion, let's consider what these words might have meant for Mary. Imagine her carrying the weight of Simeon's prophecy about the sword all these years, knowing that one day her Son would begin his messianic mission. And when he did, he would be resisted, opposed, misunderstood, plotted against, and eventually killed as Simeon foretold.

Then, one day at the Wedding at Cana, Mary approaches Jesus with this request for wine. But he responds saying, "Woman, what is it to you and to me? My hour has not yet come." In other words, what is *this wine* to you and to me? To you, the wine is just the wine for the wedding party. To me, the wine is much more. It is the messianic wine of the prophets, for to provide this wine, I will need to perform my first miracle, reveal my glory for the first time, and thus launch my public ministry. *My hour* has not yet come. But if I do perform this miracle to provide the wine, then the clock starts ticking on my hour—the story is set in motion and my movement toward my Passion and Death begins. And if I do that, then you are no longer just my mother. You are "woman"—the woman of Genesis 3:15, the woman whose Son will defeat the devil (cf. Jn 12:31; Rev 12:1–9). Are you ready for that? Is this what you want?

That would be a lot to take in. But Mary doesn't hesitate. She continues to say yes to God's will at Cana, even with the fuller knowledge of how this will all lead toward the hour of her Son's death. In the face of that stark reality, she turns to the servants and says, "Do whatever he tells you" (Jn 2:5).

Chapter Eighteen

"Do Whatever He Tells You"
(John 2:5–11)

His mother said to the servants, "Do whatever he tells you." Now six stone jars were standing there, for the Jewish rites of purification, each holding twenty or thirty gallons. Jesus said to them, "Fill the jars with water." And they filled them up to the brim. He said to them, "Now draw some out, and take it to the steward of the feast." So they took it. When the steward of the feast tasted the water now become wine, and did not know where it came from (though the servants who had drawn the water knew), the steward of the feast called the bridegroom and said to him, "Every man serves the good wine first; and when men have drunk freely, then the poor wine; but you have kept the good wine until now." This, the first of his signs, Jesus did at Cana in Galilee, and manifested his glory; and his disciples believed in him. (Jn 2:5–11)

Mary's response to Jesus's challenging statement at Cana is exemplary. Her words to the servants, "Do whatever he tells you," echo the typical response for covenant obedience in the Old Testament.

Three times at the foot of Mount Sinai, after the people hear the words of the covenant, they respond together in one voice, "All that the LORD has spoken we will do" (Ex 19:8,

24:3, 24:7).[1] Similar language is used later in Israel's history when the people renew their covenant with the Lord after they settle in the Promised Land (Jos 24:24) and when they return from exile and rebuild Jerusalem (Neh 5:12). Echoing this formula of covenant obedience in the Old Testament, Mary stands as a representative of God's people, exhibiting model faith. As Aristide Serra explains, we find "on the lips of Mary the profession of faith that the whole community of the chosen people pronounced one day in front of Sinai."[2]

There's another Old Testament passage that also has strong parallels to Mary's words at Cana. After having put Joseph in charge of distributing wheat in the time of severe famine, Pharaoh says, "Go to Joseph; what he says to you, do" (Gn 41:55). These words are almost identical to what Mary says to the servants: "Do whatever he tells you."

Some may wonder what the story of Joseph in Egypt and that of Jesus at Cana have in common,[3] but the parallels are quite striking. Each scene marks the beginning of a public leadership role, and both do so by providing a great abundance in a time of severe lack. Consider the similarities: Joseph overcomes a lack of food, feeding the people during the famine from the abundance of wheat in Egypt's storehouses. Jesus overcomes a lack of wine, providing an abundance of wine—some 120 gallons' worth![4]—in the time of shortage at the wedding feast. Genesis notes how the Spirit of God was with Joseph at the beginning of his work (Gn 41:38), while John's Gospel highlights Jesus as having the Spirit on him as he prepares to launch his public ministry (Jn 1:32). Just as Joseph was thirty years old when he began to stockpile grain for the people (Gn 41:46), so Jesus is thirty years old when he provides wine for the wedding guests (cf. Lk 3:23). And Pharaoh's words in reference to Joseph—"What he says to you, do"—come when Joseph begins exercising his leadership role in Egypt, just as Mary's words—"Do whatever he tells you"—come when Jesus launches his public ministry with his first miracle at Cana.

Trust

Mary's statement also exhibits great trust. With these words, she becomes the first person in John's Gospel who, as Moloney observes, "commands action based entirely on the word of Jesus" and does so "without offering any supporting cultural, religious, or historical motivation for such a command."[5] She simply trusts that Jesus will somehow solve the problem, leaving him completely free to act. In the words of New Testament scholar Margaret Beirne, it is "an expression of pure faith, an act of simple surrender to *whatever* he will ask or do."[6]

And her words inspire others to trust Jesus as well. Indeed, John's Gospel subtly shows us the profound impact Mary's exhortation has on the servants at the feast. They respond to her words like model disciples. The Gospel underscores how the servants do exactly what Jesus tells them. Jesus instructs them to "fill the jars with water," and in the next sentence John reports not only that they did so, but that they did so perfectly: "And they filled them up to the brim" (Jn 2:7). Then, when Jesus tells the servants to "take it to the steward of the feast," John goes out of his way to tell us that they complete the assignment: "So they took it" (Jn 2:8). By telling the story this way, the Fourth Gospel is emphasizing the perfect obedience of the servants. They do exactly what they are told to do by Jesus.[7] They are acting like model disciples, giving prompt obedience to the Word of the Lord.

But that's not all. John goes even further by using a special word to describe the servants at Cana. These workers at the

wedding feast are not called servants in the sense of slaves
(*douloi*). Rather, John calls them *diakonois*—the Greek word
from which we get "deacon" in English. In John's Gospel,
this word is used to describe not a household servant but
someone who is a servant of the Lord in the sense of being a
faithful disciple. For example, in John 12:26, Jesus says, "If
anyone serves (*diakonei*) me, he must follow me; and where
I am, there shall my servant (*diakonos*) be also." Mary's
words thus inspire the servants to respond to Jesus with the
fundamental attitude of the covenant—trusting obedience
to God's Word. Throughout their encounter with Jesus, they
respond to his Word perfectly and are portrayed as model
disciples (*diakonoi*).[8]

Jesus, the True Bridegroom

One other point to draw out is how this scene may be
associating Mary with a symbolic bridal role, one in which
she represents the faithful people of Israel who were expected
to be reunited with God, their true bridegroom.

Certainly, John explicitly identifies Jesus as the bridegroom
in 3:29, recalling the Jewish hopes for God coming like a
bridegroom to renew his covenant with his people Israel, the
bride (Is 62:4–6; Jer 2:1–2; Hos 2:16–25). But already in this
scene at Cana there are significant hints of this theme.[9] The
marriage is mentioned twice in the opening two verses of
this account, indicating that, for John, the wedding feast is
not just a trivial background detail. He makes the wedding
theme important for understanding Jesus's first miracle. But
for all the attention given to the wedding feast, it's interesting
that the bride's and groom's names are never given. Instead,
John portrays Jesus in ways that associate him with the role
of the bridegroom.

First, in first-century Jewish weddings, the responsibility for providing the wine for the feast fell on the bridegroom and his family. It was not the duty of a guest like Jesus. Yet Jesus steps into this role. Biblical scholar Adeline Fehribach sees much significance in this. She argues that readers "would have realized that Jesus's action of providing quality wine in abundance from the purification jars illustrated that he, in fact, accepted the role of the bridegroom, but that he was no ordinary bridegroom. . . . The sign Jesus performed illustrated that he was accepting the role of the messianic bridegroom and that as such he was assuming the role of Yahweh, the bridegroom of Israel."[10]

Second, that John's Gospel itself may be subtly linking Jesus with the role of the bridegroom can be detected in a small statement about the steward praising the bridegroom for serving the best wine last (Jn 2:9–10). We as readers know that this praise for the bridegroom should actually be directed to Jesus, whose miracle made the good wine possible. In this way, John's Gospel subtly associates Jesus with the bridegroom. As Brant Pitre explains,

> When the steward at Cana tastes the water that has become wine, he does not call Jesus over to thank him, because he has no idea that the wine was provided by him. Instead, the steward calls "the bridegroom" (Greek *nymphios*)—whose name is never given—in order to praise *him* for having saved the "good wine" for last (John 2:9–11). The irony is that it was the *bridegroom's* responsibility to provide the wine, but it is *Jesus* who has actually done so.[11]

Moreover, this is a point John seems to be suggesting in the peculiar way he inserts a narrative comment in this part of the story. Right after the steward of the feast calls the bridegroom and says, "You have saved the best wine for last," John as the narrator steps in to give this announcement: "This, the first of his signs, Jesus did at Cana in Galilee" (Jn 2:11).

In this move from the steward's words to the narrator's statement, John is making the point that Jesus takes on the role of the groom. As de la Potterie notes, "At this point in the text something very curious happens! We remove ourselves from the period of historical facts to that of the written text; in other words, from the time of Jesus to the time of John, and thereby from the groom of Cana to Jesus. That the *groom of Cana* had preserved the choice wine up till now, it is *this* which is transferred and applied by the evangelist *to Jesus*. It is *he*, who is the real groom."[12] De la Potterie goes on to explain that "John attributes 'the conservation of the choice wine' to Jesus who—at the level of the symbolic—takes upon himself the role of the groom. He is the real Groom, who has conserved the 'choice wine' up till now, which is for John the 'beginning' of the signs, the beginning of revelation."[13]

Mary and the Bride

If Jesus is the bridegroom in John's Gospel (3:29) and is subtly being portrayed as such at Cana, what, if anything, might this tell us about Mary? We have already seen how this account recalls the covenant made at Mount Sinai. Just as the Law was given at Mount Sinai on "the third day" (Ex 19:16) and God's glory was manifested to the people (Ex 19:16–17; 24:15–17), so Jesus launches his public ministry at this wedding that takes place "on the third day" (2:1), performing a miracle that reveals his glory (2:11). And just as the people at Sinai responded to God's words in faith, saying "all that the Lord has spoken we will do" (Ex 24:3, 7), so Mary echoes that formula of covenant obedience when she exhorts the servants, "Do whatever he tells you" (Jn 2:5). Mary thus stands as a representative of God's people, a model of faith, speaking the words of covenant faithfulness.

Aristide Serra draws out the symbolic implications of all this for Mary. Noting how in the Old Testament the Sinai covenant was depicted as a marital union between Yahweh and Israel,[14] he explains how in the Jewish tradition God is the husband, Israel is the wife, and Mount Sinai is where the marriage took place. "The response of faith pronounced by all the people 'All that the Lord has spoken we will do' is like the 'Yes' of the union of the two contracting parties."[15]

What's significant for our purposes is that Mary echoes these very words in the context of the Wedding Feast at Cana. In a scene that focuses on a wedding, has the Sinai covenant in the background, draws on hopes for the bridegroom Messiah, and portrays Jesus in the role of the bridegroom, but never mentions a bride—in such a scene as this—Mary has on her lips these words echoing what the bride Israel spoke to her bridegroom at Sinai long ago. These are words of covenant fidelity. If Jesus is the bridegroom, perhaps Mary can be seen as representing God's faithful people, the bride, whom Jesus is coming to save.[16] It may be significant "that Mary is mentioned at the beginning of the narrative even before Jesus is mentioned and that no other woman is mentioned in the narrative except the mother of Jesus (not even a single reference to the bride.)"[17] Might this suggest that we should view Mary symbolically in the role of the bride, representing the faithful people of Israel? In the words of de la Potterie, "Jesus occupies the place that had at one time Yahweh as the Spouse of Israel; and the Mother of Jesus, the 'Woman,' is perhaps the Spouse of the Lord and our Mother."[18]

Chapter Nineteen

At the Foot of the Cross
(John 19:25–27)

But standing by the cross of Jesus were his mother, and his mother's sister, Mary the wife of Clopas, and Mary Magdalene. When Jesus saw his mother, and the disciple whom he loved standing near, he said to his mother, "Woman, behold, your son!" Then he said to the disciple, "Behold, your mother!" And from that hour the disciple took her to his own home. (Jn 19:25–27)

Although this scene of Mary at the Cross in John 19:25–27 is the inspiration of much religious art, piety, and theological reflection in the Catholic tradition, just how much Marian significance can actually be drawn from this passage is often disputed in modern scholarship. While some commentators see Mary being revealed as the "New Eve" and the spiritual mother of all Christians, others argue that she is just a background figure and that John has no interest in telling us about her role in the Christian life.

J. Ramsey Michaels, for example, sums up much of the concern some interpreters have over reading too much Mariology into this scene:

[W]hat does the scene imply about the believer's relationship to Mary the mother of Jesus? Is she the spiritual mother of all believers? Is she whom Jesus twice addressed as "Woman" in some way the "the woman" in Jesus's parable who, "when she gives birth, has grief because her hour has come. But when the child is born, she no longer remembers the distress, on account of the joy that a human being is born into the world" (16:21)? Is "that hour" (v. 27) in which the Beloved Disciple takes her home her "hour" of giving birth to a new community of faith? Is she even perhaps the "woman" in the book of Revelation, "clothed with the sun, and the moon under her feet, and on her head a crown of twelve stars," who is pregnant and brings to birth a male child who will "shepherd all the nations with a rod of iron" (see Rev 12:1–6)?

Then Michaels bluntly concludes: "The answer is No, no, no, and no! None of these things are even hinted at in the text."[1]

But is that true? Is it accurate to say that these common interpretations are not "even hinted at in the text"? In this chapter, we will see that, while one would not want to overinterpret Mary's role in this passage, John 19:25–27 is, in fact, quite rich in its Marian significance, revealing Mary as a crucial figure in God's plan of salvation and the Christian life.

Focus on Mary and the Beloved Disciple

The Fourth Gospel's narrative of Jesus's Crucifixion draws particular attention to this scene of Mary at the Cross in two main ways. First, as Raymond Brown and others have noted, the episode of Mary and the Beloved Disciple emerges at the center scene in a series of episodes arranged symmetrically starting with the Crucifixion and elevation of Jesus on the Cross (Jn 19:16–18) and concluding with his body being taken down and buried in a tomb (19:38–42).[2] The following diagram sums up how this scene is the central episode in the story arc of John 19:16–42:

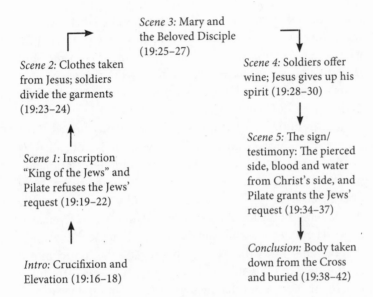

Scene 3: Mary and the Beloved Disciple (19:25–27)

Scene 2: Clothes taken from Jesus; soldiers divide the garments (19:23–24)

Scene 4: Soldiers offer wine; Jesus gives up his spirit (19:28–30)

Scene 1: Inscription "King of the Jews" and Pilate refuses the Jews' request (19:19–22)

Scene 5: The sign/testimony: The pierced side, blood and water from Christ's side, and Pilate grants the Jews' request (19:34–37)

Intro: Crucifixion and Elevation (19:16–18)

Conclusion: Body taken down from the Cross and buried (19:38–42)

Second, John's narrative presents this moment between Jesus, Mary, and the Beloved Disciple as the catalyst for Jesus realizing all was finished. Immediately upon completing his narration of this scene, John continues: "*After this* Jesus, knowing that all was now finished, said (to fulfil the Scripture), 'I thirst'" (Jn 19:28). The statement "after this" points to the new relationship forged at the Cross between the Beloved Disciple and Jesus's mother. For John, this act somehow marks the climax of Jesus's mission. As Brown explains, "The action of Jesus in relation to his mother and the Beloved Disciple completes the work that the Father has given Jesus to do and fulfills the Scripture."[3]

From Cana to the Cross

We can further appreciate the important role of Mary at Calvary when considering the similarities with her role at

Cana. In fact, there are four striking parallels between the way Mary is presented in the Wedding at Cana account, when Jesus manifested his glory for the first time and launched his public ministry, and her role in this account of Jesus's Crucifixion, when Jesus's glory is revealed most fully as he brings his saving mission to its climax.

First, in both scenes, Mary's presence is mentioned three times. Second, each time in both scenes, she is not called by her personal name "Mary" but is identified by her relationship with Jesus, as his "mother." Moreover, in both scenes, Jesus doesn't address her as "mother" or "Mary" but uses a title that is remarkably unique for a son to employ in reference to his own mother. He calls her "woman." Finally, the element that perhaps unites these two scenes most is the "hour" motif. At the start of his public ministry at Cana, Jesus introduces the theme of the hour that he says to Mary "has not yet come" (Jn 2:4). Here at the culmination of his ministry, at the Cross, Mary appears again with her Son when the hour of Jesus's Passion has arrived (cf. Jn 12:23, 31).

These parallels would prepare the reader to see Mary as much more than just a background character in John's account of the Crucifixion. Just as at Cana, the mother of Jesus has an important role to play, this time in the narrative of the Messiah's Death.

Only Filial Piety?

Yet Jesus's dying words to his mother and his Beloved Disciple ("Woman, behold your son … Behold, your mother") are sometimes interpreted only on the level of filial piety—that is, Jesus entrusting Mary into the care of his Beloved Disciple. In this view, the scene merely shows Jesus making last-minute provisions for his mother before he dies. While it was common for a man to settle legal affairs for a woman for whom he was responsible,[4] it is unlikely that filial piety is the Fourth Gospel's main concern here, especially since Jesus first speaks to Mary and instructs her, "Woman, behold your son!" (Jn 19:26), suggesting that "it is the Beloved Disciple who is given to Mary, and not vice versa."[5]

The filial piety interpretation also seems unlikely to be the primary meaning of the text because the scene comes in an account of Jesus's Death in which practically every detail is charged with great symbolism and theological import. For example, in the scene just before this one, John notes how the soldiers cast lots for Christ's tunic and then makes the point that this occurred so that the Scriptures would be fulfilled. John even quotes Psalm 22:18 to underscore the connection: "They parted my garments among them, and for my clothing they cast lots" (Jn 19:24). The passage immediately following our scene mentions that the soldiers gave Jesus "a sponge full of the vinegar on hyssop and held it to his mouth." This is a clear echo of Psalm 69:21, which states, "And for my thirst they gave me vinegar to drink."

Two more examples are found after Jesus dies. John notes that the soldiers did not break Jesus's legs and that Jesus's side was pierced (Jn 19:33–34). These details show that Jesus dies like a sacrificial Passover lamb, whose bones were not to be broken (Ex 12:46), and in a way that fulfills a prophecy from Zechariah—a prophecy that John even quotes to make the link explicit: "They shall look on him whom they have pierced" (Zec 12:10).

Think about how these small details are filled with profound meaning for John's narrative about Christ's Death. If all these other particulars—casting lots, vinegar to drink, bones left unbroken, and Jesus being pierced by a sword—are not merely background details but crucial parts of the story that are charged with deeper theological significance, it seems unlikely that Jesus's words to Mary and the Beloved Disciple merely pertain to who will look after his mother after he dies. Especially in a Gospel that is constantly turning our attention from worldly, material concerns to higher, more spiritual matters, there must be something more to this climactic scene. As Moloney explains, "At such a dramatic moment in this sophisticated and symbolic narrative the passage cannot simply mean that the Beloved disciple is to look after the widowed mother of Jesus once her only Son has died. . . . The passage affirms the maternal role of the Mother of Jesus in the new family of Jesus established at the cross."[6]

"Behold Your Son" (Jn 19:26) —Adoption or Revelatory Language?

We can begin to see the deeper meaning of this scene when we consider Jesus's words "Behold your son ... Behold your mother." On one level, these words seem to fit the pattern of language used to describe new familial relationships being forged, when someone is being adopted into another family (Ps 2:7; 1 Sm 18:21).[7] One of the stronger parallels for this is found in the book of Tobit; when Raguel describes the new relationship between his daughter and his son-in-law Tobias, he says to Tobias, "From now on you are her brother and she is your sister" (Tb 7:12). While Jesus's words point to a new kinship relationship being established, a deeper level of meaning can also be detected, for the language reflects even more a revelatory formula in John's Gospel—a pattern John uses when revealing an important point about someone. De la Potterie, Moloney, and Serra identify a fourfold pattern found multiple times in the Fourth Gospel when a character *reveals* something profound about another person.[8] The pattern can be seen as follows:

1. Characters A and B are mentioned

2. Character A sees Character B

3. A reveals something about B, introducing his statement with the word "Behold . . ." (*idou* or *ide* in the Greek)

4. A then gives a title that reveals something important about B

We can see these four elements, for example, in John 1:35–36.

1. *John* is standing with two of his disciples when *Jesus* walks by.

2. John the Baptist "*looked at* Jesus as he walked"

3. John says, "Behold . . ." (*ide*)

4. John continues, giving Jesus the title "the lamb of God."

In this passage, John is not establishing a new family relationship. He is revealing something profound about Jesus's identity and mission: he is "the lamb of God."

A similar pattern is found earlier in John 1:29. After John the Baptist *sees* Jesus coming toward him, he makes a similar revelatory declaration about Jesus: "Behold, the Lamb of God, who takes away the sin of the world!" This pattern also can be found in John 1:47, where Jesus reveals something significant about Nathanael, declaring, "Behold, an Israelite indeed, in whom is no guile!"

This technical formula sheds light on the scene of Mary and the Beloved Disciple at the foot of the Cross (Jn 19:25–27). Jesus, his mother, and the Beloved Disciple are mentioned. When Jesus *sees* his mother and the Beloved Disciple, he declares something about them, using the key word "behold" to introduce his statements. To his mother he says, "Woman, *behold*, your son!" And to the Beloved Disciple he says, "*Behold*, your mother!" The fact that Jesus's words in this scene fit the "schema of revelation" is another indication that the Fourth Gospel is concerned about much more than filial piety here. Jesus is not just forging a new familial relationship. He is *revealing* something significantly spiritual about Mary and the Beloved Disciple in this scene. As de la Potterie explains, "The dying Jesus *reveals* that his mother (as 'Woman,' with all its biblical resonance), henceforth will also be the mother of the 'disciple.' He, in turn, in representing all of Jesus's 'disciples,' hereafter shall be the son of Jesus's own mother. In other words, Jesus reveals a new dimension to the maternity of Mary, a spiritual dimension and a new role for the mother of Jesus in the economy of salvation; but at the same time, he reveals that the primary role of the disciple is to be 'son of Mary.'"[9]

How much can be gleaned from this passage regarding this new dimension of Mary's maternity and her role in God's plan of salvation requires further examination. To do that, we must consider in the next chapter the role of the Beloved Disciple.

Chapter Twenty

"Behold, Your Mother"
(John 19:25–27)

"Behold, your mother."

To understand the depths of these profound words spoken from the Cross, we must first consider the role of the person to whom these words were addressed: the mysterious character John's Gospel calls "the Beloved Disciple."

Traditionally, the Beloved Disciple has been identified as the Apostle John. But in the Fourth Gospel, this character takes on an important symbolic role as well. This Gospel often uses individual characters to symbolize larger groups. Nicodemus, for example, is described as "a man of the Pharisees" and a "ruler of the Jews" who comes to Jesus by night and fails to comprehend Christ's teachings (Jn 3:1–2). Nicodemus thus represents the many Pharisees and other Jewish leaders who do not understand Jesus and who, like Nicodemus, find themselves in the dark when it comes to Jesus's teachings. The Samaritan woman in John 4 is another individual who represents a larger group. She has trouble grasping Jesus's teaching and identity, but later comes to faith. As such, she can be seen as representing the many

Samaritans who have fallen away from Judaism but will come to believe in Christ.[1]

The Beloved Disciple also plays a representative symbolic role in the Fourth Gospel. He represents the ideal disciple. It is the Beloved Disciple who is close to Jesus, leaning on his master's breast at the Last Supper (Jn 13:25). It is the Beloved Disciple who stands as the sole Apostle accompanying Jesus to the Cross on Good Friday. While the other Apostles flee, only the Beloved Disciple remains with Jesus all the way to Calvary (Jn 19:26). It is the Beloved Disciple who is the first to believe in the Resurrection (Jn 20:8), and he is the first to bear witness to the risen Christ's Lordship (Jn 21:7, 24).

While the Beloved Disciple is traditionally associated with the Apostle John, we can also detect a deeper meaning to his role in the Fourth Gospel. He is a symbolic representative of all faithful disciples. The individual Beloved Disciple represents all who faithfully follow Christ, even in the face of the suffering of the Cross, and who believe in Jesus and bear witness to him as Lord. Indeed, this individual disciple in the Fourth Gospel represents *all* of Christ's beloved disciples.

Mary's Spiritual Motherhood?

This has important implications for understanding Mary's role in the Christian life. In one of Jesus's last acts before he dies, he entrusts this Beloved Disciple to Mary. On a basic level, this simply indicates that the Beloved Disciple has a special relationship with Mary now, like that of a son with his mother. But on a deeper spiritual level, this passage can offer important biblical support for the doctrine of Mary's spiritual motherhood of all Christians (cf. *CCC*, 968–970). In John 19, Mary becomes the mother of the Beloved Disciple, but since the Beloved Disciple represents *all* faithful disciples, we can conclude that Mary in some sense is put into a special maternal relationship with all the followers of Jesus who are represented by the Beloved Disciple, all those who have "believed in his name," have been "born anew" and "made children of God" (Jn 1:12; 3:3). Dennis Farkasfalvy explains Mary's new motherhood presented in John 19:25–27 this way: "All those symbolized by the Beloved Disciple have also been 'born' anew.... Under the Cross, then, the disciples' new status is declared. For them, becoming Mary's son means stepping into Jesus's place in the world with not only a new set of chores and responsibilities, but also with a renewed existence."[2]

When Pope St. John Paul II once commented on this scene, he explained that although Jesus does not explicitly present Mary's spiritual motherhood in these verses, the passage does point in this direction:

> Jesus's words "Behold your son" effect what they express, making Mary the mother of John and of all the disciples destined to receive the gift of divine grace. On the cross Jesus did not proclaim Mary's universal motherhood formally, but established a concrete maternal relationship between her and the Beloved Disciple. In the Lord's choice we can see his concern that this motherhood should not be interpreted in a vague way, but should point to Mary's intense, personal relationship with individual Christians. May each one of us, precisely through the concrete reality of Mary's universal motherhood, fully acknowledge her as our own Mother, and trustingly commend ourselves to her maternal love.[3]

The Woman and the Hour

The idea of Mary's spiritual motherhood of all Christians can find further biblical support when we consider two key Johannine themes that appear in this scene: "Woman" and "the hour."

Let's first look at the fundamental motif in the Fourth Gospel of "the hour." The mysterious theme of Christ's "hour" runs as a narrative thread through the Gospel of John and creates dramatic suspense for the reader. We first see this motif when Jesus launches his public ministry at the Wedding Feast at Cana and says to Mary, "My *hour* has not yet come" (Jn 2:4). At that point, Jesus does not clarify what this hour is or when it will come. He only states that it has yet to arrive.

The suspense picks up as Jesus repeatedly refers to some supreme hour that is looming on the horizon but is not quite here yet. He tells the Samaritan woman that the *hour* is coming when true worshippers will worship him in spirit and truth (4:21–23). He tells a crowd in Jerusalem that the *hour* is coming when the dead will hear the voice of the Son of God and live (5:25). He mentions his cryptic hour amid great conflict with his opponents in Jerusalem. But again, the nature and timing of this hour remain hidden. When the Jews seek to arrest Jesus, John's Gospel notes that no one was able to lay hands on him "because his *hour* had not yet come" (7:30). Similarly, after a spirited argument of Jesus with the Pharisees, the Fourth Gospel explains that no one was able to arrest Jesus because "his *hour* had not yet come" (8:20).

John keeps us on the edge of our seats throughout his Gospel by repeatedly mentioning some mysterious hour that is approaching but never quite fully here. So by the time we get halfway through the Fourth Gospel, we as readers are wondering, "What is this coming hour all about? And when will it finally arrive?"

The Hour Has Come

The turning point for this theme comes in John chapter 12. After Jesus enters Jerusalem riding on the donkey, he makes the solemn statement that his hour has finally arrived: "*The hour has come* for the Son of man to be glorified" (Jn 12:23).

He goes on to reveal what his hour is actually all about. It entails his giving up his life for us on the Cross to bring about the devil's defeat. Consider what Jesus himself says will happen in his hour:

> "Now is the judgment of this world, *now shall the ruler of this world be cast out*; and I, when, I am lifted up from the earth, will draw all men to myself." He said this to show by what death he was to die. (Jn 12:31–32)

Here, we as readers come to see that this "hour" is not simply one critical moment in Christ's life. The "hour" of Jesus is revealed in John chapter 12 to be the turning point in the history of the world! His Death on Calvary is actually his moment of triumph over the devil. For when he is "lifted up" on the Cross, "the ruler of this world"—the devil—will be cast out. Notice how Jesus's words harken back to the famous prophecy of Genesis 3:15, where God foretold that the woman would eventually have a son who would crush the head of the serpent. Thus the Fourth Gospel reveals the hour of Jesus's Passion as the hour of Satan's downfall. The hour of Jesus brings about the defeat of the devil that God promised he would accomplish in Genesis 3:15.

The New Eve

This has tremendous implications for understanding Jesus's final words to Mary at the Cross when he addresses her with the astonishing title "woman."

> When Jesus saw his mother, and the disciple whom he loved standing near, he said to his mother, "*Woman*, behold, your son!" (Jn 19:26)

We have seen from our reflections on the Wedding at Cana that it would be highly unusual for a Jewish man to call his mother "woman." In fact, there is no evidence in ancient

Judaism or Greek antiquity of a son's ever addressing his mother this way. Therefore, Jesus must have had some strategic purpose in addressing his mother with the unique title "woman."

Once we realize that, in John's Gospel, the "hour" of Jesus's Death is meant to be understood as the defeat of the devil and the fulfillment of Genesis 3:15 (cf. Jn 12:31–32), the meaning of Mary's title "woman" comes into focus. With Genesis 3:15 clearly in the background, Mary being called "woman" in this context would bring to mind one woman in particular: the woman of Genesis 3:15 whose son would defeat the serpent. Indeed, as in the Wedding at Cana account, John's Gospel again associates Mary with the first woman, Eve.[4]

Mother of All the Living

Since the Bible describes Eve as "the mother of all living" (Gn 3:20), Mary's association with "the woman" of Genesis can shed further light on her spiritual motherhood of all Christians. Here we recall the symbolism of Mary's new maternal relationship with the Beloved Disciple and how it presents Mary as the spiritual mother of all the faithful Christians whom the Beloved Disciple represents. The New Eve theme in John 19 confirms and deepens the biblical support for Mary's spiritual maternity. Just as Eve was the mother of individual children but also viewed as "the mother of all the living," so Mary, as the New Eve, becomes the spiritual mother not just of the Beloved Disciple, but of all faithful Christians whom the Beloved Disciple represents— all who are spiritually alive in Christ through grace.[5]

This is a point Pope St. John Paul II makes when reflecting on Christ's words to Mary at the Cross. With the words "Behold, your son!" Jesus indicates that Mary's maternal mission will continue in a new way. Up to this point, she has served as the Mother of the Messiah; now her motherly mission finds, as Pope St. John Paul II writes, "a 'new' continuation *in the Church and through the Church*, symbolized and represented by John [the beloved disciple]."[6] As the mother of Jesus, she now also becomes the mother of all Christians who share in Christ's life.

The Woman in Labor: Parallels with John 16:21

One other background passage that can shed light on Mary at the Cross is John 16:20–22. In Jesus's Farewell Discourse at the Last Supper, he foretells the intense trials his disciples are about to face when they see him betrayed, arrested, condemned, and crucified. But he assures them that they also will rejoice when they are reunited with him after his Resurrection. Jesus makes this point vivid for them by using the analogy of a woman giving birth to a child:

> Truly, truly, I say to you, you will weep and lament, but the world will rejoice; you will be sorrowful, but your sorrow will turn into joy. When a *woman* is in labor she has pain, because her *hour* has come; but when she is *delivered of the child*, she no longer remembers the anguish, for joy that a child is born into the world. So you have sorrow now, but I will see you again and your hearts will rejoice, and no one will take your joy from you. (Jn 16:20–22)

In this analogy, Jesus is telling his disciples that they will be like a woman in labor. Their suffering will be intense when they are separated from their Master at his death. But that sorrow won't be the end of the story. Their sorrows will turn to exuberant joy when they see Jesus again after he rises from the dead.

There are numerous parallels between this birth analogy in John 16 and the way Mary is depicted at Calvary in John 19. In the Farewell Discourse, Jesus speaks of a "woman" who gives birth in her "hour" (Jn 16:21). Notice how these same two key words are associated with Mary at the Cross: John narrates that Jesus calls his mother "woman" and "from that *hour* the disciple took her to his own home" (Jn 19:27). In addition to these two verbal correspondences, there are two thematic parallels: both passages contain the idea of *motherhood* and both relate to *Christ's Death*. Since the allegory of the woman in 16:20–21 points to the Cross, the thematic similarities (maternity, Christ's Death) and the verbal correspondences ("woman," "hour") between these two passages make it clear that John 19:25–27 is meant to be read in light of the birth allegory in John 16:20–21.[7]

And that tells us much about Mary at the Cross. There at Calvary, Mary embodies the birth pain allegory. She stands as that "woman" at the "hour" of her Son's death.[8] More than any other character in the Fourth Gospel, Mary exemplifies the mother who endures the metaphorical birth pains, which poetically depict the trials' Christ's disciples face over his passion and death.[9]

Taking Mary Home?

Finally, let's consider three points from the last sentence of this scene that tell us about the way the Beloved Disciple accepted Mary as his spiritual mother:

, "And from that hour the disciple took her to his own home" (Jn 19:27).

First, the words "from that hour" could simply have a temporal meaning, pointing to a particular moment when the Beloved Disciple took Mary. But given the major theme of Jesus's hour throughout the Fourth Gospel—a theme that is significantly in the background of this scene at the Cross (see Jn 12:22–31)—"from that hour" alludes to Christ's supreme hour of self-giving love on the Cross and his victory over the devil. Moloney argues that the "theological and dramatic significance of 'the hour of Jesus'" gives this expression a causative sense and can mean "*because of* that hour": "As a result of the lifting up of Jesus on the cross the Beloved Disciple and the Mother become one."[10] The implication is now that Christ's redemptive work on Calvary is complete; the Beloved Disciple can "take her to his own home."

But, secondly, what does it mean for the Beloved Disciple to "*take*" Mary? In John's Gospel, the Greek word for "take" (*lambanō*) has three shades of meaning.

1. When associated with a physical object, *lambanō* refers to physically taking something such as loaves of bread ("Jesus then took the loaves" [Jn 6:11]).

2. When associated with a spiritual gift, however, the word does not imply taking in the sense of physically moving something to seize it. Instead, it means "to receive," as in receiving grace (Jn 1:16) or receiving the Holy Spirit (Jn 20:22).

3. In yet another case, when the word *lambanō* is associated with a person, it means to receive someone personally—to welcome, accept or believe that person. In John's Gospel, this third sense is often used to express someone welcoming Christ in faith (Jn 1:12; 5:43; 13:20).[11]

Since our scene at the Cross in John 19:27 uses "took" (*lambanō*) in reference to the person of Mary, this third personal meaning is most likely in play here. Consequently, when the text says the Beloved Disciple "took" Mary, this does not mean merely that he took her on a journey to a specific place. Rather, it denotes a personal welcoming of Mary into his life. Recall that Jesus just put the Beloved Disciple in a new son-mother relationship with Mary ("Behold, your mother!"). Thus, the Beloved Disciple "taking" (*lambanō*) Mary points to his joyful acceptance of her in this new relationship as he welcomes her as his mother.

Welcoming Mary

Thirdly, what does it mean that "the disciple took her *to his own home*"? Though the last words are commonly translated "to his own home," the expression in the original Greek more literally means, "*into his own*" or "into the things that were his own." In fact, John's Gospel uses this expression to describe Jesus's own people (1:11), his own sheep (10:4), and his own disciples (13:1). Especially in John 13, the words "his own" describe a deep, personal communion with his disciples.

Therefore, the account of the Beloved Disciple receiving Mary into "his own" does not likely refer to his merely taking her to his house. John's Gospel is concerned with something more profound than where Mary went to live. Rather, the Beloved Disciple taking Mary into "his own" points to something deeper, something more spiritual. The Beloved Disciple welcomes Mary into a profound, personal communion, fully embracing the mother of Jesus as his own mother. He welcomes Mary as one of "his own."[12]

Pope St. John Paul II has further spiritual insight into this scene. He notes that the words "into his own" refer in John's Gospel to "the spiritual goods or gifts received from Christ: grace (Jn 1:16), the Word (Jn 12:48; 17:8), the Spirit (Jn 7:39; 14:17), the Eucharist (Jn 6:32–58)."[13]

He then concludes that the Beloved Disciple, in welcoming Mary "into his own," recognizes Mary as a great spiritual gift given to Christ's followers. By taking Mary "into his own," the Beloved Disciple welcomes Mary not simply as a mother, but as a spiritual mother who represents a profound spiritual gift to his interior life. Just as a faithful disciple welcomes the Word, the Spirit, or the Eucharist into his spiritual life, so does the Beloved Disciple welcome Mary's spiritual maternity as a treasure given to him by Our Lord. Pope St. John Paul II exhorts us to make room for Mary in our own lives, just as the Beloved Disciple did in his:

> Among these gifts which come to him from the fact that he is loved by Jesus, the disciple accepts Mary as his mother, establishing a profound communion of life with her (cf. RM 45, note 130). May every Christian, after the beloved disciple's example, "take Mary into his house" and make room for her in his own daily life, recognizing her providential role in the journey of salvation.[14]

Chapter Twenty-One

Decoding the Woman of the Apocalypse
(Revelation 12:1–17)

Now we come to the last book of the Bible, the book of Revelation, and to the mysterious woman who appears as "a great sign in heaven" in its twelfth chapter. But identifying this woman and weighing the possible Marian significance of this passage is a challenging task.[1] Some in the Catholic tradition have seen Mary as the woman "clothed with the sun, with the moon under her feet" and wearing "a crown of twelve stars." But most interpreters today—Catholic and Protestant alike—hold that the woman figure is not Mary but a symbol for God's people, whether Israel or the Church.

While there are good reasons for viewing the woman of Revelation 12 as representing God's faithful people, we also will see in this chapter that there is still room for seeing Mary in this "woman clothed with the sun."

> And a great sign appeared in heaven, a woman clothed with the sun, with the moon under her feet, and on her head a crown of twelve stars; she was with child and she cried out in her pangs of birth, in anguish for delivery. And another sign appeared in heaven; behold, a great red dragon, with seven heads and ten horns, and seven diadems upon his heads. His tail swept down a

> third of the stars in heaven, and cast them to the earth. And the dragon stood before the woman who was about to bear a child, that he might devour her child when she brought it forth; she brought forth a male child, one who is to rule all the nations with a rod of iron, but her child was caught up to God and to his throne, and the woman fled into the wilderness, where she has a place prepared by God, in which to be nourished for one thousand two hundred and sixty days. Now war arose in heaven, Michael and his angels fighting against the dragon; and the dragon and his angels fought, but they were defeated and there was no longer any place for them in heaven. And the great dragon was thrown down, that ancient serpent, who is called the Devil and Satan, the deceiver of the whole world—he was thrown down with him. (Rev 12:1–9)

Three main characters emerge in this scene: the woman, her male child, and the dragon. The woman gives birth to the male child, who is attacked by the dragon. The child is caught up to God and enthroned while the dragon is defeated and cast down (Rev 12:1–9).

Two of the three characters are easily identifiable.

1. The *dragon* is explicitly called "that ancient serpent, who is called the Devil and Satan" (Rev 12:9).

2. The *male child* is Jesus, for he is described as "one who is to rule all the nations with a rod of iron" (Rev 12:5)—a reference to the way God's Son, the Lord's anointed, is described in Psalm 2:9. Furthermore, since the child is caught up to God and sits on his throne, we can easily conclude that the child is meant to be understood as Christ.

However, the identity of the third character—the *woman*—is not as explicit. To discern her identity, we must first consider five facts we learn about the woman in Revelation 12.

Clothed with the Sun, Moon under Her Feet, Crowned with 12 Stars: First, the woman is clothed with the sun, has the moon under her feet, and is crowned with twelve stars. What is the meaning of these celestial images? In the book of Revelation, crowns symbolize the saints' reward and share in Christ's Kingship for their perseverance in faith through many tribulations.[2] The *twelve* stars are commonly seen as recalling the Twelve Apostles and the Twelve Tribes of Israel. But the significance of her being clothed with the sun and having the moon under her feet is not as apparent. One Old Testament passage that may be in the background is Song of Solomon 6:10, which describes Solomon's bride as "fair as the moon, bright as the sun."[3] Another is the lady Zion figure in Isaiah 60,[4] which depicts Zion as a mother of God's people (v. 4) filled with the radiant splendor of Yahweh's light, no longer needing the sun or moon: "Arise, shine; for your light has come and the glory of the LORD has risen upon you. . . . The sun shall no longer be your light by day, nor for brightness shall the moon give light to you by night; but the LORD will be your everlasting light" (Is 60:1, 19). With this in the background, we can see that the woman of Revelation 12:1–2 is portrayed as the eschatological Zion, shining with a light that does not come from her but radiates the glory of God.

Another Old Testament passage that has even more points of contact with Revelation 12:1 is Genesis 37:9–11, which tells of the famous dream of the patriarch Joseph.[5] In this dream, Joseph envisions the sun, moon, and eleven stars bowing down before him—a foreshadowing of how he will have authority over his father, mother, and eleven brothers when he rises to become Pharaoh's second-in-command in Egypt.

Notice the several parallels this dream has with the appearance of the woman in Revelation 12:1–2. Both are associated with the sun, moon and *stars*. Moreover, the fact that there are *twelve* stars in the woman's crown also evokes Joseph's dream in which *twelve* stars are implied— the eleven stars represent Joseph's eleven brothers bowing to Joseph, who is a *twelfth* son of Jacob.[6] Finally, although no *crown* is mentioned explicitly, the dream certainly involves the theme of royal authority that the crown symbolizes. For Joseph will obtain his unexpected position of authority over his own family when he comes to hold the most powerful position in all of Egypt, second only to Pharaoh himself (Gn 41:40, 57). With this background in mind, we can see how all three images—the sun, the moon, and the crown of stars—work together to express royal authority. Whoever this woman is, she is someone decked in regal splendor.

Birth Pains: A second fact we learn about the woman in Revelation 12 is that she delivers her child with *birth pains*.[7] This recalls the Daughter Zion prophecies of the Old Testament. As we've seen in chapter 2, Zion was the mountain of Jerusalem that was personified as a mother figure who endured labor pains before giving birth to a child. This image of lady Zion giving birth became a powerful symbol for how the faithful Jewish people would endure many sufferings from which God would come to rescue them in the messianic age (e.g. Is 26:17; 66:7–8; Mi 4:10). For example, Revelation 12 likely draws from both Isaiah 26:17, which graphically depicts the people of Jerusalem as "a woman with child, who writhes and cries out in her pangs when she is near her time,"[8] and Isaiah 66:8, where Zion gives birth to the new messianic people. As such, the woman is depicted as experiencing the labor pains lady Zion would experience in the coming of the messianic age.

Gives Birth to the Messiah: Third, as we've seen above, the woman gives birth to the one who fulfills the messianic prophecy of Psalm 2:9—he is the one who "rules all nations with a rod of iron" (Rev 12:5; cf. Ps 2:9). Moreover, the woman's child is caught up to God in Heaven, where he sits on his throne. These two details show us that the woman is the mother not of any ordinary child, but of the Messiah-King.

Conflict with the Serpent: A fourth point about the woman in Revelation 12 is that her son is portrayed as fulfilling Genesis 3:15, which foretold how the first woman would have a descendant who would defeat the devil. With the dragon identified as the "ancient serpent" (Rev 12:9), his battle with the "woman" and her messianic male child clearly evokes the strife described in Genesis 3:15. Both passages involve the ancient serpent in conflict with a woman figure and her offspring, who will eventually overcome the serpent. Moreover, the woman crying out "in her pangs of birth and in anguish for delivery" (Rev 12:2) might also recall the first woman's childbearing pains mentioned in Genesis 3:16.[9] As Brown observes, the author of Revelation 12 portrays this drama as the climactic fulfillment of Genesis 3's description of the serpent's war with the "woman" and her royal messianic offspring. "There can be no doubt that Revelation is giving the Christian enactment of the drama foreshadowed in Gen iii 15 where enmity is placed between the serpent and *the woman*, between the serpent's seed and her seed, and the seed of the woman enters into conflict with the serpent."[10]

A New Exodus: A fifth point to consider about the woman in Revelation 12 is that she experiences blessings that bring to mind *a new exodus*. After her son's victory over the devil, the woman is given two wings of a great eagle so that she might flee to the wilderness, be protected from the dragon that pursues her, and be nourished by God (Rev 12:6, 13–16). These images clearly evoke the Exodus story, when Israel was led into the wilderness, where God was portrayed like an eagle protecting the people with eagle's wings (Ex 19:4) and nourishing them with the manna. Indeed, later Old Testament passages like Isaiah 40:31—which describes the people who will return to the land as being mounted up with "wings like eagles"—gave hope for a new kind of exodus to come.

The Woman and God's People: Room for Mary?

With this background, we are prepared to consider three common views about the woman in Revelation 12.

1. *The woman is a symbol for the Church:* This ecclesial interpretation is supported by the depiction of the woman being safeguarded and nourished by God in Revelation 12:13–16, imagery that describes God protecting his people in the new covenant age.

2. *The woman is a symbol for the Old Testament people of God, Israel:* One can also appreciate this interpretation, since it makes sense out of the woman's crown of twelve stars, which can be seen as recalling the Twelve Tribes of Israel. Most of all, it makes sense out of the birth pain image, which recalls the Daughter Zion prophecies about the trials God's people would face in the coming of the messianic age and the birth of the new covenant people of God (cf. Rev 12:17).

3. *The woman is also Mary.* Although the woman is
   depicted in ways that recall God's people, both
   Israel and the Church, we must take into account
   that she is most clearly presented as the Mother
   of the Messiah, the mother of the one who will
   rule all nations with a rod of iron (Rev 12:5;
   Ps 2:9). And if that's the case, wouldn't her
   portrayal as the Messiah's mother bring to mind
   the Virgin Mary? It seems virtually impossible
   that the earliest Christians would not have seen
   Mary at all in this woman. As one commentator
   asks, "Is it conceivable that a Christian author
   of the late first century could speak about the
   Mother of Christ while prescinding entirely from
   the Virgin Mary?"[11]

Furthermore, the other two main characters in the account
are clearly individuals: the male child is Christ and the
dragon is Satan. If that's the case, it seems unlikely that the
third main character in the drama, the woman, is meant to
be understood not as an individual at all, but exclusively as a
symbol pointing to a larger collective group. If the child and
the dragon are individuals, then the woman should be seen,
at least at some level, as an individual as well.

Finally, since individuals in the Bible sometimes symbolically represent collective groups (as we saw with the
Beloved Disciple representing all faithful disciples in the
Fourth Gospel),[12] the woman here in Revelation 12 could
be viewed as *both* an individual (the mother of the messiah)
and a representative of the faithful people of God (whether
Israel or the Church or both). Mary, in fact, would be
the perfect person to do this, for she herself stands at the
threshold between the old and the new. Indeed, if there was

one woman in all of salvation history who could represent both the Old Testament and New Testament people of God , it would most certainly be the Jewish woman from Nazareth who was the first to say "Yes" to God's call in the new covenant era and receive the messiah in her womb: Mary. In the words of André Feuillet, "[T]he Virgin Mary belongs to both dispensations, the old and the new; she is situated at their meeting point. It is in her that the joining of the old people of God and the Christian Church is effected, and it is in her alone that it is possible to bring into one the diverse roles attributed to the woman of Apoc. 12, which appear otherwise incompatible."[13]

Mary and Birth Pains?

One obstacle to the Marian interpretation in the early Church was the mention of the woman's birth pains (Rev 12:2). The Church proclaimed Mary as Ever-Virgin, meaning she not only conceived of Jesus as a virgin and remained a virgin after his birth, but also *gave birth to Jesus as a virgin*. From this it was believed that the child passed through Mary's womb without causing her the normal pains of labor. But this raised questions regarding the identification of the woman of Revelation 12 with the mother of Jesus: How could this woman be the Ever-Virgin Mary if she is described as having the pains of delivering a child?[14]

Once we see, however, that the birth imagery found in Revelation 12:1–5 is not focused primarily on Jesus's physical birth in Bethlehem but is used metaphorically to point to his Death and Resurrection, the obstacle is removed and the Marian interpretation comes into clearer light. For the book of Revelation employs the childbearing pains motif *figuratively* in a way similar to what we find Jesus doing in the birth allegory in John 16:20–21—as metaphorically pointing to the Death and Resurrection of Jesus.

Indeed, the New Testament often uses *birth* imagery in general to depict Christ's Resurrection (1 Cor 15:20, 36; Col 1:18; Acts 13:33; Jn 12:24; 16:20–21), which is something the book of Revelation itself does in describing Jesus as the "first born of the dead" (Rev 1:5). Similarly, *birth pang* imagery is associated with Christ's sufferings on Calvary (Jn 16:20–21; cf. Acts 2:24). That's how it's used here in Revelation 12: the birth pain imagery in 12:3–4 metaphorically points to the suffering surrounding Jesus's Death while the delivery of the child in 12:5 describes Jesus's Resurrection.[15]

Thus, Revelation 12 should be seen as an apocalyptic retelling not primarily of the Christmas story but of the Paschal Mystery as a whole. Moreover, the fact that the particular word in Revelation 12:2 to describe the woman "in anguish" (*basanizomenē*) is never used in the Septuagint, the Apocrypha, or the writers of the Fathers to describe actual physical birth pains gives us further reason to conclude that Revelation 12 is not focusing on the physical birth of Jesus but rather using the childbearing pain imagery metaphorically.[16]

At the Cross and in the Apocalypse: The Same Woman

Now we can arrive at the strongest argument for a Marian interpretation, which involves considering the woman in Revelation 12 in light of another passage in the Johannine tradition: Mary at the Cross in John 19:25–27.

Both accounts depict the same event from different perspectives. John 19 presents what happens on Calvary *from an earthly perspective*: Jesus is crucified by the Romans while his Mother and the Beloved Disciple stand at the foot of the Cross. Revelation 12 tells of the same event, but *from a heavenly perspective*. Here, the book of Revelation helps us to see with the eyes of angels the supernatural combat that took place on Good Friday: Calvary is not just the crucifixion of an innocent man. It's the turning point of the history of the world—the ultimate battle between God and the devil. Revelation 12 helps us see that there's more to Christ's Crucifixion than Jewish leaders conspiring with Pilate to bring about Jesus's Death. No, it's Satan, the "ancient serpent," who is waging war on the Lord's Messiah. The Fourth Gospel narrates from an earthly perspective how Roman soldiers nailed Jesus to a Cross that day. But Revelation 12 reveals that it's the dragon fiercely attacking the woman's son (Rev 12:4–5), the son escaping his wrath, enthroned victorious in Heaven while the devil is defeated and cast down (Rev 12:6–9).

Both views of this scene—the earthly perspective in John 19 and the heavenly one in Revelation 12—feature the "woman." Indeed, we will see there are four key parallels between the way the woman in Revelation 12 is depicted and the way the "woman," Mary, at the Cross is portrayed in John 19. These profound parallels indicate that the book of Revelation portrays the "woman clothed with the sun" in ways that bring to mind the woman at Calvary in John 19—the woman who is very clearly the Mother of Jesus, the Blessed Virgin Mary.[17] Let's consider those four key similarities:

(1) "Woman": First, just as Revelation 12:1 presents a "woman" figure who is the mother of the Messiah (12:5), so Mary in John 19:25–27 is called "woman" and stands at the Cross as the mother of the Messiah.

(2) Birth Pains: Second, both women appear in scenes that are colored by the Daughter Zion birth pain theme. We can see this clearly with the woman in Revelation 12:1–2, who

is depicted as giving birth to her son in great anguish. We can also see birth pain imagery in the background of John's account of Mary at the Cross when the passage is read in light of something Jesus says earlier in John 16:20–21.

In his farewell discourse, Jesus tells an allegory of a woman who experiences the pains of labor and the joy of delivering her child. We saw how the allegory metaphorically expresses what Jesus's disciples will soon experience: suffering when they see him crucified and joy when he is risen from the dead.

> When a *woman* is in labor, she has pain, because her *hour* has come; but when she is delivered of the child, she no longer remembers the anguish, for joy that a child is born into the world. So you have sorrow now, but I will see you again and your hearts will rejoice, and no one will take your joy from you. (Jn 16:21–22)

Notice how the allegory mentions a "woman" in her "hour" while foretelling Christ's Passion and Death. John's portrayal of Mary at the Cross a few chapters later clearly evokes this allegory, as Mary is called "woman" (19:26) at the very *hour* of Christ's Passion (cf. Jn 12:27–31). With this birth allegory in the background of Jesus's Crucifixion in John 19, we thus find further connections between Mary at the Cross and the woman in birth pains in Revelation 12.

(3) Satan's Defeat: Third, we've seen how the woman in Revelation 12 gives birth to a male child who emerges triumphantly and is taken up to a heavenly throne while the devil is conquered and thrown out (Rev 12:7–9). This is similar to how Mary is portrayed in John 19 as standing at the Cross with her messianic Son in his "hour," which, as we have seen, in John's Gospel points to the triumphant hour of Christ's Passion, when the devil, the "ruler of this world," is cast down (Jn 12:31).[18]

(4) Twofold Maternity: Fourth, both women are described as having a twofold maternity: they are presented as the Mother of the Messiah and as being in a maternal relationship with all of Christ's faithful followers. Just as the woman in Revelation 12 is the mother not only of the individual Messiah (Rev 12:5) but also of Christians who "keep the commandments of God and bear testimony to Jesus" (Rev 12:17), so is Mary at the Cross presented not only as Jesus's mother (Jn 19:25–26), but also as the mother of the Beloved Disciple—a figure who represents all faithful disciples.

These many connections between the woman in Revelation 12 and Mary in John 19—"woman," birth pains, Satan's defeat, a twofold maternity—point to a common understanding about the woman figure in the Johannine literature.[19] Therefore, if the woman in John 19 is clearly understood to be Mary, the woman in Revelation 12 should be seen as having some reference to Our Lady as well.

Chapter Twenty-Two

Crowned in Glory
(Revelation 12:1–17)

Once we recognize there is room for seeing Mary in the woman figure in Revelation 12, we are prepared to explore what this chapter might tell us about several other aspects of her role in God's plan of salvation. Let us consider how the passage might offer more biblical support for themes we've already seen developed in other New Testament passages, such as:

- Mary, the New Eve

- Mary, the Mother of all Christians

- Mary, the Mother of Immanuel

- Mary, the Queen Mother

- Mary, the Ark of the Covenant

In the process, we will see that Mary once again appears as the first disciple—the one who goes before us, receiving in an anticipatory way what God wants to accomplish in the lives of all faithful disciples.

The "First Gospel"

First, Mary appears in Revelation 12 as the New Eve in the cosmic battle between God and the devil—a battle that is foretold at the beginning of the Bible. In a passage known as the *protoevangelium* ("first Gospel"), God gives the first prophetic foreshadowing of how the Messiah will conquer the devil and liberate the human family from sin. After the Fall of Adam and Eve, God addresses the serpent in Eden, saying,

> I will put enmity between you and the woman, and between your seed and her seed; he shall bruise your head, and you shall bruise his heel. (Gn 3:15)

This prophecy involves three main characters: the woman, the woman's seed, and the serpent. It foretells how the woman, Eve, will have a descendant ("her seed") who will bruise the head of the serpent. In the Bible, striking-the-head imagery often describes *a king defeating his enemies* (2 Sm 22:37–43; Ps 89:23; cf. Ps 110:1). Therefore, the woman's son bruising the head of the serpent tells us two important things about him: he will be a *kingly son* and he *will defeat the serpent*, the devil.

This ancient text about the devil's defeat is the key backdrop to Revelation 12, which introduces the same three characters of Genesis 3:15. The *woman* has a *royal son* who is attacked by a dragon—a figure that we've seen is explicitly identified as *"that ancient serpent, who is called the Devil and Satan"* (Rev 12:9). In this battle, the child emerges victoriously as he is taken up to Heaven and seated on a throne (Rev 12:5), while the dragon is conquered and cast down to earth (Rev 12:7–12). With the ancient serpent being defeated with the coming of the woman's royal son, Revelation 12 is clearly presenting the fulfillment of the prophecy about the devil's defeat in Genesis 3:15. The woman of Revelation 12, therefore, is being associated with the woman of Genesis, and Jesus is her royal Son whose coming brings about the serpent's defeat.

Mother of All the Living

Second, Revelation 12 presents Mary as the mother of all faithful disciples—a role that fits well with the New Eve theme. According to Genesis 3:20, Eve is called "the mother of all living." Therefore, if Mary is the New Eve, it would be fitting to see her as the new mother of all the living—the spiritual mother of all faithful Christians who are alive in Christ.

This maternal role with all Christians becomes more explicit in Revelation 12:17. Here, the woman appears not only as the mother of the Messiah, but also as the mother of other offspring, who are described as "those who keep the commandments of God and bear testimony to Jesus" (Rev 12:17). Revelation 12, therefore, reveals Mary as the mother of all who follow Christ. Similar to the Beloved Disciple in the Gospel of John, these children of the woman are depicted as loyal followers of Jesus who have a special mother-son relationship with Mary. Thus Revelation 12:17 stands out in the Bible as a Scriptural verse that offers much biblical support for Mary's maternal relationship with all Christians. She is the mother of "those who keep the commandments of God and bear testimony to Jesus." In other words, she is the mother of all faithful disciples.

The Mother of Immanuel

Third, Revelation 12 also describes the woman clothed with the sun in ways that recall the Immanuel prophecy of Isaiah

7:14, which tells of a sign that will be given to the house of David. The prophecy involves a woman who will give birth to a Davidic son. Various parallels exist between these two passages. The woman in Revelation 12 is introduced as "*a sign*" (*semeion*) echoing the sign (*semeion*) that was given to the house of David in Isaiah 7:10 (LXX). Just as the sign in Revelation is located in the heavens, so the sign offered to King Ahaz was to be as high as heaven (Is 7:10–11). And just as the sign in Revelation features a royal woman giving birth to a kingly son (12:1–2, 5), so the sign in Isaiah involves a royal woman from the house of David who would conceive and bear a Davidic heir (Is 7:14).[1]

All these connections make clear that the woman of Revelation 12 is meant to be understood as the mother of the Immanuel child prophesied in Isaiah 7:14.

A Royal Woman

Fourth, the book of Revelation can also shed light on the doctrine of Mary's queenship. Recall the magnificent introduction the woman receives in the opening verse: "And a great sign appeared in heaven, a woman clothed with the sun, with the moon under her feet, and on her head a crown of twelve stars" (Rev 12:1).

This verse describes the woman in many ways that underscore her royalty. This is most obvious with her *crown*, but her having the moon "*under her feet*" also signifies her royal position, for in the Scriptures "under-the-foot" imagery portrays royal victory over one's enemies (e.g., Ps 110:1). Furthermore, the triple image of sun, moon, and stars together recalls the royal authority Joseph had in Pharaoh's kingdom. As we saw in the previous chapter, these three exact images were found in the patriarch Joseph's dream about the sun, moon, and eleven stars bowing before him. There, the celestial images pointed the authority Joseph would have over his father and mother (symbolized by the *sun* and *moon*) and over his brothers (represented by eleven *stars*). By portraying the woman with these same three celestial images that recall Joseph's authority in Egypt, Revelation is clearly presenting the woman as having some kind of royal authority.

What might that royal status be? Two biblical themes come to mind: (1) the role of the queen mother in the Bible and (2) the share in Christ's reign promised to all faithful disciples.

First, the woman should be seen in light of the Old Testament queen-mother tradition. We saw in chapter 8 how in ancient Near Eastern kingdoms like Judah it was typically the mother who reigned as queen. We also saw how this queen-mother tradition is reflected in the Old Testament, whether it be in the way that practically every time 1 and 2 Kings introduces a new king in Judah, the king's mother is mentioned, and in the fact that the queen mother is described as a member of the royal court, wearing a crown, sitting on a throne and sharing in the king's reign (2 Kgs 24:12, 15; Jer 13:18–20). We also saw how she serves as a counselor to her son (Prv 31) and as an advocate for the people, acting as an intercessor who brought petitions from the citizens of the kingdom to her royal son (1 Kgs 2:17–20). And we considered how Mary is presented in the New Testament, particularly in the Visitation scene (Lk 1:43), in ways that recall this queen-mother background. Could this same biblical tradition illuminate the way the woman appears in the book of Revelation as well?

A number of interpreters have suggested that this is the case.[2] We've already seen how the woman is portrayed alongside her royal son and decked with regal images, indicating that she is meant to be understood as some kind of royal figure herself.[3] In his dissertation on the woman in Revelation 12, Pavol Farkas emphasizes that Revelation 12 presents a *royal* woman (12:1) giving birth to the Messiah-King (12:5). Although some interpretations of the woman see her only as a symbol for God's people, no Old Testament or early Jewish text speaks of a *queenly* figure personifying the collective people of God and giving birth to *the Messiah*.[4] However, a closer parallel exists in the Old Testament position of the queen mother, for the queen mother was a royal woman in the court known for having given birth to the Davidic king and for being intimately connected to his reign.[5] This is similar to the queenly figure in Revelation 12. She is not simply a royal woman who happens to be the mother of some king. Rather, she is presented as the mother of the *Davidic* king, the Lord's anointed who will rule all nations with a rod of iron (Rev 12:5; Ps 2:7). And she appears wearing a crown as did the queen mothers in the Davidic kingdom (Jer 13:18). As such, the queen mother is likely in the background for understanding the royal woman who gave birth to the Davidic Messiah in Revelation 12. As George Kirwin noted in his dissertation on the queen-mother theme, "The woman of Apocalypse 12 is the Mother of the Messiah-King who on the day of His birth, 'caught up to the throne of God,' is ruler of the universe. . . . Here too, she is the Queen-Mother, Mother of Christ Head and Members, Mother of the Church."[6]

Mary's Queenship Points to Our High Calling

A second consideration to keep in mind is the New Testament promise that all faithful disciples will share in Christ's reign over sin and death. Jesus himself teaches his Apostles that those who have been willing to give up everything and follow him will "sit on twelve thrones, judging the twelve tribes of Israel" (Mt 19:28–30). He also promises that if his disciples persevere through his trials, they will rule over the new Israel (Lk 22:28–30). Paul echoes this teaching, telling Timothy, "If we have died with him, we shall also live with him; if we endure, we shall also *reign* with him" (2 Tm 2:11–12). Paul even describes how a "crown of righteousness" awaits all who love Christ and persevere in faith (2 Tm 4:8).

When it comes to Mary's queenship in Revelation 12, we should see her royal splendor in this light—in the context of many others who are offered a crown in the book of Revelation. In the Apocalypse, we've seen how the crown image points to the share in Christ's kingship that is awarded to all the saints for being faithful disciples who persevere through temptations, trials, and persecution (Rev 2:10; 3:11; 4:4, 10; 6:2; 14:14). In the New Testament, Mary stands as a model disciple who hears God's Word and keeps it (Lk 1:38, 45; 8:21; 11:28). She perseveres in faith throughout her life (Acts 1:14), and is one of the few who follow Jesus all the way to the Cross (Jn 19:25–27; cf. Lk 2:34–35). It is not surprising that the book of Revelation portrays her clothed with the sun, with the moon under her feet, and wearing a crown of twelve stars on her head, sharing in Christ's reign.

Mary's royal office, therefore, should not be viewed as something separate from our lives. The Catholic doctrine of her queenship affirms that she has the utterly unique privilege of reigning with Christ over Heaven and earth. But her role as queen is not something to be merely put up high on a pedestal, admired from afar, as if it were totally detached from us lower-level Christians. Rather, her status as queen reminds us of how we're all called as Christ's followers to share in his reign over sin and death.

For us, Mary's queenship in Revelation 12 is an important "eschatological sign"—a constant reminder of the saving work God wants to do in all our lives. He calls us to be faithful disciples like the perfect disciple, Mary. And if we persevere in our walk of faith as she did, we, too, will be awarded the "crown of righteousness" as we share in Christ's glorious reign. As Pope St. John Paul II once explained,

> Thus, far from creating distance between her and us, Mary's glorious state brings about a continuous and caring closeness. She knows everything that happens in our lives and supports us with maternal love in life's trials. Taken up into heavenly glory, Mary dedicates herself totally to the work of salvation in order to communicate to every living person the happiness granted to her. She is a queen who gives all that she possesses, participating above all in the life and love of Christ.[7]

Mary in the "Place Prepared by God" (Rev 12:6)

There's a verse in Revelation 12 that may subtly point to the singular heavenly reward Mary has already received: "And the woman fled into the wilderness, where she has *a place prepared by God*" (Rev 12:6). The verb for *prepared* (*hetoimazō*) is often used in the New Testament in an eschatological context to describe the great blessings God is preparing for his faithful disciples in Heaven. The Father *prepares* the seats at Jesus's right and left hand (Mt 20:23). God is also *preparing* the kingdom for those sheep at his right hand who have been separated from the goats and blessed by him for their loving him in the least of his brethren (Mt 25:34). Paul writes of the "things God has prepared for those who love him" (1 Cor 2:9). And Peter tells of a salvation that has been prepared and will be revealed in the last times (1 Pt 1:5).

Most important is how the particular expression in Revelation 12:6 about "a place prepared" (*topon hētoimasmenon*) for the woman by God parallels what Jesus says in his farewell discourse in John 14:2–3: "In my Father's house are many rooms; if it were not so, would I have told you that I go to prepare a place (*hetoimasai topon*) for you? And when I go to prepare a place (*hetoimasō topon*) for you, I will come again and will take you to myself, that where I am you may be also."

In the context of the Johannine writings, we can see that this "place" in the "Father's house" is not about lodging at some geographical location but about the ultimate reward given to faithful disciples: dwelling with God forever in Heaven.

In Revelation 12, the woman endures the dragon's attacks but she is rescued and brought to "a place prepared by God." As such, the woman can be seen as representing all disciples who persevere through the trials of faith and are given their heavenly reward, "the place prepared by God."[8]

But to the extent we can see Mary in this woman, Revelation 12 may also subtly point to her own heavenly destiny. As the premier member of the Church and the first disciple and model follower of Jesus in Scripture, Mary may be seen in this verse as having already received her heavenly reward, anticipating what God will do for all faithful disciples. In this sense, the passage can shed some light on her unique participation in Christ's victory over sin and death, as she goes before us to the "place prepared" for his disciples in the Father's house. In his book, *Mary, Daughter of Zion,* biblical scholar Lucien Deiss even proposes that the verse may lend some scriptural support for the doctrine of the Assumption: "Here again Mary is a prefiguration of the Church. The place in the wilderness that is prepared for the Church conjures up the image of the eternal dwelling-place into which she enters on the morning of her assumption. . . . Mary stands in the vanguard of the Church on its march toward the kingdom;

in her, the desert Church that is still battling against the Dragon has already reached the shore of eternity; in her, she already contemplates, in joy and peace, the eternal face of God."[9]

Mary, Ark of the Covenant

We have seen how Luke's Gospel presents Mary as the Ark of the Covenant in the Visitation scene. There may be a hint of this theme in the book of Revelation as well.

In the verse just before the "woman clothed with the sun" is introduced, the heavenly Temple is opened, and John sees the Ark of the Covenant appearing for the first time in hundreds of years. This would have been an amazing sight for any Jew, since the Ark was the most sacred item in all of Israel. It had dwelt in the Tabernacle in the desert and in the Temple in Jerusalem, but it had disappeared during the time of the Babylonian Exile and had not been seen since. Some Jews expected that the Ark would return only in the last days when God would restore Israel and let his glory presence dwell among his people again (2 Mc 2:4–8; 2 Bar 6).

But instead of dwelling on the dramatic appearance of the Ark, the book of Revelation seems, at least at first glance, to move on quickly to something completely different in the very next verse: a mysterious sign in Heaven: a woman clothed with the sun (Rev 12:1).[10] Why talk about the woman when Israel's most sacred vessel has just appeared in the heavenly Temple? Such a sudden change in focus seems odd.

From a literary point of view, however, Revelation 11:19 and 12:1 are meant to be read together, side by side. For the appearance of the Ark in Revelation 11:19 serves not as the conclusion of the previous narrative about the seven trumpets but as an introduction to the appearance of the woman clothed with the sun (Rev 12:1). Thus, these two back-to-back verses should not be considered separately, but together.

Moreover, as Feuillet points out, the formula "and there appeared" (*kai ōphthē*) is found only three times in the book of Revelation, and all three instances are here in 11:19, 12:1, and 12:3. "Now it is difficult to dissociate the first 'and there appeared' from the others," Feuillet explains. And he concludes that "the two apparitions of the Ark of the Covenant and the Woman are seen as directly linked."[11] According to this line of interpretation, the Ark and the woman are closely associated together. The Ark that John sees in his vision in 11:19 is the woman he sees in the heavenly sign in Revelation 12:1. And since the woman is Mary, the book of Revelation may add further support for seeing Mary as a new Ark of the Covenant.[12]

◆

It is fitting that, in this final and climactic appearance of Mary in Scripture, Revelation 12 sheds additional light on a variety of topics we've already seen in previous New Testament passages. As at Cana and at the Cross, Mary is presented once again as the woman of Genesis 3:15, the New Eve whose son defeats the devil. Like the first Eve, Mary is also "the mother of all living," for she appears in this chapter as the mother of "all those who keep the commandments of God and bear testimony to Jesus" (Rev 12:17). This is, of course, related to the insight from John 19:25–27 regarding Mary's maternal relationship with the Beloved Disciple and provides further biblical support for Mary's spiritual motherhood. Revelation 12 also presents the woman as the mother of the Immanuel child foretold in Isaiah 7:14, the queen mother, and the Ark of the Covenant—themes we saw in the Annunciation and Visitation accounts in Luke 1. Finally, Mary appears as having already received her heavenly reward, dwelling in the "place prepared" for her by God, anticipating the final blessing we will all receive if we remain faithful as she did.

Chapter Twenty-Three

Mary in Other New Testament Passages:
Matthew, Mark, Luke, Acts, Paul

Our examination of Mary in the New Testament has focused on the sections that offer the most insight into her role in God's plan of salvation: the Gospel of Luke's infancy narrative (Lk 1–2), the Gospel of John's scenes involving Mary at the Wedding Feast at Cana (Jn 2:1–11) and at the foot of the Cross (Jn 19:25–27), and the account of the "woman clothed with the sun" in Revelation 12.

But there are other references and allusions to Mary in Matthew, Mark, and later chapters of Luke as well as in the Acts of the Apostles and the letters of Paul. This closing chapter will briefly consider some of those other Marian texts, starting with a perplexing statement Jesus makes about Our Lady that appears in Matthew, Mark, and Luke—but one that offers rich insight into the New Testament revelation of Mary's role as a model disciple.

"Who Are My Mother and My Brethren?" (Mk 3:31–35) (cf. Mt 12:46–50; Lk 8:19–21)

Picture the scene. While Jesus is teaching the crowds, his Mother and brethren arrive and request to see him. Here's how Mark recounts the welcome Jesus gives his family:

> And his mother and his brethren came; and standing outside they sent to him and called him. And a crowd was sitting about him; and they said to him, "Your mother and your brethren are outside, asking for you." And he replied, "Who are my mother and my brethren?" And looking around on those who sat about him, he said, "Here are my mother and my brethren! Whoever does the will of God is my brother, and sister, and mother." (Mk 3:31–35)[1]

What are we to make of this response? At first glance, Jesus might appear to modern readers as being a little cold. Instead of warmly welcoming his Mother, it seems as if he were pushing her away in favor of the people sitting and learning from him.

Another event from Jesus's public ministry is just as puzzling. An unnamed woman recognizes Jesus's greatness and expresses how blessed his Mother must be.

> A woman in the crowd raised her voice and said to him, "Blessed is the womb that bore you, and the breasts that you sucked!" But he said, "Blessed rather are those who hear the word of God and keep it!" (Lk 11:27–28)

Once again, Jesus seems to be distancing himself from Mary. The woman recognizes the honor Mary should have for being Jesus's Mother—something that is truly praiseworthy since it is through her maternity that the Son of God became man. Yet Jesus turns the attention away from mere motherhood to something he views as even more important: faithful discipleship exhibited in obeying God's Word. As Jesus explains, "Blessed rather are those who hear the word of God and keep it!"

In these two scenes from his public ministry, Jesus has the chance to single out Mary for her honorable role as his Mother. But instead, he shifts the honor to "whoever does the will of God" (Mk 3:34) and "those who hear God's word and keep it" (Lk 11:28). These are the ones who will be blessed. These are the people who are brother, sister, and mother to him. In other words, Jesus is forming a spiritual family of disciples, and the criterion for being a part of this new supernatural family is faithful obedience—hearing the Word of God and doing it. These faithful disciples will be blessed in his Kingdom, and their status is considered even greater than anything that is based merely on natural kinship.

But there is no reason Mary should be excluded from all this. Jesus's words should not be interpreted as leaving out his Mother from being counted among the "blessed" who are part of his spiritual family of disciples. According to Pope St. John Paul II, these two scenes point to a deeper kind of relationship that is being forged between Jesus and his Mother as his public ministry unfolds. Jesus "wishes to divert attention from motherhood understood only as a fleshly bond, in order to direct it toward those mysterious bonds of the spirit which develop from hearing and keeping God's word."[2]

Hearing and Keeping the Word

Let's ponder for a moment the ways in which the New Testament reveals Mary's relationship with Jesus to be not based soley on motherhood, but also that of discipleship. Keep in mind that the criteria Jesus establishes for being a part of his spiritual family of disciples are hearing the Word of God and doing it. No one else in the Gospels exhibits these qualities more beautifully than Mary!

Indeed, she's the first to hear the Word of God and do it. At the Annunciation, she hears God's message to her through the angel and completely gives her life to it. We saw this in her *fiat* when she described herself as a "handmaid of the Lord" and joyfully surrendered her life to this mission, saying "Let it be to me according to your word" (Lk 1:38).

All throughout her pregnancy and Jesus's childhood, Mary continues to be a model disciple who hears the Word of God and does it. In the Visitation scene, Mary exhibits her trust in God's Word. After hearing of Elizabeth's miraculous pregnancy from the angel, she goes "in haste" to visit her kinswoman. And when she arrives, Elizabeth praises Mary as being blessed among women for her great faith: "Blessed is she who believed there would be a fulfillment of what was spoken to her from the Lord" (Lk 1:45).

After the child is born, Mary obediently carries out the angel's command to name the child Jesus. Luke goes out of his way to underscore how the child "was called Jesus, *the name given by the angel* before he was conceived in the womb" (Lk 2:21). At the Nativity and in the finding in the Temple scene, Mary is described as someone who prayerfully mulls over the mysterious events and revelations unfolding before her—she "kept all these things, pondering them in her heart" (Lk 2:19, 51). All throughout Jesus's childhood, Mary is depicted as a model disciple, hearing God's word and striving to keep it.

Mary continues to exhibit her faithfulness in her Son's public ministry. At Cana, Mary encourages others to be obedient to Jesus's words: she instructs the servants, "Do whatever he tells you" (Jn 2:5). She is also one of the few disciples who remain close to Jesus at Calvary, where she is found "standing by the cross of Jesus" (Jn 19:25) when most of the others fled in fear. Even after Jesus's Resurrection and Ascension into Heaven, Mary remains in solidarity with the disciples in the Upper Room, praying with them in the days leading up to Pentecost (Acts 1:14).

And, finally, the book of Revelation portrays her as having received her heavenly reward for hearing God's Word and doing it all throughout her life. She appears in royal splendor with a crown, the reward given to disciples who persevere in faith and share in Christ's reign (Lk 22:28–30; 2 Tm 2:11–12). This is the reward given in the book of Revelation to all the saints who remain faithful through persecution, trials, and temptation (Rev 2:10; 3:11; 4:4, 10; 6:2; 14:14).

Thus, from beginning to end—from the Annunciation to the book of Revelation—the New Testament reveals Mary as a model, faithful disciple, consistently hearing the Word of God and doing it. No one meets the criteria for being a part of Jesus's spiritual family of disciples more than Mary.

The Gospel of Matthew: A Unique Genealogy

Matthew's Gospel opens with the genealogy of Jesus, which features forty-two generations from Abraham to Christ. In listing the names in this genealogy, Matthew employs a monotonous pattern, stating that A was the father of B, B was the father of C, all the way down the line: "Abraham was the father of Isaac, and Isaac was the father of Jacob, and Jacob the father of Judah …"

But, at the very end of the genealogical record, there's a surprise. Matthew suddenly breaks from this pattern and states: "… and Jacob the father of Joseph the husband of Mary, of whom Jesus was born, who is called Christ" (1:16). Notice how he introduces Joseph not as the father of Jesus but as the "husband of Mary." Mary becomes the center of attention as Matthew underscores that Jesus is born of her. With this unusual side-step move, Matthew goes out of the way to make sure he doesn't say Joseph is the natural father of Jesus. This is important because Matthew will soon reveal that Mary's child is conceived not by natural means but by the Holy Spirit (1:20). In this way, Matthew 1:16 subtly points to Mary's virginal conception of Christ.

Mary and the Four Other Women

Mary isn't the only woman in this genealogy. Four other women are mentioned in passing: Tamar, Rahab, Ruth, and "the wife of Uriah" (Bathsheba). Some have argued that these four women tell us something about the fifth woman, Mary. One common interpretation is that Matthew chose these four Old Testament women because they each had an "irregular union" that prepares the reader for Mary's own irregular situation of being pregnant before her union with Joseph. Rahab and Tamar were prostitutes. Ruth was a Gentile who married into the royal tribe of Judah. Bathsheba committed adultery. God's plan, however, was still at work, even through these irregular unions. By associating Mary with these women with irregular unions in the Old Testament, Matthew prepares the reader for Mary's most unique situation of bearing a child as a virgin. It has even been argued that Matthew's mention of four women with irregular unions prepares the reader for Mary's irregular situation of having a child not through her marriage—a situation that could lead some to suspect she had committed adultery.[3]

A stronger connection, however, might be found in the important role each of these women played in Israel's history and the Davidic dynasty in particular. Tamar was the mother of Perez through Judah, the patriarch whose tribe was linked with Israel's royal hopes (Gn 38:18; 49:8–12). Ruth was more immediately linked with the dynasty, serving as the great-grandmother of King David (Ru 4:13–22). Bathsheba was the wife of David and the mother of Solomon, through whom the kingship passed. Rahab is most known for her role in the conquest of Jericho that facilitated an easier access into the Promised Land (Jos 2:1; 6:17). But Matthew underscores another important (though not previously revealed) role she played in Israel's history. Listed as the mother of Boaz, Rahab is presented by Matthew as the great-great-grandmother of King David. As Menninger concludes, "What connected each of these women to Mary is the thought that they all bore children of the line of David." He goes on to explain:

> What is true of this group is true of Mary: these women bore children which were of the house of David. This common denominator links the four women of the [Old Testament] with Mary . . . If this conclusion about the four women is correct, then they were included in the genealogy in order to show that Jesus is the Davidic Messiah.[4]

A Virgin Will Conceive

Matthew 1:23 contains the first of several "fulfillment quotations" in Matthew's Gospel, and this one involves Mary. Matthew narrates that Mary's unique conception of Jesus by the Holy Spirit (1:20) fulfills the Immanuel prophecy of Isaiah 7:14. Matthew quotes the Greek text of this passage: "'Behold, a virgin [*parthenos*] shall conceive and bear a son, and his name shall be called Immanuel,' (which means, God with us)" (Mt 1:23).

Some have questioned how much this prophecy actually relates to Mary and the virginal conception of Christ. It is pointed out that the original Hebrew text describes the woman who will conceive as an *"almah"*—a word that does not translate as "virgin" but simply refers to a young woman of marriageable age. It is also argued that the prophecy of Isaiah 7:14 in its original historical setting had nothing to do with the virginal conception of the Messiah in the distant future but related to the hope God was giving the house of David during a period of dynastic crisis in the present. Foreign invaders threatened Jerusalem and the future of the dynasty was in doubt. Isaiah's prophecy foretells that the foreign threat will pass and a new son of David—an heir to King Ahaz—will assume the throne (Is 7:10–17). The foreign armies will retreat, a new king will rule in Judah, and the Davidic dynasty will continue. This royal child being called "Immanuel" is a sign that God is still "with" the dynasty through these difficult times.

These two points, however, should not dissuade us from seeing Mary and Jesus as the fulfillment of this prophecy. Though the Hebrew word used in Isaiah 7:14 (*almah*) does not emphasize virginity (*betulah* would have been the Hebrew word to specify a virgin), readers in the social and ethical milieu of ancient Israel would have assumed that a young woman of marriageable age—an *almah*—would have been a virgin.[5] Moreover, even if one might interpret the prophecy as having some relevance for the immediate future of the original audience, this should in no way rule out the ultimate fulfillment of this prophecy in Mary and Jesus. For one thing that is very clear is that Matthew interprets Isaiah 7:14 as finding fulfillment in the Christ Child and his Mother! Matthew makes explicit that the woman of Isaiah 7:14 is specifically a virgin (*parthenos*) and that Mary is identified as that virgin who conceives and bears a Son. Indeed, the child she carries in her womb is "of the Holy Spirit" (1:20) and "'his name shall be called Emmanuel' (which means, God with us)" (1:23).

Joseph "Knew Her Not Until . . ." (Mt 1:25)

Matthew concludes his opening chapter by mentioning that Joseph "took his wife, but knew her not until she had borne a son" (1:24–25). Some wonder whether this sentence implies that Joseph began to have sexual relations with Mary after Jesus was born. Such a question makes sense in the way the word "until" is used in English today. If, for example, I say "Bob worked until 5 p.m. today," it is implied that Bob stopped working at 5 p.m.

But the Greek word here translated "until" (*heōs*) does not function that way. It in no way implies a change in the state of affairs after the point in time mentioned. In 2 Samuel 6:23, for example, the Greek Old Testament uses this word *heos* to describe how Michal, the daughter of Saul, "had no child to [*heos*] the day of her death." The word merely describes her not having had children up to this moment of her death. It does not imply a change in affairs after that moment, for surely she didn't start having children after she died!

Thus, when Matthew states that Joseph did not know Mary "until" (*heos*) she gave birth to Jesus, this does not mean that Joseph and Mary began to have sexual relations after Christ's birth. It refers to their relationship up to the moment of Christ's birth without expressing any continuance or change in the situation after that point.

Matthew's statement in 1:25 simply reinforces that Joseph was not involved in Mary's pregnancy and further emphasizes her miraculous conception by the Holy Spirit. Joseph did not have sexual relations with Mary up until the moment of Christ's birth. By using the word *heos*, Matthew implies nothing about whether that status changed after Jesus's birth. The verse on its own, therefore, neither supports nor contradicts the Catholic doctrine of Mary's perpetual virginity (*CCC*, 499–510).

Mary with the Magi (Matthew 2:1–11)

In Matthew's infancy narrative, Joseph is much more prominent than Mary. The genealogy of Jesus is traced through Joseph's ancestors, not Mary's. The angel appears to Joseph three times, but not once to Mary. Joseph is the one leading the Holy Family first to Bethlehem, then to Egypt, and then back to Nazareth. But there is one moment when Mary takes center stage and Joseph fades into the background: when the Magi come to worship the Christ Child. Matthew relates that "going into the house they saw the child with Mary his mother, and they fell down and worshiped him" (Mt 2:11). Joseph is not even mentioned in the passage. As R. Aragon explains, "Her mention in this moment, along with the omission of Joseph, underlines that Mary is a person especially important for the narrator, and that is why he puts her in this very high position."[6]

The many Davidic kingdom themes in this passage may also shed light on Mary's sudden prominence. The child is called "king of the Jews" (2:2). The star guiding the Magi brings to mind the star associated with the royal scepter coming to Jacob in Balaam's oracle (Nm 24:17). The passage is centered on Bethlehem, which is where David was born (1 Sm 17:12) and the city from which the future Davidic king would come (Mi 5:2). Finally, the Magi bringing gifts of gold, frankincense, and myrrh while paying Jesus homage echoes the words in Psalm 72:10–11 about the nations coming to worship the royal son.

With these many Davidic kingdom overtones in this scene, some have suggested that the sudden focus on the mother and child may bring to mind the close association between the queen mother and her royal son.[7] As Brown has observed, "[S]ince the magi story puts so much emphasis on homage paid to a Davidic king in Bethlehem of Judah, 'the child with his mother' might evoke the peculiar importance given to the queen-mother (*gebirah*, 'the Great Lady') of a newborn or newly installed king in the Davidic dynasty."[8] Valentini concludes that Matthew intends to associate the mother with the royal glory of her son in the homage the Magi offer Jesus as the King. "Adoring the Lord-King, [the Magi] offer their homage also to the noble *gebirah*."[9]

The Brothers and Sisters of Jesus

The New Testament several times mentions the "brothers and sisters" of Jesus.[10] One might think these biblical references would contradict the Catholic doctrine of Mary's perpetual virginity. But a closer look at this issue will reveal that there is no contradiction and even some biblical support for the traditional understanding.

First, we must realize that there was no word for "cousin" in the Hebrew language. It was common to use the word "brother" to refer to cousins or other males in the extended family. The Greek Old Testament reflects this understanding when it employs the Greek word for brother (*adelphos*) to describe relationships that are not between siblings. The word *adelphos* is used to describe a cousin (1 Chr 23:21–22), an uncle (Gn 13:8), and men not united by kinship bonds at all, but brought together in covenant (2 Sm 1:26).

This background sheds light on the New Testament descriptions of Jesus's "brethren." The word used is *adelphoi*, which does not necessarily refer to brothers by blood but can be used more broadly to denote various extended family and even covenant relationships. So the fact that the New Testament mentions the *adelphoi* of Jesus does not necessarily mean Jesus had physical brothers and sisters.

But we can go a step further. We can see that Matthew has extended family in mind when he actually lists some of the names of Christ's "brothers." Two of those names— James and Joseph—are later identified in 27:56 as the sons of a different Mary (see also Mk 15:40; Jn 19:25). This understanding is in harmony with the Passion narrative in the Fourth Gospel, which tells how Jesus entrusts Mary to the care of the Beloved Disciple before he dies. This is not something Jesus would do if he had natural brothers and sisters to look after his mother (Jn 19:25–27). This interpretation also reflects the view of the majority of the Church Fathers who commented on this topic. Most of them saw the New Testament references to Jesus's "brethren" (*adelphoi*) pointed not to physical brothers and sisters, but to members of his extended family.

Mary at the Upper Room

> "All these with one accord devoted themselves to prayer, together with the women and Mary the mother of Jesus, and with his brethren." (Acts 1:14)

This verse is the last time Mary's name appears in the New Testament. And the final image of Mary on earth is one of prayer and communion. Luke presents Mary at prayer and at one with the disciples, at the center of the Church, awaiting the coming of the Spirit at Pentecost.

Her being listed here might, at first glance, seem to be an insignificant point, just a background detail. But we can detect her importance for Luke in the fact that he singles her out from all the other women disciples and relatives of Jesus. In addition to the Apostles listed in the previous verse (1:13), Mary is the only other person whose name is given in this group of people gathering in the Upper Room after Christ's Ascension. What is her important role in this scene? A few points can be drawn out.

First and foremost, Mary's presence with the Apostles underscores her perseverance in faith. Mary gave her initial "Yes" at the Annunciation (Lk 1:38). We've seen her reaffirm that throughout her pregnancy and her Son's birth, childhood, public ministry, and Passion. Now we see her continuing to be among the faithful disciples after the Ascension as the Apostles await the promised Holy Spirit that will come at Pentecost. From her first to her last appearance in Luke-Acts, Mary has consistently stood out as a model, faithful disciple.

Second, we can see some parallels with her role in the Annunciation scene. The same Holy Spirit that overshadowed Mary is about to be poured out on Jesus's disciples and the 3,000 people who are baptized at Pentecost (Acts 2). In fact, Luke seems to be making this very connection by using two key words in both the Annunciation scene and the account of Jesus promising the Spirit just before his Ascension in Acts 1:8: "power" and "come upon." The same Holy Spirit—"the *power* of the Most High" that "*will come upon*" Mary at the Annunciation (Lk 1:35)—is about to "*come upon*" the Apostles when they receive "*power*" from on high, the Holy Spirit at Pentecost (Acts 1:8; cf. Lk 24:49).

Third, the Church has seen Mary's role in prayer and in communion with the disciples as bearing much fruit.[11] Mary's presence at prayer with the disciples before Pentecost can be seen in parallel with her role at Cana. At Cana, she interceded and opened the doors for the first miracle and the launch of Jesus's public ministry. In the Upper Room, her prayers contribute to the birth of the Church as she prays for the outpouring of the Holy Spirit. According to Pope St. John Paul II, Mary, in her motherly love for her Son's disciples, prays for the Spirit she already received to enter their hearts at Pentecost. "Just as the Incarnation of the Spirit had formed the physical body of Christ in her virginal womb, in the upper room the same Spirit came down to give life to the Mystical Body."[12]

"Born of Woman" (Gal 4:4)

> But when the time had fully come, God sent forth his Son, born of woman, born under the Law, to redeem those who were under the Law, so that we might receive adoption as sons. And because you are sons, God has sent the Spirit of his Son into our hearts, crying, "Abba! Father!" So through God you are no longer a slave but a son, and if a son then an heir. (Gal 4:4–7)

Paul describes how in the fullness of time God sent his Son, who was "born of woman, born under the law." This is one of the earliest New Testament allusions to the mother of Jesus and the New Testament's first intuition of Mary's importance in salvation history.

Indeed, this initial, brief mention of the mystery of the "woman" appears in the context of a passage packed with other soteriological, Trinitarian, and Christological reflections from Paul. "In the fullness of time"—at the climax of salvation history—God sends his Son to liberate those born under the Law so that he can send the Son's Spirit. Then they can be adopted as God's children and receive their heavenly inheritance. Notice how the Trinity is at work in this passage, Father, Son and Holy Spirit. Also noteworthy are the soteriological themes of the Son redeeming those born under the Law so they may receive the indwelling of the Spirit and become children of God and heirs.

In the middle of this concise summary of God's saving work is the mention of the woman. And she plays an important role in the story. In the fullness of time, "God sent forth his Son, born of woman, born under the law."

Here Paul is underscoring Christ's humanity. "Born of woman" was a Jewish expression that described a person's humanness. It occurs in the book of Job to describe the fragility and weakness of the human condition.[13] Job 14:1, for example, states, "Man that is born of a woman is of few days, and full of trouble." It's used in a similar way in the Dead Sea Scrolls.[14] Jesus himself uses the expression twice in the New Testament to depict John the Baptist as a member of the human family: "Truly, I say to you, among those born of women there has risen no one greater than John the Baptist" (Mt 11:11; cf. Lk 7:28).

Paul's statement that the Son of God was "born of woman" is, therefore, a sign of the Incarnation—the Son truly took on human flesh.[15] According to Joseph Ratzinger, Paul uses the expression "born of woman" to underscore how Jesus "participated in the complete ordinariness of being human, that he entered fully into the human condition."[16] And the woman plays an important role in this drama: At the turning point of the history of salvation, *a woman offers human flesh to the Son of God* so he can enter the human condition, liberate us from slavery, and make us children of God. Paul does not at all elaborate on this point, but the fact that he mentions the woman from whom the Son of God is born is significant. As Moloney explains, "The point is made: there was a woman crucial to the life of Jesus—his mother."[17]

But there is a paradox here at the center of this passage. The Son of God is also "born under the law." This emphasizes that Jesus is born of a Jewish woman, into the Jewish people of God. He does not rescue God's people from the outside, but enters fully into the life of Israel as one born under the Law. So here's the paradox: How can one born under the Law liberate those who are slaves under the Law? Even more, how can someone who is part of the weak human condition, "born of woman," be the source of such a great redemption that fills us with God's Spirit and makes us God's children? In short, how can someone who is a child of Adam have the power to make us children of God—unless he has profound divine power to do so? These questions go beyond what Paul explicitly states in the text at hand. Italian biblical scholar Alberto Valentini sums up the issue well when he asks, "How is it possible that someone 'born of a woman,' frail and weak, can confer the status of children of God if not for a mysterious divine power that the text does not make explicit, but needs to be affirmed on the basis of other texts less concise and more detailed?"[18]

In Galatians 4:4, Paul does not elaborate on the nature of Jesus's divine sonship nor on the role of Mary in the Son becoming man. But these are topics other New Testament texts will expound upon. Here we have only what Ratzinger calls "a remote prelude" or "faint cadences of the future theology of the Christmas mystery."[19] One might think of this verse as a subtle introduction of Mary's role as the "woman" and Mother of Jesus. Other New Testament texts (many of which were considered throughout this book) develop these themes with much deeper and more extended reflection than what Paul offers in this verse.

Appendix

What Kind of Annunciation?
(Luke 1:28–38)

Attentive readers of the Bible will notice that Gabriel's announcement to Mary has many elements that sound familiar. On one hand, some have seen Luke's account of the Annunciation as following the pattern of other Old Testament birth announcements—such as the ones given to Hagar, Sarah, or Samson's parents—that focus on someone who is coming to perform great deeds for the Lord. Others have said that Luke's account should be viewed in light of Old Testament biblical commissioning stories, in which someone such as Moses, Gideon, Abraham, or Jeremiah is being called to serve in the Lord's plan of salvation in a crucial way.

What does this background mean for Mary? Is Luke trying to show us that Mary is being commissioned for some great mission like the great heroes of the Old Testament? Or is Luke's main concern to highlight that she will give birth to an important child in God's plan of salvation? Let's consider both of these possibilities.

A Birth Announcement?

Many interpreters have drawn attention to how the announcement of Christ's birth to Mary in Luke 1:26–38 recalls the way God or God's angelic messengers announce the birth of a son in the Bible.[1] While reading the account of the Annunciation to Mary, one might think of the Old Testament announcements given to Hagar about the birth of Ishmael (Gn 16:7–14), to Hannah about the birth of Samuel (1 Sm 1:9–20), or to Sarah about the birth of Isaac (Gn 18:9–15). The strongest parallels are found in the announcement of Isaac's birth to Abraham in Genesis 17 and the announcement of Samson's birth to his parents (Jgs 13:2–7).

New Testament scholar Raymond Brown, for example, sees in these and other Old Testament birth announcements a genre that he calls "Biblical Annunciation of Birth." This genre generally includes the following five elements:

1. *An appearance of an angel* (or the Lord himself) to the parents (Gn 17:1; Jgs 13:3);

2. The parent *responding in fear* (Gn 17:3; Jgs 13:22);

3. *The announcement of the conception of a child* (Gn 17:15, 19; Jgs 13:3–4);

4. The parent raising *a question or objection* regarding the announcement (Gn 17:17; Jgs 13:8, 17); and

5. The parent being given *a sign* to reassure him or her (Jgs 13:9; 18–21; possibly Gn 17:20–21).[2]

Luke's narrative of the Annunciation to Mary also includes each of these five elements:

1. An angel appears to Mary (1:28);

2. She is "greatly troubled" (1:29);

3. The angel announces the conception of Jesus (1:31);

4. Mary asks a question about this conception (1:34); and

5. The angel gives Mary the sign of her barren kinswoman miraculously conceiving a child in her old age (1:36–37).

According to Brown, the correspondence between these five steps in Luke 1:26–38 and the five-part pattern of Old Testament birth announcements suggests that the "Biblical Annunciation of Birth" literary form helped shape Luke's account of the Annunciation to Mary. This pattern for birth announcements was used in the Bible to prepare readers for the coming of someone who was destined by God to play a crucial role in God's salvific plan. Seeing the Annunciation to Mary as a biblical birth announcement story raises our expectations about the divine intervention taking place and the significance of the child whom Gabriel announces is to be born: Jesus.

A Commissioning Story?

While the Annunciation to Mary scene would likely recall famous Old Testament stories about God or an angel announcing the birth of a marvelous child, Luke 1:26–38 also recalls Old Testament commissioning narratives in which an individual is called by God to serve in his redemptive plan. Benjamin Hubbard, in his thorough examination of this theme in twenty-seven Old Testament passages, in Ancient Near Eastern literature, and in Luke-Acts, identifies seven features often found in Old Testament commissioning stories:

1. *Introduction:* Gives the setting in which the commissioning takes place;

2.   *Confrontation* (or *Theophany*): God or an
     angel appears and addresses the person about to be
     commissioned;

3.   *Reaction:* The person responds in fear or a sense of
     unworthiness;

4.   *Commission:* The person is given a specific
     mission from God that involves taking on a new
     role in his or her life;

5.   *Protest* (or *objection/question*): The person objects
     by claiming to be unworthy to fulfill the mission or
     raises a question about the message in some way;

6.   *Reassurance:* The person is given encouragement
     with words such as "fear not" or God "will be with
     you"; and

7.   *Conclusion:* The commissioning narrative often
     ends with a remark about how the person begins
     to carry out the work. [3]

All of these elements are found in the accounts of the commissioning of Moses (Ex 3:1–4:17), Gideon (Jgs 6:11–24), Elijah at Mount Horeb (1 Kgs 19:1–19), and Isaiah (Is 6). And almost all are found in the commissioning of Abraham (Gn 15:1–6), Jacob (Gn 28:10–22), Samuel (1 Sm 3:1–4:1), Jeremiah (Jer 1:1–10), and Ezekiel (Ez 1:1–3:15).[4]

The commissioning narrative that most clearly resembles Luke's Annunciation to Mary scene is the one involving Gideon, who was chosen by the Lord to rescue the people from the Midianites.[5] We can see numerous parallels in these two scenes. Both Gideon and Mary are greeted by an angel and told "the Lord is with you" (Jgs 6:12; Lk 1:28). Both are instructed not to be afraid (Jgs 6:23; Lk 1:30) and are presented as having "found favor" with God (Jgs 6:17; Lk 1:30). After having been given their mission, both raise questions about their missions, and each receives clarification and a sign to reassure him or her about the calling. Both in the end express their consent to God's call for them.[6]

One way in which the accounts of Gideon and Mary can be seen as containing the seven elements of the commissioning-type story is summarized in the chart on pages 238 and 239.

Another approach to understanding the parallels can be found in the work of G. del Olmo, who offers a simpler structure for Old Testament vocation narratives that makes the connections between Gideon's call in Judges 6:11–24 and Mary's in Luke 1:26–38 clear. Rodriguez summarizes Olmo's five key aspects of the typical vocational narrative—(1) Introduction; (2) Theophany; (3) Mission; (4) Sign; and (5) Conclusion—and uses these five parts to show the parallels between the call of Gideon and the call of Mary:

	Gideon's Vocation (Judges 6:11–24)	Mary's Vocation (Luke 1:26–38)
Introduction	v. 11	vv. 26–27
Theophany	vv. 12–13	vv. 28–29
Mission	vv. 14–16	vv. 30–35
Sign	vv. 17–21a	vv. 36–38a
Conclusion	vv. 21b (22–24)	v. 38b[7]

Seven Elements of the Comissioning Story

Judges 6:11–24: Call of Gideon	Luke 1:26–38: Annunciation to Mary
Introduction: Gideon is under the oak tree at Ophrah, discreetly beating out wheat in the wine press to hide it from the Midianites (v. 11).	*Introduction:* It is the sixth month of Elizabeth's pregnancy. Gabriel is sent to Nazareth of Galilee to Mary who is betrothed to Joseph (vv. 26–27).
Theophany: The angel appears to Gideon and says "The Lord is with you" (v. 12).	*Theophany:* The angel appears to Mary and says, "The Lord is with you" (v. 28).
Reaction: Gideon struggles with this angelic greeting, wondering how God can be with the Israelites when they are suffering under the hands of the Midianites (v. 13). Gideon is also in awe over having seen God's messenger face-to-face and worried that he will now die as a result (v. 22).	*Reaction:* Mary is "greatly troubled at the saying" of the angel and wonders "what sort of greeting this might be" (v. 29).
Reassurance: God tells Gideon "do not fear" and reassures him he will not die (v. 23). Gideon is also reassured that God will be with him to smite the Midianites (v. 16).	*Reassurance:* Mary is reassured by the angel "Do not be afraid" because she "has found favor with God" (v. 30).
First Commissioning Message: Gideon is given his mission: to rescue Israel from the Midianites. "Go in this might of yours and deliver Israel from the hand of Midian; do I not send you?" (v. 14).	*First Commissioning Message:* Mary is given her mission: to become the Mother of the royal Son of David, the Messiah-King: "You will conceive in your womb and bear a son, and you shall call his name Jesus. He will be great, and will be called the Son of the Most High; and the Lord God will give to him the throne of his father David, and he will reign over the house of Jacob for ever; and of his kingdom there will be no end" (vv. 31–33).

Seven Elements of the Comissioning Story (continued)

Judges 6:11–24: Call of Gideon	Luke 1:26–38: Annunciation to Mary
Objection: How? Gideon asks how this military victory will be possible for a lowly man like he, coming from the weakest family in the weakest clan of his tribe: "Please, Lord, how can I deliver Israel?" (v. 15).	*Objection: How?* Mary asks how this conception will be possible for her since she does "not know man" (v. 34).
Reassurance (in the form of clarification): Gideon receives further reassurance of how he will be able to deliver Israel. God will be with him to accomplish this: "But I will be with you" (v. 16).	*Reassurance* (in the form of clarification): "The Holy Spirit will come upon you, and the power of the Most High will overshadow you" (v. 35).
Second Commissioning Message: Gideon is told not only that he will rescue Israel, but that he will crush the oppressing Midianites: "And you shall smite the Midianites as one man" (v. 16).	*Second Commissioning Message:* Mary receives further clarification of her maternal mission: The child she will conceive will not only be the Messiah; he will be the Son of God (v. 35).
Reassurance (in the form of a sign): Gideon requests a sign to assure him that he is speaking with God, and the sign is given (vv. 17–21).	*Reassurance* (in the form of a sign): Mary is given the sign of her elderly, barren kinswoman Elizabeth having conceived a son, "for with God, nothing will be impossible" (vv. 36–37).
Conclusion (showing the consent of Gideon): Gideon builds an altar to God and names it "The LORD is Peace" (v. 24).	*Conclusion* (showing the consent of Mary): Mary consents saying, "Behold, I am the handmaid of the Lord; let it be to me according to your word" (v. 38).

Conclusion: The Vocation of Mary

So is Luke 1:26–38 an announcement of birth story or a commissioning story? We have seen elements of both. The combination of the two aspects has led Brown to conclude that "the annunciation of Jesus's birth in Luke also involved the beginning of Mary's confrontation with the mysterious plan of God—in other words, a type of commissioning of Mary as the first Christian disciple."[8] Similarly, de la Potterie calls it "a mixed form" synthesizing both literary genres.[9] In fact, the two can be seen as working together. The announcement of birth aspect sheds light on the content of Mary's vocation: her mission is to be the Mother of the Messiah-King (1:31–33), the divine "Son of God" (1:35) who is coming to Israel.[10]

One key point about Mary that we can take away from this analysis is that Luke does want his readers to view this scene as a commissioning of Mary—not just an announcement about the birth of Jesus. A number of Catholic and Protestant commentators alike have made this point.[11] While the passage certainly has a Christological focus, this does not mean Luke is uninterested in Mary's role in the coming messianic age.[12] The extensive parallels with the Old Testament passages narrating the commissioning of Jeremiah, Moses, and especially Gideon (there is no other Old Testament passage that has more links with Luke's Annunciation to Mary scene) support seeing Luke 1:26–38 in a similar light as a vocation-commissioning story.

Also pointing in this direction is the fact that the angel Gabriel greets Mary in a way that no one else in the entire Bible is ever greeted (1:28). And he employs key terms in his dialogue with her that were commonly used in the Old Testament when someone was being called by God for an important mission.

Gabriel tells Mary "the Lord is with you" (1:28), an expression that was used by God or God's angelic messengers to address someone who was being called by God to some great task in which the future of Israel was at stake (Gn 26:24; 28:15; Ex 3:12; Jgs 6:16; Jer 1:8). The expression provides assurance that God will be with the person to help him or her carry out the mission. Mary being addressed this way underscores that some mission is being entrusted to her.

Similarly, Mary having "found favor with God" (1:30) draws attention to the role God is giving Mary. As we saw in chapter 4, this expression denotes a favor given to an inferior and sometimes includes the conferral of a distinguished role. It can describe someone to whom much has been entrusted (Gn 39:4, 21). Thus, Mary's having found favor with God indicates that much is being entrusted to her. She is standing in the footsteps of other great heroes in Israel like Noah (Gn 6:8), Abraham (Gn 18:2–3), Moses (Ex 33:12–17), Hannah (1 Sm 1:18), and David (2 Sm 24:25), who found favor with God and through whom God graciously accomplished something special.

By presenting the vocation of Mary, Luke is drawing the reader's attention to Mary herself and to the important role she will play in God's plan.[13] Like Gideon, Mary is being called to a formidable task in which the future of God's people is at stake. Hence, as de la Potterie argues, since the vocation of Gideon story is a primary model for the Annunciation to Mary scene, Luke puts the accent on "*the vocation of Mary*, by which she is invited to take part in the realization of the plan of salvation willed by God. The Annunciation account attracts our attention to the role of Mary in the Incarnation of the Son of God."[14]

Notes

Introduction

1. As a leading New Testament Greek lexicon of the late twentieth century concluded, "Little is known about the life of this Mary." Walter Bauer, F. Wilbur Gingrich, et. al., eds. *A Greek-English Lexicon of the New Testament and Other Early Christian Literature* (Chicago: University of Chicago Press, 1979), 491.

2. See, for example, the ecumenical work *Mary in the New Testament*, ed. Raymond Brown, et. al. (Philadelphia: Fortress, 1978), 97–102, 167–77; Jaroslav Pelikan, *Mary Through the Centuries* (New Haven: Yale University Press, 1996), 7–21; Beverly Gaventa, *Mary: Glimpses of the Mother of Jesus* (Columbia, SC: University of South Carolina Press, 1995), 69–72; Joel Green, "The Social Status of Mary in Luke 1,5–2,52: A Plea for Methodological Integration," *Biblica* 73 (1992): 457–71; Dwight Longenecker and David Gustafson, *Mary: A Catholic-Evangelical Debate* (Grand Rapids: Brazos Press, 2003), 21–22.

3. Gaventa, *Mary*, 56. See also Brown, *Mary in the New Testament*, 137–43.

4. Benedict XVI, encyclical letter *Deus caritas est* (2006), no. 41.

5. Raymond Brown, *Biblical Exegesis and Church Doctrine* (New York: Paulist Press, 1985), 97.

6. "There is no convincing evidence that Luke specifically identified Mary with the symbolism of the Daughter of Zion or the Ark of the Covenant." Brown, *Mary in the New Testament*, 134.

7. "One cannot prove any of these symbolic interpretations; possibility is the *most* one can accord them." Brown, *Mary in the New Testament*, 217.

8. See chapter 2 ("'Rejoice!': Mary as Daughter Zion"), chapter 9 ("Ark of the Covenant"), and chapter 20 ("Behold, Your Mother").

9. Brown, *Mary in the New Testament*, 127–8.

10. Ignace de la Potterie, *Mary in the Mystery of the Covenant* (New York: Alba House, 1992), xxiii.

11. De la Potterie, *Mary in the Mystery of the Covenant*, 203.

12. Vatican II, *Dogmatic Constitution on Divine Revelation*, 24.

13. Joseph Fenton, "Our Lady's Queenship and the New Testament Teachings," in *Alma Socia Christi* Congressus Mariologicus Romae (Rome: Academia Mariana, 1950), 68–86.

14. Edward Sri, *Queen Mother: A Biblical Theology of Mary* (Steubenville, OH: Emmaus Road, 2005), 32.

15. See Sri, *Queen Mother*. We will treat this topic also in this present work in chapter 8.

16. Pontifical Biblical Commission, *Interpretation of the Bible in the Church*, II, B, 2 (my emphasis).

17. The main difference between the two kinds of typology examined here is this: "Extra-biblical typology" involves the creative discernment of the theologian who perceives connections between the Old Testament, the New Testament, and the Christian faith; whereas what one might call "inter-biblical typology" can be observed in the New Testament writer's interpretation of the Old Testament. In the latter case, it is the New Testament itself that points out how a particular Old Testament figure foreshadows a reality in the New.

18. Similar to the PBC, Brown draws attention to the "types that have been pointed out by the NT" and "already existing scriptural

patterns" as criteria for recognizing an authentic typical sense. Raymond Brown, "Hermeneutics," in *Jerome Biblical Commentary*, ed. Raymond Brown, et. al. (Englewood Cliffs, NJ: Prentice Hall, 1968), 619. See also Raymond Brown, *An Introduction to the New Testament* (New York: Doubleday, 1997), 41. Brown is also open to the possibility of extra-biblical typologies (those which are not established by the New Testament) provided they are found in a consensus of the Fathers, the liturgy, or Church doctrine. Although he recognizes these as authentic typologies, Brown still gives a certain primacy to those types that are supported by the Scriptures themselves.

19. Stefano Manelli, *All Generations Shall Call Me Blessed: Biblical Mariology* (New Bedford, MA: Academy of the Immaculate, 2005), 82–83.

20. For some of these parallels, see, for example, John Nolland, *Luke 1–9:20* (Dallas: Word, 1989), 74–76; Brant Pitre, *Jesus and the Jewish Roots of Mary* (New York: Image, forthcoming 2018), 61–65; John McHugh, *The Mother of Jesus in the New Testament* (London: Darton, Longman & Todd, 1975), 56–63. We will develop these connections extensively in chapter 9.

Chapter One – Mary's Life before the Annunciation

1. William Petersen, "Nazareth" in *Anchor Bible Dictionary*, ed. David Noel Freedman (New York: Doubleday, 1992), vol. 4, 1050.

2. I. Howard Marshall, *The Gospel of Luke* (Grand Rapids: Eerdmans, 1978), 64.

3. Joel Green, *The Gospel of Luke* (Grand Rapids: Eerdmans, 1997), 84.

4. See Joachim Jeremias, *Jerusalem in the Time of Jesus* (Philadelphia: Fortress Press, 1969), 365–68; Raymond Brown, *The Birth of the Messiah* (Garden City, New York: Doubleday, 1977), 324. All references to Brown's *The Birth of the Messiah* will be from this 1977 edition unless otherwise noted.

5. It also relates (as we will see in chapter 4) to the Immanuel prophecy of Isaiah 7:14: "A virgin shall conceive and bear a son, and shall call his name Immanuel. . . ."

6. Joseph Fitzmyer notes that the name was probably a shortened form of Yosip-yah, which means "May Yahweh add." Joseph Fitzmyer, *The Gospel According to Luke I–IX* (New York: Doubleday, 1983), 344.

7. Green, *Luke*, 84–85.

8. 1 Sm 20:16; 1 Kgs 12:19; 13:2; 2 Chr 23:3. Mark Strauss, *The Davidic Messiah in Luke-Acts: The Promise and its Fulfillment in Lukan Christology* (JSNTSup 110) (Sheffield: Sheffield Academic Press, 1995), 87. The virgin birth in no way would diminish Joseph's fatherhood, since his legal paternity would have been viewed as a realistic fatherhood which would have brought Jesus into Joseph's family heritage. See also Marshall, *The Gospel of Luke*, 157. In commenting on the genealogy in Luke 3, which speaks of Jesus as being "the son (as was supposed) of Joseph . . . the son of David," Marshall explains: "There is no inconsistency in Luke's mind between the account of the virgin birth and the naming of Joseph as one of the parents of Jesus. From the legal point of view, Joseph was the earthly father of Jesus, and there was no other way of reckoning his descent. There is no evidence that the compilers of the genealogies thought otherwise."

9. Green, *Luke*, 84–85.

10. Fitzmyer, *Luke I–IX*, 344. Manelli, *All Generations Shall Call Me Blessed*, 161.

11. See, for example, Brown, *Birth of the Messiah*, 248–53, 292–98, 408–10; Fitzmyer, *Luke I–IX*, 313–15; Robert Tannehill, *The Narrative Unity of Luke-Acts* (Philadelphia: Fortress, 1995), 15–20.

12. Green, *Luke*, 83.

13. Ibid.

14. Tannehill, *Narrative Unity*, 16.

15. "The similarity of structure and content between the two scenes invites the reader to consider the differences between them all the more closely." R. Alan Culpepper, "Luke" in *The New Interpreter's Bible*, ed. Leander E. Keck, et al. (Nashville: Abingdon, 1995), 51.

16. Zechariah and Elizabeth in Luke 1:5–9; Simeon in Luke 2:25–27; Anna in Luke 2:36–38. See Joel Green, "The Social Status of Mary," 457–71.

17. Green, "The Social Status of Mary," 470.

18. Ibid, 468. Luke Johnson makes a similar point: "That she should have 'found favor with God' and be 'highly gifted' shows Luke's understanding of God's activity as surprising and often paradoxical, almost always reversing human expectations." Luke Johnson, *The Gospel of Luke* (Collegeville, MN: Liturgical Press, 1991), 39. This surprising choice of Mary of Nazareth to be the mother of Israel's Messiah anticipates the theme of reversal that will be developed more in the Magnificat (see chapter 10).

19. F. Scott Spencer, *The Gospel of Luke and Acts of the Apostles* (Nashville: Abingdon Press, 2008), 103.

20. Ibid, 104.

21. Ibid.

Chapter Two – "Rejoice!": Mary as Daughter Zion

1. The same call for the land to be glad and rejoice in Joel 2:21 is given to the children of Zion in Joel 2:23. In Lamentations 4:21, *chaire* is being used ironically in a parody of this theme as Edom is told to rejoice while the Daughter of Zion is told in the next verse that God will bring an end to her suffering in exile and punish the "daughter of Edom" (4:22). Arthur Just notes, "Therefore all the occurrences in the LXX of this form of the imperative are at least in

proximity to the theme of the daughter of Zion." Arthur Just, *Luke 1:1–9:50* (St. Louis: Concordia Publishing House, 1996), 66. See also de la Potterie, *Mary in the Mystery of the Covenant*, 14; John McHugh, *Mother of Jesus*, 39.

2. "In Hebrew the word *beqirbek* can mean 'in your midst' when it is used of a city (as in Zephaniah's text), but the same word when used of a woman can mean 'in your womb' (Gen 25:22). Luke would then understand the Zephaniah prophecy about the Lord coming into the *midst* of his people as fulfilled by the Lord-Savior coming into the womb of Mary." George Montague, *Our Father, Our Mother* (Steubenville, OH: Franciscan University Press, 1990), 107.

3. Joseph Ratzinger, *Jesus of Nazareth: The Infancy Narratives* (New York: Image, 2012), 28.

4. De la Potterie, *Mary in the Mystery of the Covenant*, 15.

5. "Mary here is greeted with a mini-oracle of salvation." Nolland, *Luke 1–9:20*, 50.

6. De la Potterie, *Mary in the Mystery of the Covenant*, 16. Such a view would fit well with how Luke presents Mary as a representative figure in the Magnificat, where the celebrated blessings bestowed on her (1:46–50) are commonly seen as anticipating the blessings God desires to bestow on all of Israel (1:51–55). Since the woman Zion figure of the Old Testament represented the faithful Israelites, Mary's association with Daughter Zion in Luke 1:28 could be seen as laying the foundation for Luke's further development of this representative role for her as she embodies the hopes of Israel—a theme to be discussed more in chapter 10.

7. See, for example, Brown, *Mary in the New Testament*, 130–32.

8. Mt 26:49; 27:29; 28:9; Mk 15:18; Jn 19:3.

9. See Jas 1:1, where it is used as a greeting in the opening of this letter.

10. Brown, *Birth of the Messiah*, 324.

11. "The occurrence, in such a Semitically colored narrative, of the Greek greeting formula *chaire* ('Hail') instead of the Semitic 'Peace!' is so surprising that one hesitates to accept it at its face value." Wilfrid Harrington, *The Gospel of Luke* (Westminster, MD: Newman Press, 1967), 45; Ratzinger, *Jesus of Nazareth: The Infancy Narratives*, 26.

12. Joseph Paredes, *Mary and the Kingdom of God* (Middlegreen: St. Paul Publications, 1991), 67. He goes on to explain: "The Greek greeting *chaire* appears several times in the first three Gospels (cf. Mt 26:49; 27:29; Mk 15:18; Jn 19:3). However, whenever Luke's Gospel refers to a greeting, except in the annunciation, the greeting is always the Hebrew word *shalom* (Luke 10:5; 24:36)" (79). Similarly, McHugh: "Now if Luke's only concern in 1:28 was to express a conventional greeting from Gabriel to Mary, why did he choose to write this greeting in the Greek, not the Semitic, form? Why did Luke not write 'Peace unto thee!', since he was so visibly striving to imitate a Semitic style and to imprint on the reader's mind a lively picture of a thoroughly Jewish world?" McHugh, *The Mother of Jesus in the New Testament*, 38.

13. Lucien Deiss, *Mary Daughter of Sion* (Collegeville: Liturgical Press, 1972), 54; S. Lyonnet, "ΧΑΙΡΕ ΚΕΧΑΡΙΤΩΜΕΝΗ" *Biblica* 20 (1939), 130–31; E. G. Mori, "Annunciazione del Signore" in *Nuovo Dizionario di Mariologia* (Milan: Edizioni San Paolo, 1986), 73; de la Potterie, *Mary in the Mystery of the Covenant*, 14–17; Johnson, *Luke*, 37; McHugh, *The Mother of Jesus in the New Testament*, 38. A number of Protestant scholars have reached this conclusion as well. See Green, *Luke*, 87; Nolland, *Luke 1–9:20*, 49–50; cf. Robert Tannehill, *Luke* (Nashville: Abingdon Press, 1996), 48.

14. Green, *Luke*, 87; Nolland, *Luke 1–9:20*, 49–50.

15. In Lamentations 4:21, this three-fold pattern is used in a parody to mock Edom: the cause for this ironic rejoicing is the cup of judgment that is about to fall upon Edom.

16. As we will see in greater detail in chapter 4, Gabriel's description

of Mary's child echoes the promises given to King David in 2 Samuel 7:11–16, where David was told that God would give David a royal son who will bear a "great" name, establish "the throne of his kingdom forever," and receive a "kingdom" that will be "made sure forever."

17. This would prepare the reader (and Mary as a character in Luke's narrative) for Gabriel's explicit announcement of the coming of the Messiah-King, Jesus.

18. Montague, *Our Father, Our Mother*, 107.

Chapter Three – Full of Grace

1. *Kecharitōmenē* is a passive perfect participle of the causative verb *charitoun*, which is the verbal form of the noun *charis* (meaning "favor" or "grace"). In the active voice, *charitoun* means "to grace" or "to favor" or even "to make graced." As a passive perfect participle, it means to be favored or graced or "to be made graced."

2. For a summary of these approaches, see Ernesto Della Corte, "Κεχαριτωμένη (Lc 1,28) Crux Interpretum" *Marianum* 52 (1990), 101–148.

3. Brown, *Birth of the Messiah*, 325–27. Similarly, Fitzmyer argues that Mary "is favored by God to be the mother of the descendant of David and the Son of the Most High." Even though the word might express a state of divine favor, "that favor is to be understood of the unique role that she is to perform in conceiving God's Messiah." Fitzmyer, *Luke I–IX*, 245–6.

4. Brown, *Birth of the Messiah* (1993 edition), 634 (emphasis added). The hesitation some scholars have had in seeing *kecharitōmenē* as involving an internal reality pointing to Mary's personal holiness can be illustrated by Brown's two editions of *Birth of the Messiah*. In the original 1977 version, Brown held that *kecharitōmenē* in 1:28 is linked to Mary's unique maternity. It refers to the grace or favor of being chosen to be the Mother of God's

Son. He is completely silent on the effect this grace might have on Mary's soul. Brown leaves the impression that this is just an exterior favor—God looked kindly on Mary. He also makes no mention of Mary already having been a recipient of God's grace, as the perfect tense indicates. In his 1993 updated edition of *Birth of the Messiah*, Brown responded on this point to his critics, especially Ignace de la Potterie, who argued that *kecharitōmenē* does involve a profound effect on the soul and that this effect already had taken place in Mary before the Annunciation. In regards to *timing*, Brown then admitted that "*kecharitōmenē* does involve an already existing state of Mary in God's favor." And in regards to the *content and meaning* of this grace bestowed on Mary, Brown acknowledged that this favor does involve some transforming effect in her. But he still does not elaborate on that effect, and seems uncomfortable with approaches that ponder how much Marian theology one might draw out of this word in Luke's Annunciation account, as noted.

5. "Nel nostro caso con il passivo del perfetto participio l'accento non è su Dio che agisce, ma soprattutto sull'*effetto* che ne è seguito in Maria." Ernesto Della Corte, "Κεχαριτωμένη (Lc 1,28) Crux Interpretum," 106. See also: de la Potterie, "Κεχαριτωμένη en Lc 1,28 Étude philologique" *Biblica* 68 (1987), 365; Deyanira Flores, "Mary, the Virgin 'Completely and Permanently Transformed by God's Grace': The Meaning and Implications of Luke 1:28 and of the Dogma of the Immaculate Conception for Mary's Spiritual Life" *Marian Studies* 65 (2004), 88; François Rossier, "*Kecharitomene* (Lk. 1:28) in the light of Gen. 18:16–33: A Matter of Quality" *Marian Studies* 65 (2004), 161.

6. Fitzmyer, *Luke I–IX,* 345; Green, *Luke,* 87; René Laurentin, *A Short Treatise on the Blessed Virgin Mary* (Washington, NJ: AMI Press, 1991), 20; Eugene LaVerdiere, *The Annunciation to Mary* (Chicago: Liturgy Training Publications, 2004), 75.

7. Lucien Deiss, *Mary, Daughter of Sion,* 61. Josef Dillersberger, *The Gospel of Saint Luke* (Westminster, Maryland: Newman Press, 1958), 20–21.

8. Rossier, "Kecharitomene," 163.

9. The rare use of this verb—found in the NT only in Luke 1:28 and Ephesians 1:6—"supposes in the evangelist a special intention: he wants to express something extraordinary." Pietro della Madre di Dio, "Gratia plena" *Ephemeridaes Carmeliticae* 11 (1960), 109. (As cited in Ernesto Della Corte, "Κεχαριτωμένη (Lc 1,28) *Crux Interpretum*," 108.)

10. Origen, *Homilies on Luke*, PG 13, 1815–1816.

11. De la Potterie, "Κεχαριτωμένη," 379. De la Potterie notes how verbs ending in –όô (like the verb *charitóô* of which *kecharitōmenē* is the perfect passive feminine participle singular) are causative, denoting an action that has a transforming effect on the object. He gives a series of examples, including *doulóô* (to enslave), *éleuthéróô* (to render free), *kakóô* (literally, to make bad), and *tuphlóô* (to blind). De la Potterie explains, "These verbs, then effect a change of something in the person or the thing affected." Along these lines, *charitóô*, as a causative verb, expresses "a *change* brought about by grace." De la Potterie, *Mary in the Mystery of the Covenant*, 17–18. See also Della Corte, "Κεχαριτωμένη (Lc 1,28) *Crux Interpretum*," 106–8, 141; Rene Laurentin, *The Truth of Christmas* (Petersham, Massachusetts: St. Bede's Publications, 1982), 18–19; Flores, "Mary, the Virgin 'Completely and Permanently Transformed by God's Grace,'" 87; Rossier, "Kecharitomene," 160; Brown, *Birth of the Messiah* (1993), 632, n. 153.

12. De la Potterie, "Κεχαριτωμένη en Lc 1,28: Étude exégetique et théologique," 483.

13. Della Corte, "Κεχαριτωμένη (Lc 1,28) *Crux Interpretum*," 134–35; Rossier, "Kecharitomene," 161; de la Potterie, *Mary in the Mystery of the Covenant*, 18–20; Deiss, *Mary, Daughter of Sion*, 62–63.

14. De la Potterie critiques the position of Brown and Fitzmyer, who hold that *kecharitōmenē* in Luke 1:28 points to the grace of the divine maternity. "That appears impossible to us, for the maternity of Mary must yet begin. Here . . . the *perfect* passive participle

is used by Luke to indicate that the transformation by grace
has already taken place in Mary, well before the moment of the
Annunciation." De la Potterie, *Mary in the Mystery of the Covenant*,
18. For de la Potterie, the grace envisioned in Luke 1:28 was not the
grace of the divine maternity that she is about to receive, but the
grace already given to Mary to prepare her for this calling.

15. Paul Haffner, *The Mystery of Mary* (Gracewing: Hillenbrand
Books, 2004), 57.

16. Graystone also holds that Mary being full of grace is not merely
anticipatory, but also refers to her personal holiness: "Its functional
significance does not, cannot, exclude prior reference to Mary's personal holiness and status, in the past, as in the present and future."
Geoffrey Graystone, *Virgin of all Virgins: The Interpretation of Luke
1:34* (Rome: Pontifical Biblical Institute, 1968), 87. Similarly,
Manuel Miguens: "As the case of Joseph (Gn 39:4) reveals, the
'grace' of choice which is found is not separated from an objective
fitness in the subject which renders this subject 'pleasing, graceful'
in someone's eyes." Manuel Miguens, *Mary, The Servant of the Lord*
(Boston: St. Paul Editions, 1978), 43.

Chapter Four – The Mother of the Messiah

1. This is quite different from what Luke says about Gabriel's
appearance to the priest Zechariah in the Temple. When Luke describes Gabriel appearing to the priest Zechariah in the Temple, he
notes that Zechariah "was troubled when he saw him, and fear fell
upon him" (Lk 1:12).

2. W.C. van Unnik, "*Dominus Vobiscum*: The Background of a
Liturgical Formula" in *New Testament Essays: Studies in Memory of
Thomas Walter Mason 1893–1958* (Manchester: University Press,
1959), 276, 289. While the phrase is used many times in the OT,
only twice is it employed as a greeting similar to what we find in
the angel's announcement to Mary: the angel's words to Gideon
(Jgs 6:12) and Boaz's words to the reapers in the field (Ru 2:4). In

both Old Testament cases, as in Luke 1:28, the verb, however, is not given. The text simply says *ho kyrios meta sou*, so it is up to the translator to supply a verb. Should the verb be subjunctive ("May the Lord be with you") or declarative ("The Lord is with you")? The context is key. A subjunctive verb is typically supplied in Boaz's greeting in Ruth 2:4 ("May the Lord be with you") because the parallel response of the reapers clearly expresses a wish, not a declaration ("The Lord bless you"). On the other hand, Gideon responds to the angel's *ho kyrios meta sou* by saying, "If the Lord is with us, why then has all this befallen us?" (Jgs 6:13). This implies that Gideon understood the angel's words to be a declaration that God was with him, not simply a wish. Hence, most translate the angel's words in Judges 6:12 as "the Lord is with you."

Similarly, the context of Gabriel's words to Mary in Luke 1:28 points to them being seen as a declaration of God's presence with Mary, not merely a wish. As we saw in the previous chapter, God's presence working in Mary has already been emphasized in the title given to her, *kecharitōmenē*. Moreover, as Fitzmyer notes, Luke 1:28 has more similarities to the angel's words to Gideon in Judges 6:12 (which is declarative) than it does to the subjective wish of Boaz in Ruth 2:4. Fitzmyer, *Luke I–IX*, 346. Both the Annunciation to Mary and the scene with Gideon involve an appearance of an angel and similar words and themes are found in both accounts. Both are instructed not to be afraid and are presented as having "found favor" with God (Jgs 6:17; Lk 1:30). Both are commissioned for an important task in God's saving plan; after having been given a mission, each raises a question about the mission and then receives clarification and a sign to reassure him or her about the calling. Both in the end express their consent to God's call.

3. "This is no conventional or pious greeting but announces a dynamic power of God's own presence. . . . The promise or statement of the presence of God runs like a thread through OT history . . . and here reaches a certain culmination." Nolland, *Luke 1–9:20*, 50.

4. Edward Sri, *Walking with Mary* (New York: Image, 2014), 46.

5. Ratzinger, *Jesus of Nazareth: The Infancy Narratives*, 33.

6. This expression recalls the assurance given by heavenly visitors in the Old Testament (Gn 15:1; 26:24; Dn 10:12, 19). It's also used this way in Luke's Gospel by Gabriel himself when he appears to Zechariah (Lk 1:13) and by the angels appearing to the shepherds at the Nativity (Lk 2:10).

7. Sometimes the expression is used when people are making a request. Gideon, for example, asks the angel, "If now I have found favor with you, then show me a sign . . ." (Jgs 6:17). This is also the case with Hannah (1 Sm 1:18), David (2 Sm 15:25), and others (see Gn 18:3; Ex 33:12–13, 16).

8. In Luke 1:30 we have an explicit heavenly affirmation of God's favor for Mary, and this is exceptional. As Gordon Wenham points out, "It very rare for it to be said outright that a man has found favor in God's sight." Gordon Wenham, *Genesis 1–15* (Dallas: Word, 1987), 145. In fact, Moses is the only other person to receive a heavenly pronouncement of finding favor with God (Ex 33:17). Noah comes close to meeting this criterion as well. Though not directly stated by God or an angel, Noah finding favor with God is stated in the narrative of Genesis (Gn 6:8). See also Darrell Bock, who notes that in the Old Testament the expression often involves a request fulfilled on condition, but here in Luke 1:30 it is given without any request. Darrell Bock, *Luke 1:1–9:50* (Grand Rapids: Baker Academic, 1994), 111.

9. Gn 14:14–20, 22; Nm 24:16; Ps 7:17; 2 Sm 22:14. Darrell Bock, *Proclamation from Prophecy and Pattern: Lukan Old Testament Christology* (JSNTSup 12) (Sheffield: Sheffield Academic Press, 1987), 64.

10. Fitzmyer notes how Luke uses this title for God more than any other New Testament author: Luke 1:35, 76; 6:35; 8:28; Acts 7:48; 16:17. Fitzmyer, *Luke I–IX*, 348.

11. "According to the angel's words, Jesus will be 'Son of the Most High,' a designation synonymous with 'Son of God.' This will be made clearer in v. 35." Green, *The Gospel of Luke*, 89.

12. Cf. 2 Sm 7:14; 1 Chr 17:13; 22:10; 28:6; Ps 2:7; 89:26–27. In fact, Luke associates Jesus's kingship and sonship elsewhere (cf. Lk 4:41; 22:29, 67–70; Acts 9:20–22). "This was one form of the hope of Israel; cf. Ps. So. 17:23, 'Lord raise up for them their king, the Son of David'—which was based on the promise in 2 Sm 7:12–14 of a son of God from David's line on the throne of his kingdom. For literal fulfillment, Jesus as the Son of David (Lk 18:38; 20:41) must have David as well as God for *his father*." Christopher Evans, *Saint Luke* (London: SCM Press, 1990), 162.

13. See, for example: Edward Schillebeeckx, *Mary, Mother of the Redemption* (New York: Sheed and Ward, 1964), 9; Richard Nelson, "David: A Model for Mary in Luke?" *Biblical Theology Bulletin* 18 (Oct. 1988), 139; Alberto Valentini, "Editoriale: L'Annuncio a Maria," *Theotokos* 4 (1996), 286.

14. Brown, *Birth of the Messiah*, 310–1. Brown also shows how Gabriel quotes that promise from 2 Samuel 7 "in a slightly rephrased manner" (which he notes was customary at the time, as is seen in the Dead Sea Scrolls). Brown, "The Annunciation to Mary, the Visitation, and the Magnificat," *Worship* 62 (1988), 253.

15. Brown, *Birth of the Messiah*, 310.

16. McHugh, *The Mother of Jesus in the New Testament*, 54. Similarly, Strauss concludes: "The description of the birth in v. 31 is verbally similar to Gen. 16:11 and Isa. 7:14 (cf. Judg. 13.3, 5), and may be a conscious allusion to the latter with the name 'Immanuel' changed to Jesus." Strauss, *The Davidic Messiah in Luke-Acts*, 88.

17. Fitzmyer, *Luke I–IX*, 336. It is surprising that even with these many parallels, Fitzmyer and others do not think that Luke 1:31 is drawing specifically on Isaiah 7:14. It is argued that these phrases in Luke's Annunciation scene that correspond to Isaiah 7:10–17 also have connections with other Old Testament passages and fit into the typical annunciation scene pattern in the Old Testament. For example, Fitzmyer argues that the description of Mary as "a virgin betrothed to a man" in Luke 1:27 is much closer to Deuteronomy 22:23 than to Isaiah 7:14 (336, 343). Further, "the house of David"

is a stereotyped phrase from the wider Old Testament (e.g. 1 Kgs 12:19; 2 Chr 23:3), not just from Isaiah 7:14 (344). Also, "The Lord is with you" is found throughout the Old Testament, but was used specifically as a greeting in Ruth 2:4 and Judges 6:12. When considering Luke 1:31, Fitzmyer argues: "The message to Mary is couched in rather stereotyped OT phraseology for announcing the conception and birth of an extraordinary child" (346). Here, the language seems to echo not just Isaiah 7:14, but Genesis 16:11 as well: "Behold, you are with child, and shall bear a son; you shall call his name Ishmael" (cf. Jgs 13:3, 5). See also Brown, *Birth of the Messiah*, 300; Nolland, *Luke 1–9:20*, 51; Bock, *Luke 1:1–9:50*, 112. They conclude that we cannot know whether Luke was drawing either upon Isaiah 7:14 specifically or on those common themes found in other birth annunciation narratives of the Old Testament. Nevertheless, these possible allusions to a variety of passages and annunciation accounts in the Old Testament should not rule out the importance of Isaiah 7:14. After all, there is no single Old Testament passage that has more verbal similarities to Luke 1:31 *and* brings together the various Davidic themes which the Lukan Annunciation account emphasizes.

18. Green, *Luke*, 85, n. 15; See also Strauss, *The Davidic Messiah in Luke-Acts*, 88, n. 1.

19. Green, *Luke*, 85.

20. Strauss, *The Davidic Messiah in Luke-Acts*, 88, n. 1. Another link between the two texts is seen in the fact that both the woman of Isaiah 7:14 and Mary are singled out as the ones who are to name the royal child. The husbands are not mentioned in this regard. Valentini, "L'Annuncio a Maria," 285. Unlike Matthew's Gospel, in which Joseph is highlighted as the one giving the name to the child (Mt 1:21), Luke portrays Mary as the one who "shall call his name Jesus" (Lk 1:31). Valentini concludes: "Diversamente da Lc 1,13 (cf Mt 1,21), è lei che attribuisce il nome (come in Is 7,14 TM): l'averlo sottolineato è un discreto accenno alla maternità verginale." Similarly, Montague sees an allusion to Isaiah 7:14 in the words "and *you* shall call him" (Lk 1:31), thus establishing another link between the virgin

Mary in Luke and the young woman in Isaiah 7:14 who will bear the royal child and "*who shall call his name* Immanuel." Montague, *Our Father, Our Mother*, 95–96.

Chapter Five – The Mystery of Mary's Question

1. See Brown, *Birth of the Messiah*, 123–24, on betrothal in first-century Judea and Galilee.

2. David Landry, "Narrative Logic in the Annunciation to Mary (Luke 1:26–38)," *JBL* 114 (1995), 65. See also Tannehill, who notes the oddity of Mary's question: "Mary's response 'How can this be?' ignores the fact that she will soon be living with her husband. For some reason she assumes that this child will not be conceived in the normal way." Tannehill, *Luke*, 49. Similarly, Marshall, *The Gospel of Luke*, 69: "Mary's question is puzzling, since, if the promised child is to be a descendant of David, she is already betrothed to a member of the house of David and can expect to marry him in the near future and bear his child."

3. For example, Brown, *Birth of the Messiah*, 307–8; Fitzmyer, *Luke I–IX*, 348–51; Brown, *Mary in the New Testament*, 111–5.

4. Landry, "Narrative Logic in the Annunciation to Mary (Luke 1:26–38)"; Leon Morris, *The Gospel According to Luke* (Grand Rapids: Eerdmans, 1975), 73. See also Bock, *Luke 1:1–9:50*, 119–120. When summarizing various interpretations of Luke 1:34, Bock seems most open to this immediate pregnancy view.

5. Brown, *Birth of the Messiah*, 307.

6. Ibid.

7. Fitzmyer, *Luke I–IX*, 350.

8. Brown, *Birth of the Messiah*, 308.

9. Brown outlines five steps: (1) the appearance of an angel or the Lord; (2) the visionary responding in fear; (3) the divine message;

(4) an objection by the visionary; and (5) the giving of a sign to help assure the visionary. The annunciations are about the births of Ishmael (Gn 16:7–13), Isaac (Gn 17:1–19; 18:1–15), Samson (Jgs 13:3–23), John the Baptist (Lk 1:11–20), and Jesus (Lk 1:26–47; Mt 1:20–21). See Brown, *Birth of the Messiah*, 156. See also my Appendix for more on this.

10. Fitzmyer, *Luke I–IX*, 350; Brown, *Birth of the Messiah*, 307–8.

11. "The problem of why Mary would mention her virginity as an obstacle to conception (since she could have had sexual relations with Joseph to beget a child after the Annunciation) disappears once we shift away from the psychological quest—Luke phrases Mary's objection the way he does because he has the tradition that the divine plan excluded a human begetting of the child." Brown, *Birth of the Messiah*, 308.

12. Schaberg attempts to explain Mary's question not as being about the physical impossibility of conceiving a child as a virgin. Rather, she argues that Mary's question is about how the Messiah can be born illegitimately to a humiliated woman who had sexual relations with a man who was not her husband. Schaberg begins by asking what many commentators have pondered throughout the centuries: Why would a betrothed woman object to an announcement that she will conceive a child? She proposes that Mary was raped or seduced by a man other than Joseph. She finds initial support for this in Mary's question itself. Schaberg translates *andra* (man) as referring specifically to Joseph: "How will this be since I do not have sexual relations with my *husband*?" Second, she argues that the language describing Mary going to visit Elizabeth "with haste" (1:39) sometimes has a tone of terror or flight, which could indicate a crisis situation in regards to Mary's pregnancy. Jane Schaberg, *The Illegitimacy of Jesus* (San Francisco: Harper & Row, 1987), 90. Schaberg rests more of her argument on Mary's self-description in 1:48, where the word *tapeinosis* is used. Schaberg argues that this word normally means "humiliation" (97) and points to Mary having been humiliated by having been raped or seduced by a man

who was not her husband. In the Magnificat, Mary praises God for having overcome her humiliation by making her the mother of the Messiah (102–3).

Landry critiques Schaberg's view that 1:34 has nothing to do with the physical impossibility of Mary conceiving a child as a virgin. First, when 1:34 is read in the context of this scene, the reader is likely to recall how Mary was introduced as a virgin twice in 1:27. Thus, the reader is prepared to see Mary's question as having something to do with her virginity. Second, Luke's narrative seems to draw attention to the physical impossibility of Mary becoming pregnant as a virgin. The angel two verses later compares Mary's situation with Elizabeth, who "in her old age" is already in her sixth month of pregnancy, and then concludes his message by saying, "With God nothing is impossible." Just as Elizabeth's physical situation of old age was not too big of an obstacle to be overcome by God, so Mary's virginal status can be overcome by God, who desires to make her the mother of this child. Moreover, the angel's words underscore the magnitude of the miracle of Mary conceiving this child. There is nothing impossible about a woman becoming pregnant when she is raped or seduced. Landry thus concludes that some physical miracle is expected to take place. Landry, "Narrative Logic," 72–73. Brown also critiques Schaberg's interpretation, arguing that "it is very weak exegetically to contend that an author expressed his central concern so incompetently that his contemporary audience would miss it." It is also very unlikely that Luke as an author was "so incompetent that it took nineteen hundred years for someone to recognize the central meaning he intended in a major passage—a meaning that even after its discovery most others still cannot recognize." Brown, *Birth of the Messiah* (1993 edition), 637.

13. Jane Schaberg, *The Illegitimacy of Jesus*, 87.

14. "The question is an essential part of the form *and* of the story line." Schaberg, *The Illegitimacy of Jesus*, 87.

15. Landry, "Narrative Logic," 70.

16. Ibid, 75. Landry argues that his position is confirmed in the

Nativity scene where Luke describes Mary as still being "betrothed" (Lk 2:5). However, Luke likely calls Mary "betrothed" in 2:5 to emphasize that her marriage was not consummated yet. This in itself helps underscore that Mary was not pregnant by natural means. See Green, *Luke*, 128.

17. John Collins, "Our Lady's Vow of Virginity," *CBQ* 5 (1943), 373.

18. See Nolland, *Luke 1–9:51*, 53.

19. Furthermore, we do not yet know how far along into betrothal Mary and Joseph are.

20. Landry, "Narrative Logic," 76, n. 38.

21. Ibid.

22. As will be discussed further in chapter 23, this prophecy is ultimately fulfilled in the birth of Jesus (cf. Mt 1:23).

23. Denis Farkasfalvy, *The Marian Mystery* (New York: St. Paul's, 2014), 29.

24. St. Gregory of Nyssa, *On the Holy Generation of Christ*, PG 46, 1140 C–1141 A. As translated in Luigi Gambero, *Mary and the Fathers of the Church* (San Francisco: Ignatius Press, 1999), 157.

25. John Paul II, General Audience (August 7, 1996). As translated in John Paul II, *Theotokos* (Boston: Pauline Books and Media, 2000), 124.

26. McHugh, *The Mother of Jesus in the New Testament*, 194–96.

27. Josephus, *War of the Jews*, 2.160–61.

28. Philo, *On the Contemplative Life*, 68.

29. *Targum Pseudo-Jonathan* on Leviticus 16:29; Mishnah, *Yoma* 8:1. Pitre also refers to Jacob Milgrom's comment on Numbers 30:13: "[L]iterally, 'you shall afflict yourselves', chiefly by fasting, as testified by Isaiah 58:3, 5, 10. But other acts of self-denial are also implied

and are understood by the rabbis as follows: 'Afflict yourselves from food and drink, bathing, anointing, putting on sandals, and sexual intercourse' (Targ. Jon. Mishnah, *Yoma* 8:1). Indeed that the psalmist must specify . . . 'I afflicted myself with a fast' (Ps. 35:13) means that there are other forms of self affliction." Jacob Milgrom, *The JPS Torah Commentary: Numbers* (Philadelphia: Jewish Publication Society, 1990), 246. In Brant Pitre, *Jesus and the Jewish Roots of Mary* (New York: Image, forthcoming 2018), 116.

30. Pitre, *Jesus and the Jewish Roots of Mary*, 117.

31. Ibid, 117–18. "Although it's possible that ancient Israelite husbands everywhere were so fed up with their wives' constant fasting that a law had to be created to deal with it . . . it is much more likely that women's vows of sexual abstinence were a cause for conflict. Indeed, it is very easy to imagine a situation in which the husband might later change his mind and decide to make his wife's vow 'null and void' (Nm 30:15)."

32. Ibid, 119.

33. John Paul II, General Audience (August 21, 1996). As translated in John Paul II, *Theotokos*, 127–8.

Chapter Six – Mary's *Fiat*

1. See chapter 4.

2. Strauss, *The Davidic Messiah in Luke-Acts*, 90–91.

3. Brown, *Birth of the Messiah*, 314.

4. Nolland, *Luke 1–9:20*, 54. See also Fitzmyer, *Luke I–IX*, 351, who notes that the verb *eperchesthai* is linked with *pneuma* in other Septuagintal passages, but the sense of the word *pneuma* is different. Numbers 5:14 and 30 describe a spirit of jealousy coming upon a man. Job 4:15 depicts a tempting spirit discouraging Job.

5. The Holy Spirit *coming upon* (*epeleusethai epi*) Mary and the Spirit's association with the "*power*" (*dynamis*) of God in Gabriel's Annunciation to Mary (Luke 1:35) anticipates the "power" (*dynamin*) of the Holy Spirit that Jesus in the Ascension says will "come upon" (*epelthontos*) the disciples in Acts 1:8. Green, *Luke*, 90.

6. Bock, *Proclamation from Type and Pattern*, 63.

7. The same can be seen in the rest of the New Testament. Apart from Acts 5:15, *episkiazein* is used only in accounts of the Transfiguration (Lk 9:34; Mk 9:7; Mt 17:5) with reference to the divine glory being physically present in the cloud.

8. Nolland, *Luke 1–9:20*, 54.

9. Strauss, *The Davidic Messiah in Luke-Acts*, 94.

10. Ibid, 93.

11. "The 'holy Spirit' coming upon her and the 'power of the Most High' overshadowing her are parallel expressions for God's intervention. The result of it will be that the child will not be merely the Davidic Messiah, but God's own Son." Fitzmyer, *Luke I–IX*, 339–40.

12. Nolland comments that the purpose of the angel telling Mary that "nothing is impossible with God" is to call Mary to an amazingly high level of faith, trusting that God could do for her what had never been done before and what seems to be impossible. Nolland, *Luke 1–9:20*, 57, 59.

13. "[T]he final word is always given to the supernatural voice." Nolland, *Luke 1–9:20*, 57. See also table in Brown, *Birth of the Messiah*, 156.

14. Paredes, *Mary and the Kingdom of God*, 75–6.

15. De la Potterie, *Mary in the Mystery of the Covenant*, 35.

Chapter Seven – The Visitation—Why the Haste?

1. John Paul II, General Audience (October 2, 1996). As translated in John Paul II, *Theotokos*, 139.

2. "The entire Nativity section in Luke is marked by the motifs of 'journeying' and 'sojourning.'" Octavian Baban, *On the Road Encounters in Luke-Acts* (Milton Keynes, UK: Paternoster, 2006), 174. David Moessner, *Lord of the Banquet* (Minneapolis: Fortress, 1989), 294.

3. Moessner, *Lord of the Banquet*, 294.

4. Bovon, *A Commentary on the Gospel of Luke 1:1–9:50* (Minneapolis: Fortress Press, 2002), 58; Fitzmyer, *Luke I–IX*, 362, 359; Arthur Just, *Luke 1:1–9:50*, 72; Calogero Milazzo, *Israele, Maria, la Chiesa*, Commento a Luca 1–2 (Rome: Città Nuova, 2010), 29–30.

5. Bovon, *A Commentary on the Gospel of Luke 1:1–9:50*, 58. Joel Green argues that Luke's use of the term here might indicate that Luke is narrating Mary's travel as having an important role in salvation history, "relating her journey to her primary identification as servant of the Lord (1:38) and to the narrative need to identify Gabriel's 'sign.'" Green, *Luke*, 95.

6. Nolland, *Luke 1–9:20*, 65.

7. Bovon, *A Commentary on the Gospel of Luke 1:1–9:50*, 58.

8. Bock, *Luke 1:1–9:50*, 134.

9. Ibid; Brown, *Birth of the Messiah*, 331.

10. Bock, 134.

11. See Fitzmyer, *Luke I–IX*, 362; Nolland, *Luke 1:1–9:20*, 65–66.

12. Culpepper, *Luke*, 54; Nolland, *Luke 1:1–9:20*, 65–66.

13. Bruno Maggioni, "La Madre del mio Signore: Esegesi di Lc 1, 39–45," *Theotokos* 5 (1997), 15.

14. Milazzo notes how Zechariah, Mary, and the shepherds receive a sign, but only Mary and the shepherds respond positively and only they are described as going in haste. Zechariah, who responds negatively, is described as simply returning to his home. Milazzo, *Israele, Maria, la Chiesa*, 30.

15. Culpepper, *Luke*, 54.

16. Nolland, *Luke 1–9:20*, 66.

Chapter Eight – The Queen Mother

1. "When Elizabeth addresses Mary as 'the mother of my Lord,' she switches from second to third person; moreover 'the mother of my Lord' resembles the expression 'my Lord, the king,' the latter being used in a consistent and highly stylized manner in 1 S 22–24 and 2 S 3–24 more than thirty times." Farkasfalvy, *The Marian Mystery*, 33, n. 37.

2. For a more extensive treatment on this topic, see my *Queen Mother: A Biblical Theology of Mary's Queenship*, 45–53. See also: Niels-Erik Andreasen, "The Role of the Queen Mother in Israelite Society," *CBQ* 45 (1983), 179–94; Scott Hahn, *Hail Holy Queen* (New York: Doubleday, 2001), 69–86; L. Schearing, "Queen" in D. Freedman, ed., *The Anchor Bible Dictionary*, vol. 5 (New York: Doubleday, 1992), 583–88; Roland De Vaux, *Ancient Israel* (New York: McGraw-Hill, 1961), 115–19; George Kirwin, *The Nature of the Queenship of Mary* (Ann Arbor, Michigan: UMI Dissertation Services, 1973), 297–312.

3. Montague, *Our Father, Our Mother*, 92.

4. Manuel Miguens, *Mary: "The Servant of the Lord"* (Boston: St. Paul Editions, 1978), 65.

5. Timothy Gray, "God's Word and Mary's Royal Office," *Miles Immaculatae* 13 (1995), 377.

6. P. De Boer, "The Counselor," *VTSup* 3 (Leiden: Brill, 1955), 54; Andreasen, "The Role of the Queen Mother in Israelite Society," 190–91.

7. De Boer, "The Counselor," 60–61; Andreasen, "The Role of the Queen Mother in Israelite Society," 194.

8. Emphasis added.

9. See François Rossier, *L'intercession Entre les Hommes dans la Bible Hébraique,* Orbis Biblicus et Orientalis 152 (Gottingen: Vandenhoeck & Ruprecht, 1996), 189. Also, see Gray's note on this passage: "The fact that Solomon denies the request in no way discredits the influence of the [g]ebirah. Adonijah wanted Abishag the Shunammite for the treacherous purpose of taking over the kingdom from Solomon." Gray, "God's Word and Mary's Royal Office," 381, n. 16. Taking the king's concubine was a sign of usurping the throne in the ancient Near East. For example, see how Absalom (Adonijah's older brother), in his attempt to take the throne from David, took his concubines (2 Sm 16:20–23). Gray continues, "Thus *the wickedness of Adonijah's intention is the reason for denial, which in no way reflects negatively upon the [g]ebirah's power to intercede. The narrative bears out the fact that the king normally accepted the [g]ebirah's request,* thus Solomon says, 'Ask, I will not refuse you.' To say then that this illustrates the weakness of the [g]ebirah's ability to intercede would be to miss the whole point of the narrative, which tells how Adonijah uses the queen mother's position in an attempt to become king." Gray, "God's Word and Mary's Royal Office," 381, n. 16, emphasis added. For more on the political symbolism of usurping a member of a king's harem, see de Vaux, *Ancient Israel,* 116.

10. Bock, *Proclamation from Prophecy and Pattern,* 69–70.

11. Bock continues: "But in view of Luke's later development of this term, clearly something more is in mind here, though this deeper intention is *not clear by this text alone.* It only emerges from later Lucan usage." Bock, *Proclamation from Prophecy and Pattern,* 70.

12. Brown, *Birth of the Messiah*, 344.

13. Miguens, *Mary: Servant of the Lord*, 61.

14. Barnabas Ahern, "The Mother of the Messiah" *Marian Studies* 12 (1961), 28; George Kirwin, *The Nature of the Queenship of Mary*, 29, n. 72; G. Del Moral, "La Realeza de María segun la Sagrada Escritura," 176; Miguens, *Mary: Servant of the Lord*, 60–62.

15. See Origen *Fragmenta Origenis, Ex Maccarii Chrysocephali Orationibus in Lucam*, PG 13, 1902; Ephrem, *Ed. Assemani*, III, 524; Jerome, *Homilia in die Dom. Paschae*, ed. D. Morin, *Anecdota Maredsolan*, t. III, pars. II, 414; Augustine, *In Joannis Evangelium VIII*, PL 35, 1456.

Chapter Nine – Ark of the Covenant

1. For a helpful introduction to this theme in the New Testament, see Scott Hahn, *Hail Holy Queen*, 49–67. For his treatment of this topic specifically in Luke's Visitation scene, see 63–64.

2. According to the first-century Jewish historian Josephus, "The inmost part of the temple ... was also separated from the outer part by a veil. *In this there was nothing at all.* It was inaccessible and inviolable, and not to be seen by any; and was called the Holy of Holies." Josephus, *War* 5.219. As translated in *The Works of Josephus*, William Whiston (Peabody, MA: Hendrickson, 1987), 707. Similarly, according to Tacitus, the Roman general Pompey who conquered Jerusalem actually entered the Temple and found "the place stood empty with no similitude of gods within, and that the shrine had nothing to reveal." Tacitus, *Histories* 5.9. As translated in *The Complete Works of Tacitus*, ed. Alfred John Church, William Jackson Brodribb, Sara Bryant. Edited for Perseus. (New York: Random House, 1942), www.perseus.tufts.edu.

3. Brant Pitre, *Jesus and the Jewish Roots of Mary*, 55–58.

4. For further discussion of some of these parallels, see Nolland, *Luke 1–9:20*, 74–76.

5. 1 Chr 15:28; 16:4, 42; 2 Chr 5:13.

Chapter Ten – Magnificat

1. Green, *Luke*, 98.

2. Nolland, *Luke 1–9:20*, 75.

3. Green, *Luke*, 98.

4. See Joel Green, *New Testament Theology: The Theology of Luke* (Cambridge: Cambridge University Press, 1995), 79–84.

Chapter Eleven – Mary at the Nativity: Keep and Ponder

1. Tacitus, *Histories* 4.74. As translated in *The Complete Works of Tacitus*, ed. Alfred John Church, William Jackson Brodribb, Sara Bryant. Edited for Perseus. (New York: Random House, 1942), www.perseus.tufts.edu.

2. It may also subtly point to Mary having remained a virgin even after she lived under the same roof as Joseph.

3. One difficulty with this view is that when Luke wishes to speak of an actual inn, as he does in the parable of the Good Samaritan (Lk 10:34), he does not use the word *katalyma*. Furthermore, when Luke does use the word *katalyma*, it refers to the guest room where Jesus celebrates the Last Supper, not a commercial inn where travelers would sleep with the livestock (22:11).

4. Justin Martyr (AD 165), *Dialogue 78*; Origen (AD 254), *Against Celsus* I 51. See also Brown, *The Birth of the Messiah*, 401.

5. St. Jerome, *Epistle* 58, to Paulinus, iii 5; CSEL 54:531–32.

6. Ratzinger, *Jesus of Nazareth: The Infancy Narratives*, 67.

7. Ben Witherington, "The Birth of Jesus" in *Dictionary of Jesus and the Gospels*, ed. J. Green, et. al. (Downers Grove, Illinois: InterVarsity Press, 1992), 70.

8. John Paul II, General Audience (November 20, 1996). As translated in John Paul II, *Theotokos*, 147.

9. Green, *Luke*, 124. Iconographic depictions of this scene have theologically interpreted the details of the child being wrapped in swaddling clothes and laid in a manger in ways that point to Christ's sacrifice on the Cross. See also Ratzinger, *Jesus of Nazareth: The Infancy Narratives*, 68. "The child stiffly wrapped in bandages is seen as prefiguring the hour of his death: from the outset, he is the sacrificial victim, as we shall see more closely when we examine the reference to the first-born. The manger, then, was seen as a kind of altar."

10. Gaventa, *Mary*, 59–60.

11. John Paul II, General Audience (November 20, 1996). As translated in John Paul II, *Theotokos*, 146.

12. Francis Moloney, *Mary: Woman and Mother* (Eugene, Oregon: Wipf & Stock, 1988), 24.

Chapter Twelve – Mary at the Presentation

1. Here's an example to illustrate the point: It would be one thing if I told you that Tom drove to work today. It would be another thing if I said, "When Tom drove to work today, he made a complete stop at all red lights, according to the State of Colorado Traffic Code, Section 604 (1)(c): 'Vehicular traffic facing a steady circular red signal alone shall stop at a clearly marked stop line.' Tom also gave the right of way to other drivers whenever he was turning left, according to section 702: 'The driver of a vehicle intending to turn to the left within an intersection . . . shall yield the right-of-way to any vehicle approaching from the opposite direction.'" In this approach, I would clearly be emphasizing Tom's obedience to the details of the law.

2. John Paul II, General Audience (December 11, 1996). As translated in John Paul II, *Theotokos*, 155.

3. Cf. Brown, *Birth of the Messiah*, 447.

4. Fitzmyer, *Luke I–IX*, 423.

5. Andre Feuillet notes how "[t]he presentation of Jesus in the Temple thus appears as a prelude to the sacrificial offering of the Passion of which the Fourth Gospel speaks." Andre Feuillet, *Jesus and His Mother* (Still River, Massachusetts: St. Bede's Publications, 1974), 46.

6. Ratzinger, *Jesus of Nazareth: The Infancy Narratives*, 82–3.

Chapter Thirteen – Mary and the Return of Glory

1. In fact, in the time of Jesus, one of the major Jewish feasts, the Feast of Tabernacles, involved lighting four candelabras in the Temple at night for seven days. According to some interpreters, this ritual, which illuminated the entire outer court of the Temple, recalled how God's glory used to shine in the sanctuary (Ez 10:4). At the same time, it looked to the future, expressing the hope that the glory of the Lord would soon return to Israel. See Alfred Edersheim, *The Temple: Its Ministry and Services* (Peabody, MA: Hendrickson, 1994), 226. On the Israelite hope for God's glory-presence to return to the Temple in general, see N.T. Wright, *The New Testament and the People of God* (Minneapolis: Fortress, 1992), 269.

2. Brown, *Birth of the Messiah*, 453.

3. René Laurentin, *Structure et Théologie de Luc 1–2*, 123–4. As translated in André Feuillet, *Jesus and His Mother*, 46.

4. See Brown, *Birth of the Messiah*, 270–1; Nolland, *Luke 1–9:20*, 35; McHugh, *The Mother of Jesus in the New Testament*, 25–27.

5. See, for example, Eric Burrows, *The Gospel of the Infancy and Other Biblical Essays* (London: Burns Oates & Washbourne, 1940),

41–42: "The chronological scheme from the beginning to the Presentation in the Temple ... is 6 months + 9 months + 40 days. If the conventional value of 30 days be given to the month (as in the chronological scheme of Gen. 7, 11.24; 8,4) we have $30 \times (6 + 9) + 40$ days = seventy weeks! Possibly L saw in this surprising coincidence with the number of Dan. 9, 24 a sort of secondary fulfillment in miniature of that verse, taken in the abstraction: seventy weeks from the return of Gabriel at the time of oblation (perhaps the evening oblation) to the sacring and offering of Christ in the Holy City." See also: Nolland, *Luke 1–9:20*, 35; McHugh, *The Mother of Jesus in the New Testament*, 25–27.

Chapter Fourteen – Pierced by a Sword

1. Ratzinger, *Jesus of Nazareth: The Infancy Narratives*, 85.

2. The image of many falling probably evokes the stone metaphor used in the Old Testament, where the Lord is depicted in Isaiah 8:14–15 as a sanctuary and stone causing the fall of many in Israel who refuse to acknowledge the Lord of Hosts. "And he will become a sanctuary, and a stone of offense, and a rock of stumbling to both houses of Israel. . . . And many shall stumble thereon; they shall fall and be broken."

3. Scott Cunningham, *Theology of Persecution in the Gospel of Luke-Acts*. JSNTSup. 142 (Sheffield: Sheffield Academic Press, 1997), 47.

4. Since this saying of Jesus in Luke 12:2 comes in the context of him critiquing the Pharisees specifically (see 12:1), the *dialogismoi* Simeon says will be revealed by Jesus may point more specifically to the hostile opposition of the Pharisees in 5:22; 6:8; and 20:14. Simeon's words also may recall the proud mentioned by Mary in the Magnificat: "He has scattered the proud *in the imagination of their hearts*" (1:51), which described a deep-seated pride rooted in the inmost hearts. The proud will have their thoughts revealed.

5. Ratzinger, *Jesus of Nazareth: The Infancy Narratives*, 86.

6. Fitzmyer, *Luke I–IX*, 429.

7. The sentence begins with the emphatic adverb *kai*, which is followed by the genitive singular of the personal pronoun *sou*, which itself is followed by another intensifier (*de*), and the pronoun *autes*. See Fitzmyer, *Luke I–IX*, 429: "Stress is thus put on Mary's individual lot."

8. See Nolland, *Luke 1–9:20*, 121.

9. Evans, *Luke*, 219. He translates this sentence literally: "And more-over (or 'but') of thee further thyself the soul…"

10. Nolland, *Luke 1–9:20*, 121; Fitzmyer, *Luke I–IX*, 429.

11. Nolland, *Luke 1–9:20*, 121.

12. Nolland, *Luke 1–9:20*, 121–2. Other Protestant scholars also see this verse as pointing to Mary sharing in the sufferings of her Son. See, for example, Morris, *The Gospel According to Luke*, 89; Marshall, *The Gospel of Luke*, 123; C. Marvin Pate, *Moody Gospel Commentary: Luke* (Chicago: Moody Press, 1995), 88; Tannehill, *Luke*, 73.

13. Michael Goulder, *Luke: A New Paradigm*. JSNTSup, 20 (Sheffield: Sheffield Academic Press, 1989), 259. Also: Nolland, *Luke 1–9:20*, 122.

14. Brown, Fitzmyer, and others interpret the sword in 2:35 as referring to the sword of destruction passing through Israel in Ezekiel 14:17. Brown, *Birth of the Messiah*, 463–66; Fitzmyer, *Luke I–IX*, 429–30; Brown, *Mary in the New Testament*, 154–7. In their view, the sword is an instrument of discrimination, singling out "some for destruction and others for mercy." Fitzmyer, *Luke I–IX*, 430. But the sword in Ezekiel 14 is not a discriminating sword. It's an act of judgment which brings utter destruction in the land, not mercy. Ezekiel 14:21 in fact lists the sword as one of God's "four sore acts of judgment" alongside famine, evil beasts, and

pestilence afflicting the land of Israel. Though there are two verbal links between Luke 2:35 and Ezekiel 14:17 LXX (*romphaiai* = sword and *dierchesthai* = go through) just as there are two verbal links between Luke 2:35 and Psalm 22:21, LXX), the thematic correspondence is stronger between Simeon's prophecy and Psalm 22. We have already seen that the sword passing through Mary in Luke 2:35 is linked with the rejection of the child who is set for the fall and rise of many in Israel and will be a sign that is opposed. The righteous man in Psalm 22 who suffers at the hands of his enemies and who cries out for God to save his *soul* from the *sword*, therefore, easily relates to Jesus as the rejected sign in Simeon's oracle—the one who will be opposed and cause many to fall. The sword of Ezekiel 14 may be in the background of Simeon's oracle not as a sword of discernment but as an allusion to how Jesus is taking on himself the curses of Israel. The sword of judgment in Ezekiel 14 draws from the imagery of the curses in Leviticus 26, where the same four acts of judgment—the sword, pestilence, wild beasts, and the land not bearing fruit (famine)—are listed as chastisements for God's people if they persist in their infidelity and remain unrepentant (Lv 26:20–25). Again, it's clear that this is not a sword discriminating the faithful from the unfaithful but a sword of judgment on the unrepentant people. To the extent Ezekiel 14 is in the background, we can see Simeon foreshadowing how Jesus enters into the punishment and takes on this sword.

15. Goulder, *Luke: A New Paradigm*, 260.

16. Ibid, 259.

17. John Paul II, *Redemptoris Mater* (Boston: Pauline Books and Media, 1987), 16.

18. In the other cases when Luke uses the word "soul" (*psyche*), it doesn't refer to a particular person but describes saving life (6:9; 9:24; 17:33; 21:19), loving God with all your soul (10:27), or hating one's life in the sense of making discipleship a priority over all other relationships (14:26).

Chapter Fifteen – Finding Her Son in the Temple

1. Bock, *Luke 1–9:50*, 264.

2. Fitzmyer, *Luke I–IX*, 441.

3. "The joy of finding him is overcome by the realization that he would have done something so agonizing to his parents." Fitzmyer, *Luke I–IX*, 442.

4. See Gaventa, *Mary*, 68.

5. Fitzmyer, *Luke I–IX*, 443.

6. Ratzinger, *Jesus of Nazareth: The Infancy Narratives*, 124.

7. Cf. Green, *Luke*, 157.

8. Ratzinger, *Jesus of Nazareth: The Infancy Narratives*, 125.

9. Ibid, 125.

10. John Paul II, General Audience (January 15, 1997). As translated in John Paul II, *Theotokos*, 167.

11. Ratzinger, *Jesus of Nazareth: The Infancy Narratives*, 124.

12. Ibid, 123.

Chapter Sixteen – Mary at Cana

1. She's always referred to as "the mother of Jesus" (Jn 2:3) or "his mother" (Jn 2:12; 19:25), or addressed by her son as "woman" (Jn 2:4; 19:26).

2. Francis Moloney, *The Gospel of John* (Collegeville, MN: Liturgical Press, 1998), 71.

3. Ibid, 67.

4. Vatican II, *Dogmatic Constitution on the Church*, 58.

5. John Paul II, General Audience (March 5, 1997). As translated in John Paul II, *Theotokos*, 177.

6. John Paul II, *Redemptoris Mater*, 21 (emphasis added).

7. De la Potterie, *Mary in the Mystery of the Covenant*, 183.

8. Similarly, John the Baptist publicly proclaimed that he saw the Spirit descend as a dove from Heaven on Jesus. If many people heard of this extraordinary sign through John the Baptist's testimony, Mary might have come in contact with this as well.

9. Brown, *Mary in the New Testament*, 188.

10. Leon Morris, *The Gospel According to John* (Grand Rapids: Eerdmans, 1995), 158.

11. Brown, *Mary in the New Testament*, 188.

12. Jean Galot, *Mary in the Gospel* (Westminster, Maryland: Newman Press, 1965), 108.

13. Feuillet, *Jesus and His Mother*, 121.

14. Galot, *Mary in the Gospel*, 116.

15. John Paul II, General Audience (February 26, 1997). As translated in John Paul II, *Theotokos*, 174.

Chapter Seventeen – The Woman, the Hour, and the Wine

1. De la Potterie argues instead that the Old Testament prophetic image of Daughter Zion is the key background to Mary being called "woman" at Cana: "[T]his symbolic figure, described by the prophets, is concretized at once in a daughter of Israel, Mary, who thus becomes the personification of the messianic people in eschatological times." While it may be true that Mary is the personification of Daughter Zion (see Vatican II, *Dogmatic*

Constitution on the Church, 55) and other New Testament passages would support this (see my comments on Luke 1:28; John 19:25–29; and Revelation 12:1–6 in chapters 2, 20, and 21), de la Potterie does not demonstrate how John is depicting Mary as Daughter of Zion in this scene at Cana with the title "woman." It's not clear that the passage is primarily alluding to the Daughter Zion passages. Moreover, Daughter Zion is never called "woman" in the Old Testament, though Eve is. As we will see below, the New Eve interpretation has a much stronger basis at least in the Wedding at Cana narrative than does de la Potterie's Daughter Zion proposal. De la Potterie, *Mary in the Mystery of the Covenant*, 203.

2. Gaventa, *Mary*, 86.

3. "There are . . . *no known examples* of a son's using such a term to address his mother, and so this vocative must have more significance than it would when, for instance, Jesus used it to address Mary Magdalene." Ben Witherington, *John's Wisdom* (Louisville: Westminster John Knox Press, 1995), 79. Emphasis in original. Cf. Raymond Brown, *The Gospel of John* (New York: Doubleday, 1966), 99.

4. See Scott Hahn, *Hail Holy Queen*, 34–35.

5. De la Potterie, *Mary in the Mystery of the Covenant*, 165.

6. Some interpret these words not as Jesus making a statement of fact but rather as him raising a rhetorical question, "Has not my hour come?"—a position that is at least philologically possible. De la Potterie, for example, argues that translating 2:4 as a statement ("My hour has not yet come") does not fit with the conclusion of the scene in which John says, "He manifested his glory." If the hour of Jesus's glory has not begun at Cana, how could his glory be manifested in this scene? "If on the other hand one reads the text as a question, then something of importance already had begun to be realized *here*. This is the 'beginning' of a prolonged event which must be developed further: that of the self-revelation of Jesus." De

la Potterie, *Mary in the Mystery of the Covenant*, 187. De la Potterie, however, does not address later statements of Jesus in the Fourth Gospel that make explicit that Jesus's hour has not yet begun. Over a year after the Wedding at Cana, John twice states, "His hour had not yet come" (7:30; 8:20). Perhaps a better approach is to see that *at this precise point* in John's narration of this scene, Jesus hasn't begun to reveal his glory. He has not yet performed a miracle. But with the unfolding of the story and Jesus's miraculous changing of water into wine, the movement toward Jesus's hour has been initiated and his glory *starts* to be revealed. This glory will continue to be revealed with each sign (miracle) Jesus performs, culminating with the full arrival of his hour in Jerusalem in his Death and Resurrection.

7. Philo, *De Benedictionibus* 121–123 (cf. *De Vita Mosis II*, 204); *De Somniis* II, 246-249; *Legum allegoriae* III, 82. Also *Targum Cantica* 7, 3. Aristide Serra, *Le Nozze di Cana* (Padua: Edizioni Messaggero, 2009), 257–58.

8. 2 Bar 29:5. As translated by A.F.J. Klijn in *The Old Testament Pseudepigrapha*, vol. 1, ed. James Charlesworth (New York: Doubleday, 1983).

9. See *Targum Cantica*, 8:1–2. As translated in de la Potterie, *Mary in the Mystery of the Covenant*, 194.

10. "[W]henever one approaches Jesus about material things, He invariably responds by working to bring His hearer to a higher plane." Feuillet, *Johannine Studies* (Staten Island, NY: Alba House, 1964), 30.

11. Serra, *Le Nozze di Cana*, 289–90 (emphasis in original).

12. De la Potterie, *Mary in the Mystery of the Covenant*, 185–86. Similarly, Feuillet: "Because Jesus, seeing everything from the point of view of the mission which His Father has entrusted to Him, interprets His mother's intervention as a request for the messianic wine, He could only consider it premature, 'You are asking for something which I do not yet intend to give; my Hour is not yet come.'" Feuillet, *Johannine Studies*, 31–32.

Chapter Eighteen – "Do Whatever He Tells You"

1. The fact that Mary says these words in a scene introduced as having taken place "on the third day" strengthens this connection to Sinai, for in the Jewish tradition the giving of the Law at Sinai was associated with "the third day" (Ex 19:16). Francis Moloney, *Belief in the Word: Reading John 1–4* (Eugene, Oregon: Wipf & Stock, 1993), 77.

2. Aristide Serra, *Maria a Cana e sotto la Croce* (Rome: Centro di Cultura Mariana "Madre della Chiesa," 1991), 36.

3. De la Potterie, for example, objects: "At first glance, this comparison seems justified, because the two expressions are materially almost identical. Nevertheless, we have to admit that such a comparison does not really mean that much: the scenes have nothing in common and they unfold in contexts which are totally different (Joseph with Pharaoh, and Mary at Cana in Galilee)." De la Potterie, *Mary in the Mystery of the Covenant*, 189.

4. As explained in chapter 17.

5. Moloney, *Belief in the Word*, 84. He further explains: "The woman, the mother of Jesus, is the *first* person, in the experience of the reader, to manifest trust in the word of Jesus. Her relationship with Jesus transcends the limitations displayed by the disciples, who attempted to understand him within their own categories in 1:35–51."

6. Margaret Beirne, *Women and Men in the Fourth Gospel*. JSNTSup 242 (2003), 59.

7. "Jesus commands: 'Fill the jars with water' (v. 7a), and these words are obeyed to the letter (v. 7b). The attendants do what the mother told them to do (v. 5). The narrator tells the reader that the jars were fulfilled 'to the brim.' ... Jesus instructs the attendants ... to draw the jars that had been filled, and to take it to the steward (v. 8b). Again, the narrator reports silent obedience to the word of Jesus: 'So they took it' (v. 8c). They continue to respond to the mother's imperative (v. 5)." Moloney, *Belief in the Word*, 85–86.

8. De la Potterie, *Mary in the Mystery of the Covenant*, 190.

9. "The next time the reader will encounter the word 'bridegroom' (*nymphios*) will be in 3:29. At this stage of the Gospel (2:9–10), the reader can only wonder at the sudden introduction of a new character. A bridegroom who does nothing but is only spoken to by the steward. A gap has been created for the reader. It will be filled in 3:29 where, in the reader's next (and only other) encounter with the word, it is explicitly applied to Jesus." Moloney, *Belief in the Word*, 87.

10. Adeline Fehribach, *The Women in the Life of the Bridegroom: A Feminist Historical-Literary Analysis of the Female Characters in the Fourth Gospel* (Collegeville, MN: The Liturgical Press, 1998), 30.

11. Brant Pitre, *Jesus the Bridegroom* (New York: Image, 2014), 44.

12. De la Potterie, *Mary in the Mystery of the Covenant*, 177.

13. Ibid.

14. Hos 2:16–25; Is 50:1; 54:4–8; 62:4–5; Jer 2:1–2; 3:1–13.

15. Aristide Serra, *Le Nozze di Cana*, 427.

16. "Though this episode takes place in a wedding context, the evangelist never mentions the bride. The mother of Jesus is presented as one of the main characters of the episode in the first verse. And Jesus is the central figure of the episode. We note that the spouses are not introduced in these first verses whereas Jesus and his mother are, and thus it is very clear that these two characters (Jesus and Mary) in the episode are to be symbolically taken as the spouses." Denis Kulandaisamy, "The First Sign of Jesus at the Wedding at Cana: An Exegetical Study on the Function and Meaning of John 2:1–12," *Marianum* (2006) vol. 169–170, 101.

17. Kulandaisamy, "The First Sign of Jesus at the Wedding at Cana," 101.

18. Ignace de la Potterie, "La Madre di Gesú e il misterio di Cana,"

Civiltà Cattolica 130 (1979), 436. As translated in Kulandaisamy, "The First Sign of Jesus at the Wedding at Cana," 101.

Chapter Nineteen – At the Foot of the Cross

1. J. Ramsey Michaels, *The Gospel of John* in *The New International Greek Testament Commentary* (Grand Rapids: Eerdmans, 2010), 958–59.

2. Brown, *The Gospel of John*, 910–11. See also Moloney, *Mary: Woman and Mother*, 41–45; Montague, *Our Father, Our Mother*, 114–15.

3. Brown, *The Gospel of John*, 923.

4. Craig Keener points out that from what we know of Jewish customs, such an act might be expected, even from a crucified man. Craig Keener, *The Gospel According to John* (Peabody, MA: Hendrickson, 2003), 1144–45.

5. Feuillet, *Johannine Studies*, 287.

6. Moloney, *The Gospel of John*, 504.

7. "You are my son; today I have begotten you" (Ps 2:7); "Today you will be my son-in-law" (1 Sm 18:29).

8. De la Potterie, *Mary in the Mystery of the Covenant*, 217–18; Moloney, *Mary: Woman and Mother*, 45–46; Serra, *Maria a Cana e presso la croce*, 89–91. Also: Michael de Goedt, "Un scheme de revelation dans le Quatrième Evangile," *New Testament Studies* 8 (1961–62), 142–50.

9. De la Potterie, *Mary in the Mystery of the Covenant*, 218.

Chapter Twenty – "Behold, Your Mother"

1. Craig Koester, *Symbolism in the Fourth Gospel: Meaning, Mystery, Community* (Minneapolis: Ausburg Fortress, 2003), 33–77.

2. Farkasfalvy, *The Marian Mystery*, 45–46.

3. John Paul II, General Audience (April 23, 1997). As translated in John Paul II, *Theotokos*, 190.

4. "An exegesis unfriendly or suspicious to symbolism would eagerly point out that Jesus calls 'woman' not only his mother, but also the Samaritan woman (Jn 4:21) and Mary Magdalene (Jn 20:13 and 15), and then, on that basis, question any symbolic meaning attached to the word. But the symbolism at hand is not merely philological. 'Woman' in John 2:4 and the same word in 16:21 are linked by a 'woman and her hour,' an hour of anguish at giving birth. Similarly, the word 'woman' under the Cross refers to an incipient filial relationship: a birth. This is why we can only approve and admire the early Church Fathers (starting with Justin Martyr), who expanded on this link by pointing out the connection between Mary and Eve." Farkasfalvy, *The Marian Mystery*, 46. See also Brown, *The Gospel of John*, 926.

5. The New Eve background to this scene can help address one significant question that the authors of *Mary in the New Testament* raise about the interpretation of this scene as pointing to Mary's role as the mother of all Christians: According to these authors, the spiritual maternity view "requires the mother of Jesus in 19:25–27 to be treated as an individual (Mary) while the beloved disciple is treated as a general symbol of every Christian. An ordinary symbolic pattern would treat both as individuals or both as general." Brown, *Mary in the New Testament*, 215–16. But such a strict approach to parallel symbolism does not seem to be what the Fourth Gospel is presenting in John 19:25–27. The author of Genesis, for example, is comfortable with Eve, the individual woman of Genesis, being presented as both the mother of an *individual* son, Cain (Gn 4:1), and *as mother of a collective group*, "the mother of all living" (Gn 3:20). Similarly, Jesus at the Cross associates Mary with the woman of Genesis, Eve. And, like Eve, Mary is brought into a maternal relationship with an individual— the individual Beloved Disciple (John)—and at the same time she is brought into a maternal relationship with a larger collective group— the group of faithful disciples whom the Beloved Disciple represents.

6. John Paul II, *Redemptoris Mater*, 24.

7. "The scene at the foot of the cross has these details in common with xvi 21: the use of the words 'woman' and 'hour'; the theme of maternity; and the theme of Jesus' death." Brown, *The Gospel According to John*, 925. "The various literary points of contact between these two passages allow us to suppose that the evangelist, in writing the text of Jn 16:21, had in mind the Hour of Jesus and the 'Woman' whom he gave as 'mother' to his disciple." De la Potterie, *Mary in the Mystery of the Covenant*, 222. See also: R. H. Lightfoot, *St. John's Gospel* (London: Oxford University Press, 1956), 317; Feuillet, *Jesus and His Mother*, 119; *idem.*, "The Messiah and His Mother," 287–8; Valentini "Il 'Grande Segno' di Apocalisse 12: Una Chiesa ad immagine della Madre di Gusu," Marianum 59 (1997), 58–59; Brown, *Mary in the New Testament*, 237.

8. The connection between these two passages can add further support to the New Eve interpretation of Mary at the Cross in John 19:25–27, for there are numerous parallels between the birth allegory in John 16:20–22 and the woman of Genesis, Eve. Both the mother in the birth allegory and Eve are called "woman" and both are mothers associated with the hour of messianic victory (Gn 3:15; Jn 16:22). But both will first experience the pains of birth (Gn 3:16; Jn 16:20). Two key words in the birth allegory also harken back to the woman of Genesis. Jesus says the woman in labor feels "pain" (*lypēn*), just as God said to Eve he would "greatly multiply [her] pain" (*lypas*) in childbirth (Gn 3:16). Similarly, Jesus says that the mother will rejoice that a *man* (*anthropos*) (not a child, *teknon*) is born into the world, just as Eve said "with the help of the Lord I have begotten *man* (*anthropos*)" (not a child, *teknon*). These parallels indicate that the woman in Jesus's birth allegory is meant to be understood in light of Eve, the woman of Genesis. If John's Gospel is connecting the woman of the birth allegory with the woman of Genesis, then the fact that John 19:25–27 portrays Mary as embodying the birth allegory gives the mother of Jesus a further association with the New Eve motif.

9. Sri, *Walking with Mary*, 140. See also Jean Galot, *Mary in the Gospel*, 202: "More than all the others, Mary verified this picture of the woman who is about to give birth, because more than all

the others she would be subject to grief at the time of the passion, and then filled with joy by the triumph of her son. . . . Mary fulfills in a unique way this figure which serves to describe the disciples' participation in the Passion."

10. Moloney, *The Gospel of John*, 503. He further explains: "The theological and dramatic significance of 'the hour of Jesus' can give the proposition *apo*, followed by the genitive case, a causative sense, meaning 'because of that hour.'"

11. De la Potterie, *Mary in the Mystery of the Covenant*, 225–28; Montague, *Our Father, Our Mother*, 128–29; Serra, *Maria a Cana e presso la croce*, 112–13.

12. De la Potterie, *Mary in the Mystery of the Covenant*, 227–28; Montague, *Our Father, Our Mother*, 128–29. See also Moloney, who argues that this passage represents the reversal of Christ's rejection in the Prologue, which describes Jesus coming into his own (*eis ta idia*) but not being received by his own: "The disciple leads the Mother *eis ta idia*. The situation described in the Prologue, when the Word came *eis ta idia* but was not received (1:11: *ou parelabon*) has been reversed. Because of the cross and from the moment of the cross a new family of Jesus has been created. The Mother of Jesus, a model of faith, and the disciple whom Jesus loved and held close to himself are one as the disciple accepts the Mother (19:27: *elaben . . . autēn*) in an unconditional acceptance of the word of Jesus" (Moloney, *The Gospel of John*, 503–4).

13. John Paul II, General Audience (May 7, 1997). As translated in John Paul II, *Theotokos*, 193.

14. John Paul II, General Audience (May 7, 1997). As translated in John Paul II, *Theotokos*, 193.

Chapter Twenty-One – Decoding the Woman of the Apocalypse

1. For a more in-depth treatment of this complex passage, see my *Queen Mother*, 88–103.

2. Rev 2:10; 3:11; 4:4, 10; 14:14.

3. In Isaiah 62, Zion is described as Yahweh's bride, as "a crown of beauty" and "a royal diadem" (Is 62:3–5, 11).

4. De la Potterie, *Mary in the Mystery of the Covenant*, 247–48.

5. We've seen how Song of Solomon 6:10 and Isaiah 60:1 mention the sun and moon. But these passages do not allude to the other details in the woman's depiction in Revelation 12: the stars, the number twelve, or a crown. Joseph's dream, however, touches on all these elements. See Brown, *Mary in the New Testament*, 230.

6. "Strictly speaking, Joseph is not explicitly identified as a star in Genesis 37, though Philo, *Dreams* 2.113 refers to Joseph as the twelfth star in that dream." G. K. Beale, *The Book of Revelation* (Grand Rapids: Eerdmans 1999), 625.

7. If such a depiction is related to Mary, it would not necessarily be opposed to the traditional Catholic view that Mary remained a virgin while giving birth to Jesus and thus did not experience birth pains. As we will see more below, the New Testament and John's Gospel in particular uses birth pain imagery metaphorically not to describe a physical birth, but Christ's Death and Resurrection (Jn 16:20–21). Similarly, the book of Revelation itself uses birth imagery to portray Christ's Resurrection (Rev 1:5). Thus, Revelation 12 is focusing not primarily on Jesus's birth in Bethlehem, but on the metaphorical birth of his Death and Resurrection.

8. "The imagery of the nation as a woman giving birth to the Messiah already appears in Isaiah 26:18 LXX and more strikingly in the Qumran *thanksgiving Hymn E*." Beasley-Murray, *The Book of Revelation* (Grand Rapids: Eerdmans, 1974), 198. Moreover, Fekkes notes: "If John has borrowed from Isaiah 26—and we must conclude that this is extremely likely—it provided him with the language and context to explain the condition of the woman (pregnant), the intensity of her labour (full of pain and anguish), and the nearness of the birth (imminent)." Jan Fekkes, *Isaiah and Prophetic Traditions in the Book of Revelation* (JSNTSup 93)

(Sheffield: Sheffield Academic Press, 1994), 182. "[W]hereas one or more of these expressions is found in a number of biblical passages, the particular combination of ideas chosen by John comes strikingly close to the birth metaphor related in Isa. 26.17" (181).

9. The image from the prophets of Zion giving birth to the messianic people with great pain—which, as we will see, is a key background to the woman of Revelation 12 (see below)—itself may draw from the birth pangs of Genesis 3:16. Beale, *The Book of Revelation*, 630–31. Also: W. Harrington, *Understanding the Apocalypse* (Washington: Corpus Books, 1969), 165. And the reference in Revelation 12:17 to the dragon attacking the woman's other offspring (*spermatos autēs*) may add further support for seeing Revelation 12 as alluding to the strife between the serpent's seed and the woman's seed (*spermatos autēs*) in Genesis 3:15 (LXX). G. B. Caird, *Commentary on the Revelation of St. John the Divine* (London: A & C Black, 1984), 160: "This is a conscious echo of the words of God to the serpent in Eden." A. Feuillet, *Jesus and His Mother*, 22: "We have here almost certainly a literary contact with the Greek translation of Gn. 3:15." Beale, *The Book of Revelation*, 679: "Rev. 12:17 is also a partial fulfillment of the promise in Gen. 3:15 where God prophesies that the individual (messianic) and corporate seed of the woman will bruise fatally the head of the serpent." Beale argues that Genesis 3:15–16 is explicitly alluded to in Revelation 12:17 (630). See also: J. Massyngberde Ford, *Revelation*. (Garden City, New York: Doubleday, 1975), 205.

10. "The figure of Eve in Gen iii 15 is the background for the description of the woman in Rev xii." Brown, *The Gospel According to John*, 107–8

11. Feuillet, *Jesus and His Mother*, 23.

12. Other examples: Adam represented all humanity in Romans 5:12–19; Jacob stood for all of Israel in Psalm 44:4.

13. Feuillet, *Jesus and His Mother*, 27. Also, the ecclesial interpretation *by itself*, however, does not make sense out of all

the data, for Revelation 12:1–5 portrays the woman as the mother of the Messiah. If the woman represents the Church, we must ask, how could the Church give birth to Christ? "The collective Woman of Apoc. 12:6, that is to say, the Christian Church which survives in the desert, cannot be exactly the same as the Woman who existed before the birth and the Passion of Christ, that is, the old people of God" (27). Rather, it should be the other way around. At the same time, seeing the woman *exclusively* as daughter Zion/ faithful Israel fails to explain Revelation 12:13–16, which portrays the woman fleeing into the desert, to be protected and nourished by God *after* the messianic child has been enthroned in Heaven. These verses clearly describe what God does for his people of the *new* covenant—after Christ's coming—not Israel of the old covenant era. As Beale concludes, "It is too limiting to view the woman as representing only a remnant of Israelites living in trial at the last stage of history, since the following verses show that the woman symbolizes a believing community extending from before the time of Christ's birth to at least the latter part of the first century A.D. [12:13–17]." Beale, *The Book of Revelation*, 631. Moreover, while the daughter Zion prophecies foretell the birth of a new messianic people (Is 66:7), they do not speak of a collective mother giving birth to the individual Messiah. Feuillet, *Jesus and His Mother*, 21.

14. Laurentin, *A Short Treatise on the Virgin Mary*, 44.

15. "The scene described in Revelation 12:4–5 can be read in light of John 16:21–3, where the passion and resurrection of Jesus are depicted in terms of the sorrow and joy of the birth process; and that same scene in Revelation can also be read in light of John 19:25–27, where the emphasis is on the extension of the community of faithful followers of Jesus. What John describes in a historico-interpretive fashion, Revelation describes in terms of a symbolic vision." Farkasfalvy, *The Marian Mystery*, 46–47. See also Ivone Gebara & Maria Clara Bingemer, *Mary: Mother of God, Mother of the Poor* (New York: Orbis Books, 1989), 85.

16. Feuillet, *Johannine Studies*, 262.

17. Feuillet identifies three particular characteristics that are common to the woman in John 19 and the woman of Revelation 12 but do not occur in the other Gospels: calling the mother of the Messiah "woman"; presenting her as having other children besides the Messiah; and her spiritual motherhood being linked to Christ's Death on the cross. He also adds the defeat of Satan as another common point between the two scenes and concludes, "It becomes indubitable that we have here also a basic Johannine tradition, common to both the fourth Gospel and the Apocalypse" Feuillet, *Johannine Studies*, 286.

18. An additional link between Revelation 12 and John 19 could be how Satan is conquered by the blood of the Lamb and the Word of testimony in Revelation 12:11, which parallels the climax of John's Crucifixion account. There, the author gives *testimony* ("his testimony is true"), which tells how the *blood* came out of Jesus, who is presented as the true Passover *Lamb* whose bones have not been broken (Jn 19:33–34). I am grateful to my colleague John Sehorn for this insight.

19. Indeed, the text begs to be read in light of John 19. It's clearly Johannine even if one does not hold Revelation is written by John.

Chapter Twenty-Two – Crowned in Glory

1. For a more extensive treatment of the Isaiah 7:14 background to Revelation 12, including verbal parallels between Isaiah 7:10, 14 and Revelation 12:1–2, see Beale, *The Book of Revelation*, 630–31: "The language of 12:1–2 may be patterned partly after the typological prophecy of the mother and child in Isa. 7:10, 14" (630).

2. Oscar Lukefahr, *Christ's Mother & Ours* (Liguori, Missouri: Liguori, 1998), 40–2; Henri Cazelles, "Note D'Exegese Sur Apocalypse 12," In *Mater Fidei et Fidelium* Marian Library Studies, vol. 17–23 (1985-91), 133; Pavol Farkas, *La Donna di Apocalisse 12:*

Storia, Bilancio, Nuove Prospettive. Tesi Gregoriana: Serie Teologia,
25. (Rome: Editrice Pontificia Università Gregoriana, 1997), 210–12;
Domenico Bertetto, *Maria La Serva del Signore* (Napels: Edizioni
Dehoniane, 1988), 440; Kirwin, *The Nature of the Queenship of
Mary*, 296–7; Gray, "God's Word and Mary's Royal Office," 386–87;
Kearney, "Gen. 3:15 and Johannine Theology," *Marian Studies* 25
(1974): 105.

3. "She is a queen without saying it," P. Farkas, *La Donna di
Apocalisse 12*, 211. See also Angel Luis, *La Realeza de Maria*, "La
Realeza de María en los Últimos Veinte Años." EstMar 11 (1951),
31: "In the Apocalypse she shines brilliantly with majesty and
greatness, crowned with a royal diadem, and as the Mother of 'a
royal son who has to rule all nations with an iron hand,' a son who
is 'caught up to God and to His throne.' Once more the Mother of
the King offers herself to our eyes showing forth the attributes of
her exalted queenship." Also: Adela Yarbro Collins, *The Combat
Myth in the Book of Revelation* (Missoula, Montana: Scholars Press,
1976), 71; *idem., The Apocalypse* (Wilmington, Delaware: Michael
Glazier, 1979), 85; Bernard Le Frois, "The Woman Clothed with the
Sun," AER 76 (1952), 167.

4. "Supponendo che l'autore si era ispirato all'immagine anticotesta-
mentaria della donna partoriente (il popolo), rimane sempre
la difficoltà: la donna di Ap 12 è descritta come una regina e l'immagine della regina partoriente il Messia totalmente manca nell'AT."
Farkas, *La Donna di Apocalisse 12*, 210.

5. Ibid, 211.

6. Kirwin, *The Nature of the Queenship of Mary*, 297.

7. John Paul II, General Audience (July 23, 1997). As translated in
John Paul II, *Theotokos*, 211–12.

8. Throughout the Bible, the word *topon* often describes the sacred
place where one encounters God, the Temple. It's used this way in
the Greek Old Testament, translating the Hebrew word *māqôm* forty

times describing the Temple (many times with the adjective "holy"or "holy place") and twenty other times in reference to the land in association with the Temple. Beale, *The Book of Revelation*, 649. The word *topos* is used similarly in the New Testament to describe the Temple in Matthew 24:15; Acts 6:13–14; 21:28; and John 4:20; 11:48. At the culmination of the book of Revelation, John sees that there is no Temple, for the Temple is the Lord God Almighty and the Lamb (Revelation 21:22). The heavenly Temple is nothing less than God himself, the communion between the Lord and the Lamb.

9. Deiss, *Mary: Daughter of Sion*, 158.

10. Beale, *The Book of Revelation*, 621; Feuillet, *Jesus and His Mother*, 29.

11. Feuillet, *Jesus and His Mother*, 29. See also Protestant New Testament scholar Craig Koester, who notes that the repeated word "appeared" (*ōpthē*) "links the manifestation of the ark" with the vision of the woman in 12:1. The woman "appears" in Heaven just like the Ark does. Koester, *Revelation and the End of All Things* (Grand Rapids: Eerdmans, 2001), 524.

12. For more on the Ark-Woman theme in Revelation 11–12, see Scott Hahn, *Hail, Holy Queen*, 49–55.

Chapter Twenty-Three – Mary in Other New Testament Passages

1. Matthew and Luke give a similar account: Matthew 12:46–50; Luke 8:19–21.

2. John Paul II, *Redemptoris Mater*, 20.

3. "However, if Matthew's main concern is to counter misunderstandings about Mary's pregnancy, one wonders why he would use Rahab and Tamar, two prostitutes, and Bathsheba, with whom

David committed adultery, as examples to defend Mary from the charge of sexual sin." Curtis Mitch and Edward Sri, *The Gospel of Matthew* (Grand Rapids: Baker Academic, 2010), 39.

4. Richard Menninger, *Israel and the Church in the Gospel of Matthew.* (New York: Peter Lang, 1994), 76. See also Susan Ackerman, "The Queen Mother and the Cult in the Ancient Near East" in K. King, ed., *Women and Goddess Traditions* (Minneapolis: Fortress, 1997), 197; Manelli, *All Generations Shall Call Me Blessed*, 144–45.

5. Brown, *Birth of the Messiah*, 147.

6. R. Aragon, "La Madre con el Nino en la Casa," EphMar 43 (1993), 54–55.

7. Valentini, *Maria Secondo le Scritture* (Bologna: EDB, 2007), 79–87; Brown, *Birth of the Messiah*, 192, n. 32; Vincent Branick, "Mary in the Christologies of the New Testament," *Marian Studies 32* (1981), 38; Serra, "Regina," 1073; Juan Luis Bastero de Eleizalde, "Fundamentos Cristológicos de la Realeza de Maria," EstMar 51 (1986), 208; Sri, *Queen Mother*, 75–77.

8. Brown, *Birth of the Messiah*, 192, n. 32.

9. Valentini, *Maria Secondo le Scritture*, 85.

10. Mt 12:46; 13:55; Mk 3:31; 6:3; Lk 8:19; Jn 2:12; Acts 1:14; Gal 1:19.

11. Vatican II, *Lumen Gentium*, 59; John Paul II, General Audience (June 25, 1997).

12. John Paul II, General Audience (May 28, 1997). As translated in John Paul II, *Theotokos*, 198–99.

13. Jb 14:1; 15:14; 25:4.

14. 1QS XI, 21; cf. 1QH XIII, 14; XVIII, 12–13.16.23–24.

15. Valentini, *Maria secondo le Scritture*, 38.

16. Ratzinger, *Daughter Zion*, 38.

17. Moloney, *Mary: Woman and Mother*, 5.

18. Valentini, *Maria secondo le Scritture*, 36.

19. "More is not to be found in this text. Of course, when the entire context is considered and its thought is, as it were, extrapolated toward future development, one can perhaps, in a modest way, already catch the faint cadences of the future theology of the Christmas mystery." Ratzinger, *Daughter Zion*, 38–39.

Appendix – What Kind of Annunciation?

1. See, for example, Brown, *Birth of the Messiah*, 156–59; Fitzmyer, *Luke I–IX*, 335–9; Brown, *Mary in the New Testament*, 112–5.

2. Brown, *Birth of the Messiah*, 156–59. Brown's schema further specifies eight other features that come with the third element of the divine message: (a) the visionary is addressed by name; (b) a qualifying phrase describes the visionary; (c) the visionary is urged not to be afraid; (d) a woman is with child or is about to be with child; (e) she will give birth to a (male) child; (f) the name by which the child is to be called is revealed; (g) an etymology interprets the name; (h) the future accomplishments of the child are indicated. Brown, *Birth*, 156. However, aspects of this fuller schema are missing in all the examples Brown offers and even the basic five-fold structure is not clearly represented in all the examples Brown offers. See Edgar W. Conrad, "The Annunciation of Birth and the Birth of the Messiah" CBQ 47 (1985), 569, 659; Tannehill, *Luke*, 43.

3. Benjamin J. Hubbard, "Commissioning Stories in Luke-Acts: A Study of their Antecedents, Form and Content" *Semeia* 8 (1977): 103–26. See also LaVerdiere, *The Annunciation to Mary*, 26–27.

4. With these, there is some type of response to the presence of God or to the commissioning itself, but not both. See Hubbard's explanation of how the reaction and protest aspects "are the two elements appearing with the least frequency. However ... either one or the other of these elements usually is found in a commissioning

account. We will see that the same is true of the NT pericopes to be analyzed. There is, then, a general tendency for the individual to *respond* either to the (holy) *presence* of the deity/commissioner ... or to his *commission* itself." Hubbard, "Commissioning Stories in Luke-Acts," 105, emphasis in original. This seems to be the case with these particular commissioning stories.

5. De la Potterie, *Mary in the Mystery of the Covenant*, 7–10.

6. See Brown, *Birth of the Messiah*, 157, n. 70; Green, *Luke*, 87, n. 28.

7. As one can see, these five parts are almost exactly the same as five of the seven parts of Hubbard's seven-part scheme. The two elements from Hubbard's structure not included by Olmo—reaction and objection—are the ones that do not always appear *together* (though almost always one is present) in each of the twenty-seven vocational stories Hubbard examined. See A. Aparicio Rodrìguez, "The Vocation of Mary," in Joseph Paredes, *Mary in the Kingdom*, 83. Rodrìguez cites the work of G. del Olmo, *La vocación de líder en el antiguo Israel. Morfología de los relatos bíblicos de vocación* (Salamanca, 1973), 113–32.

8. Brown, *Birth of the Messiah* (1993), 629. Though Brown admits the commissioning aspect, he considerably downplays this because he is concerned that highlighting the Marian vocational element will overshadow the central Christological message of this scene. "That most of the verses in Luke 1:26–38 concern Jesus (what he will do; who he is) and that the annunciation scene is prefaced to a Gospel about Jesus should make it evident that the primary purpose of this scene is not mariological—indeed, this revisionist approach makes me see why some might think we Catholics have our priorities confused" (630). Although interpreters must maintain the Christological focus of this passage, we will see below that there is no reason the vocational aspect cannot be affirmed alongside it.

9. However, he argues that Luke 1:26–38 is fundamentally more a vocation story that harkens back to the call of Gideon for its model and puts "the accent on *the vocation of Mary*, by which she is

invited to take part in the realization of the plan of salvation willed by God. The annunciation attracts our attention to the role of *Mary* in the Incarnation of the Son of God." De la Potterie, *Mary in the Mystery of the Covenant*, 10.

10. A. Aparicio Rodríguez argues that the Annunciation to Mary scene contains an announcement of birth, but this aspect "allows us to capture the content of the vocation." A. Aparicio Rodríguez, "The Vocation of Mary," as cited in J. Paredes, *Mary and the Kingdom of God*, 84. Along similar lines, John Nolland argues that the vocation-commissioning pattern is the one at the forefront for Luke since the Annunciation to Mary has stronger points of contact with the Old Testament accounts of this type than it does with the announcement-of-birth type. He concludes that the annunciation to Zechariah and the Annunciation to Mary both recall Old Testament birth announcements, but "in the second case, the birth oracle form has been heavily modified in the direction of a call narrative form (Judg 6:11–24; Exod 3; Jer 1:4–10 . . .), and the account overall is best seen as a call, to which Mary responds as an obedient servant of God (Luke 1:38)." John Nolland, *Luke 1–9:20*, 41. Tannehill may be right in viewing biblical birth announcement stories as a "subtype" of the commissioning stories, which may help explain why both elements are found in this account. Tannehill calls these stories "Promise and Commission Epiphanies." Tannehill, "The Gospels and Narrative Literature," 65. Tannehill elsewhere argues that the commissioning-type story fits better with the Annunciation to Mary than does the five-part Announcement of birth structure proposed by Brown and explains that "In the Lukan scenes, however, the commission includes an announcement of birth, thus making the scenes similar to the stories cited by Brown." Tannehill, however, concludes that in the Lukan scenes of the annunciations to Zechariah and to Mary, the commissioning aspect is applied "primarily to the promised child, for in both cases we have a significant description of the child's future role in the plan of God." Tannehill, *Luke*, 43–44. On this point, however, Tannehill does not take into account how the parent's vocation is bound up in the promised child and his mission.

11. Paredes, 65–66; Hubbard, 117: "Mary is being commissioned as the mother of the Messiah"; Tannehill, *Luke*, 43–44; Green, *The Gospel of Luke*, 55–56; Calogero Milazzo, *Israele, Maria, la Chiesa: Commento a Luca 1–2* (Rome: Città Nuova, 2010); Nolland, *Luke 1–9:20*, 24–25.

12. Rodríguez affirms that Gabriel's announcement concerns the coming of Jesus, but he emphasizes that "it is no less true that Mary is not merely a decorative figure here." After demonstrating the many parallels this scene has with the vocation of Gideon, Rodríguez concludes that Luke 1:26–38 likewise should be viewed as the vocation of Mary. "In the scene of Gideon, the central image is the salvation of Israel from the hands of the Midianites and yet the scene is not called 'The Annunciation of the Salvation of Israel' but 'The vocation of Gideon for the salvation of Israel.' Similarly, in Luke's narrative, Jesus is the central character but the scene must not be called 'The Annunciation of the birth of Jesus' but 'The vocation of Mary to be the mother of Jesus.'" A. Aparicio Rodríguez, "The Vocation of Mary," in J. Paredes, *Mary and the Kingdom of God*, 84–85.

13. Joel Green notes how Luke's use of the commissioning form can be seen in the angelic announcements made to Zechariah, the shepherds, and, important for our topic, Mary. In these cases, "the interpretive focus would fall above all on the recipients of the message—Zechariah, Mary, and the shepherds—and so on their role in the realization of God's purpose." Green, *Luke*, 55–56. Green mentions one aspect of the commissioning story that is not explicitly found in Luke's annunciation scenes: the mention of God *sending* the person being called. "Even though the Lukan material lacks the commission-oriented language typical of commission scenes (e.g., Judg 6:14; Jer 1:7–10), as becomes apparent throughout Luke-Acts, Luke's point here seems to be that the miraculous, redemptive activity of God calls forth human response and partnership" (56).

14. De la Potterie, *Mary in the Mystery of the Covenant*, 10.

Acknowledgments

I am grateful to the many colleagues, students, clergy, and religious with whom I've discussed the Marian texts in Scripture over the last twenty years at Benedictine College, the Augustine Institute, FOCUS (Fellowship of Catholic University Students), and the Missionaries of Charity. The students in the various Biblical Mariology classes I've taught since 2004 have particularly helped me deepen my understanding of the Marian passages in the Bible as we studied these texts together. I'm grateful to Curtis Mitch and Michael Barber for reviewing certain sections of the book and to Ben Akers, John Bergsma, Fr. Pablo Gadenz, Fr. Luigi Gambero, Mark Giszczak, Tim Gray, Scott Hahn, Mary Healy, Brant Pitre, John Sehorn, and many others for various helpful conversations about Mary in Scripture throughout the years.

Special thanks goes to Brant Pitre for allowing me to review and cite a pre-published manuscript of his wonderful book, *The Jewish Roots of Mary*; to Curtis Mitch, whose exegetical wisdom has impacted my thoughts on numerous Marian passages throughout the years and, no doubt, has helped make this a better book; and to the faculty and staff at the

Marian Library and International Marian Research Institute at the University of Dayton, where some of the initial research for this project was conducted.

I'm also grateful to the Augustine Institute for granting me the sabbatical in 2017 which gave me the time to finish this more in-depth project. Thanks also to the Augustine Institute faculty for helping us arrive at the title and to Grace Hagan and Jeff Cole for editing this work.

Most of all, I thank my wife Elizabeth for her prayers and encouragement during the writing of this book and to my children, Madeleine, Paul, Teresa, Karl, Luke, Josephine, Chiara, and Elinor. May Mary lead us all ever closer to her Son.

About the Author

Dr. Edward Sri is a theologian, author, and well-known Catholic speaker who appears regularly on EWTN. Each year he speaks to clergy, parish leaders, catechists, and laity from around the world.

He has written several Catholic best-selling books, including *Men, Women and the Mystery of Love* (Servant); *A Biblical Walk through the Mass* (Ascension); *Walking with Mary* (Image); and *Who Am I to Judge?: Responding to Relativism with Logic and Love* (Augustine Institute–Ignatius Press).

Edward Sri is also the host of the acclaimed film series *Symbolon: The Catholic Faith Explained* (Augustine Institute) and the presenter of several popular faith formation programs, including *A Biblical Walk through the Mass* (Ascension Press); *Mary: A Biblical Walk with the Blessed Mother* (Ascension Press); and *Follow Me: Meeting Jesus in the Gospel of John* (Ascension Press). He also served as the content director for several Augustine Institute sacramental preparation programs, including *Beloved: Finding Happiness in Marriage*; *Forgiven: The Transforming*

Power of Confession; and *Reborn: You, Your Child, and the Sacrament of Baptism.*

He is a founding leader with Curtis Martin of FOCUS (Fellowship of Catholic University Students) and currently serves as FOCUS vice president of formation.

Dr. Sri is also the host of the podcast *All Things Catholic* and leads pilgrimages to Rome and the Holy Land each year. He holds a doctorate from the Pontifical University of St. Thomas Aquinas in Rome and is an adjunct professor at the Augustine Institute. He resides with his wife Elizabeth and their eight children in Littleton, Colorado.

You can connect with Edward Sri through his website www.edwardsri.com or follow him on Facebook, Twitter, and Instagram.